EDWARDS IN OUR TIME

D0890911

Edwards in Our Time

Jonathan Edwards and
the Shaping of American Religion

Edited by

SANG HYUN LEE *and* ALLEN C. GUELZO

WILLIAM B. EERDMANS PUBLISHING COMPANY
GRAND RAPIDS, MICHIGAN / CAMBRIDGE, U.K.

© 1999 Wm. B. Eerdmans Publishing Co.
255 Jefferson Ave. S.E., Grand Rapids, Michigan 49503 /
P.O. Box 163, Cambridge CB3 9PU U.K.

All rights reserved

Printed in the United States of America

04 03 02 01 00 99   7 6 5 4 3 2 1

Library of Congress Cataloging-in-Publication Data

Edwards in our time: Jonathan Edwards and the shaping of American religion /
edited by Sang Hyun Lee and Allen C. Guelzo
p.   cm.
Includes bibliographical references.
ISBN 0-8028-4608-4 (alk. paper)
1. Edwards, Jonathan, 1703-1758 — Influence.
2. Theology — United States — History — 20th century.
I. Lee, Sang Hyun, 1938-   . II. Guelzo, Allen C.
BX7260.E3E38   1999
230'.58'092 — dc21   99-15036
CIP

Contents

CONTENTS

PART II: ETHICS

PART III: PREACHING AND REVIVAL

PART IV: ESCHATOLOGY

Editors' Preface

Although Jonathan Edwards is now acknowledged by many as America's premiere philosopher-theologian, the serious consideration of his thought as a compelling resource for today's issues has only begun. Such work of appropriation of his thought is of course made possible by the impressive historical, textual, and interpretive scholarship on Edwards over the past fifty years, especially the critical edition of Edwards's works by Yale. The present collection of essays, originating from the 1996 national conference in Philadelphia, is intended to make a contribution to the timely and challenging enterprise of taking Edwards seriously in our own time.

The Editors would like to thank Harry S. Stout and Kenneth P. Minkema, the General Editor of *The Works of Jonathan Edwards* and the Executive Editor of *The Works*, respectively, for conceiving the 1996 conference in Philadelphia and for providing guidance and encouragement both for the conference and for the publication of this collection. Prof. Stout has also written a stimulating introduction to this volume. The planning committee for the 1996 conference consisted of Allen C. Guelzo, Daryl Hart, Sang Hyun Lee, Kenneth P. Minkema, and Harry S. Stout.

Those who responded to the papers at the conference made significant contributions to the discussion although their remarks are not published here. The commentators were Richard R. Niebuhr of Harvard Divinity School, Stephen Crocco of Princeton Theological Seminary, George Marsden of the University of Notre Dame, and John F. Wilson of Princeton University.

EDITORS' PREFACE

The sponsoring institutions for the 1996 conference were *The Works of Jonathan Edwards,* Princeton Theological Seminary, Eastern College, Westminster Theological Seminary, The McNeil Center for Early American Studies at the University of Pennsylvania, and The Presbyterian Church (U.S.A.) Department of History. We are grateful to The Pew Charitable Trusts and Princeton Theological Seminary for funding the conference, and to President Thomas W. Gillespie of Princeton Theological Seminary for financial support for the publication of this volume.

The Editors would also like to thank Mr. Charles Van Hof of Eerdmans for his expeditious and helpful overseeing of the publication process as well as Virginia Landgraf, a doctoral student at Princeton Theological Seminary, for compiling the index.

SANG HYUN LEE
ALLEN C. GUELZO

Introduction

HARRY S. STOUT

A perennial question in twentieth-century philosophy is whether "perennial questions" actually exist. The skeptics say no: philosophical questions that seem universal across the ages are in fact radically conditioned by particular temporal, geographical, and cultural circumstances. Though the problems addressed by Plato or Kant may be similar to problems addressed by philosophers today, the modes of inquiry are so different that in the end we are left only with "individual answers to individual questions."[1]

Even if truly perennial problems elude us, however, perennially popular thinkers do exist, and no American philosopher-theologian better exemplifies this than Jonathan Edwards (1703-58). The extent of research on Edwards's thought in the last fifty years is nothing short of phenomenal, and this renaissance shows no signs of abatement.[2] One

---

1. Quentin Skinner, "Meaning and Understanding in the History of Ideas," in James Tully, ed., *Meaning and Context: Quentin Skinner and His Critics* (Princeton, N.J.: Princeton University Press, 1988), 65; originally published in *History and Theory* 8 (1969): 3-53.

2. On the current state of the field, see two review essays: Michael J. McClymond, "The Protean Puritan: *The Works of Jonathan Edwards*, Volumes 8 to 16," and Roland A. Delattre, "Recent Scholarship on Jonathan Edwards," both in *Religious Studies Review* 24 (1998): 361-75. See also the two bibliographies compiled by M. X. Lesser: *Jonathan Edwards: A Reference Guide* (Boston: G. K. Hall & Co., 1981); and *Jonathan Edwards: An Annotated Bibliography, 1979-1993* (Westport, Conn.: Greenwood Press, 1994).

explanation for the thriving industry in Edwards's studies is the wealth of extant manuscript evidence. With more than 1,200 sermons, thousands of pages of philosophical and theological notes, more than 200 letters, not to mention handwritten annotations of the entire Bible, the Edwards papers offer a major window into the intellectual culture of the eighteenth-century Atlantic world.[3]

The other explanation for Edwards's popularity, as indicated by the essays in this volume, is the artistic creativity and intellectual force of his speculations. Though the essayists here eschew blatant hagiography—Edwards does not emerge unscathed from these pages—they nevertheless regard him as a wellspring for contemporary philosophical and theological reflection. Edwards's universe, to be sure, was vastly different from our own, and the scholars represented here are not insensitive to the cultural incommensurability of New England in the eighteenth century and the globally networked world we inhabit at the dawn of a new millennium. Yet the remarkable feature of Edwards, and what places him in the canon of great post-Reformation thinkers, is his enduring ability to speak across the ages.

The essays in this collection originated as papers for a national conference, "Edwards in Our Time," held in Philadelphia, Pennsylvania, 3-5 October 1996. This was the fourth national symposium on Edwards in recent years, following events at Wheaton, Illinois (1984); New Haven, Connecticut (1990); and Bloomington, Indiana (1994). The primary focus of the Philadelphia conference was Edwards as pastor, philosopher, and theologian. The first three gatherings also resulted in published collections of essays.[4] All the Philadelphia papers are included here except for that by Joseph A. Conforti, which appears

---

3. The two most important Edwards collections are at the Beinecke Rare Book and Manuscript Library, Yale University, New Haven, Connecticut, and the Franklin Trask Library, Andover Newton Theological School, Newton Centre, Massachusetts. Major portions of both of these collections appear in *The Works of Jonathan Edwards*, the definitive multi-volume critical edition, published by Yale University Press since 1957.

4. The Wheaton conference papers appear in *Jonathan Edwards and the American Experience*, ed. Nathan O. Hatch and Harry S. Stout (New York: Oxford University Press, 1988); the New Haven conference papers in *Benjamin Franklin, Jonathan Edwards, and the Representation of American Culture*, ed. Barbara B. Oberg and Harry S. Stout (New York: Oxford University Press, 1993); and the Bloomington conference papers in *Jonathan Edwards's Writings: Text, Context, Interpretation*, ed. Stephen J. Stein (Bloomington: Indiana University Press, 1996).

as Chapter 6 of his book, *Jonathan Edwards, Religious Tradition, and American Culture* (Chapel Hill: University of North Carolina Press, 1995).

In the Philadelphia keynote address, John E. Smith painted one particularly compelling picture, among endless possible portraits, of the "perennial Edwards." His address (Chapter 1) highlights three particularly durable elements in Edwards's thought: his notion of religious affections, which challenges the presumed dichotomy between the head and the heart in religion; his philosophical realism, as opposed to nominalism, which posits a single humanity united with Adam through the continuous creation of God; and his conception of history, in which God's work of redemption proceeds on the individual level in an endlessly recurring pattern and on the world-historical level in a dynamic succession of interrelated dispensations.

Smith's wide-ranging essay sets the tone for the rest of the chapters, which explore the continuing relevance of Edwards's thought under four major themes. In Part I ("God, Being, and Nature"), Sang Hyun Lee and Stephen H. Daniel both conclude that Edwards's ontology—the branch of philosophy devoted to theories of existence—was far ahead of its time and therefore speaks as much to philosophers and theologians today as it did to Edwards's contemporaries.

Lee shows the considerable subtlety of Edwards's ontological speculations and their relevance to ongoing discussions of God's being. Edwards conceived of God as at once fully actual and fully dispositional, or simultaneously being and becoming. In probing the complexities of God's "disposition," Edwards anticipated much later discussions of God's dynamic involvement in the world. The ontological status of the temporal world, moreover, is intimately linked to God's own being. Edwards elaborated a kind of modified idealism in which objects in nature have what Lee calls a "virtual" reality—a particular disposition caused by God to occur at a particular space and time. Material objects become fully actual only as types (images or shadows) of divine things, just as perceiving beings become fully actual only when they know and love God. Lee thus finds resources in Edwards for contemporary ecological theology: humans participate with the material environment in the glorification of the divine being.

Daniel takes Lee's "dispositional ontology" one step further by asking *why* Edwards's God has a disposition to communicate, whether *ad intra* (within the Trinity) or *ad extra* (with creation). Daniel's provocative answer is that God, for Edwards, does not exist apart from communication; indeed, God is the discursive space in which everything else has its identity. In holding this view, Edwards resembles not only Karl Barth but more recent "postmodern" theologians who have rejected what Daniel calls the Aristotelian-Cartesian-Lockean "substantialist ontology" (or language of subjects and predicates) still dominating much theology. The upshot of Edwards's God-as-discourse is that God is inseparable from his revelation, which provides the grammar and syntax for interpreting all other texts. Edwards's (and Barth's) solution to the age-old conundrum of God's being is thus to immerse themselves in the divine semiotics of Scripture.

The question of being flows naturally into the question of ethical existence, and in Part II ("Ethics"), Roland A. Delattre and Allen C. Guelzo mine the depths of Edwards's writings on human responsibility, unearthing rich resources for contemporary reflection. Both highlight Edwards's radically theocentric ethical perspective, though Guelzo shows that the preeminence of divine will over human initiative is a perilous thing to elaborate and that Edwards failed to build a logically impermeable case for traditional Calvinism. For Guelzo, however, even in failure, Edwards was capable of articulating enduring questions and leaving a substantial legacy.

Delattre, who focuses on the big picture of Edwards's ethics, finds therein an alternative to the two ethical approaches long regnant in philosophy: deontology, which attempts to theorize duty and right action, and teleology, which focuses on the consequences or ends of our actions. On Delattre's reading, Edwards's ethical agenda resembles that of H. Richard Niebuhr two centuries later, namely, to claim an intimate link between ethics and aesthetics and to develop an aesthetics of responsibility. This aesthetics of responsibility entails cordial consent to the beauty of God and participation in God's beautifying activity in the world. "Beauty is our home if ever we have a home," Delattre concludes, and this poetic refrain might well order the ethics of any "authentically religious life," not just the Christian's. God, as the source of all beauty, thus becomes for Edwards and Niebuhr and Delattre the "center of gravity" for ethics; any ethical system that takes humanity as its starting point is self-limiting and deficient.

Edwards's thoroughgoing theism is nowhere more evident than in his most famous work, *Freedom of the Will*, which Guelzo regards as the opening salvo in a peculiarly American, and surprisingly perennial, philosophical debate. Guelzo identifies Edwards as a "compatibilist" but one for whom divine determinism "clearly had the upper hand" over human liberty. Edwards's complicated attempt to reconcile free will and necessity seemed untenable to many nineteenth-century thinkers, who argued either for Arminian liberty or deistic mechanism, and in the early twentieth century, pragmatists like William James advocated free will not because of its inherent truth or falsehood but because it seemed congruent with the goals of an open and democratic society. Such optimism fell victim to two world wars, the resiliency of analytic philosophy, and the rise of the neurosciences. In this new environment, a number of theologians—some of them evangelical heirs of Edwards—began to argue that a viable theism requires an open-ended, rather than the deterministic deity Edwards described. Meanwhile, a variety of secular thinkers, from analytic philosophers to neuroscientists, aggressively promoted a hard determinism that even Edwards himself would have denied. Stepping back from the past two and a half centuries of debate, Guelzo aptly concludes that even if Edwards's answers to the free will problem no longer command the attention of theologians and scientists, he nevertheless "asked the right questions about human ability at the dawn of the liberal era."

The long argument on the will is among the most rarefied pursuits in philosophy and theology, but in stepping into this fray, Edwards never lost sight of the more immediate concerns of daily ministry. In Part III ("Preaching and Revival"), Walter V. L. Eversley and Helen P. Westra assess the practical side of Edwards's career and offer us a mixed account of his legacy for today's clergy.

For Eversley, Edwards's tenure as a pastor illustrates the abiding tension in American Protestantism between conversionism and sacramentalism. Conversionism emphasizes the immediacy and individualism of the "second birth" experience; it typically occurs in the context of revival. Sacramentalism emphasizes the order and continuity of baptism and communion; it seals the Christian community with the means of God's grace. Edwards did not regard conversionism and sacramentalism as contradictory; indeed, he intimately linked the two when he abandoned the open communion policy of his grandfather and predecessor, Solomon Stoddard, in favor of admitting only those persons who had experienced genuine conversion. Eversley concludes that Edwards's policy was pastorally ungenerous and politically disastrous. He sees in Edwards's unsuccessful attempt to serve the two masters of conversionism and sacramentalism a lesson for contemporary pastors: the ecclesial context inevitably will dictate which of these two means is most effective for evangelism.

Westra focuses on the conversion side of the conversion-sacrament dialectic, concurring with Joseph Conforti, Michael Crawford, and others that revival was for Edwards the central element in the great drama of redemption.[5] From her wide reading in his sermons, Westra finds ample evidence that Edwards conceived of history in terms of a divinely ordained, recurring pattern of revival-declension-revival. Edwards's chief pastoral duty was therefore to conform his ministry to this divine design—to announce his parishioners' apostasy with unflinching resolve and to inspire a continual renewal of their covenant with God. In managing the cycle of revival at Northampton, Edwards incorporated local events—his grandfather's death, his uncle's suicide, the collapse of the meetinghouse gallery—into his sermons as providential warnings of impending judgment. Edwards interpreted these local events as texts, which he skillfully wove together with biblical texts into a narrative of decline and revival under God's providence. As an interpreter of the cycle of revival, Edwards remains a model for contemporary revivalists, who seek to discern a similar pattern in salvation history.

The end of salvation history is finally the concern of Robert W. Jenson and Gerald R. McDermott, who in Part IV ("Eschatology") examine the relevance of Edwards's end-time speculations for theologians in today's pluralistic age. Both Jenson and McDermott find much to admire in Edwards, but they admire him for different reasons. Jenson is attracted to the pre-Enlightenment impulse in Edwards's thought: the notion that God's reason and our reason may not be identical, which requires Christians to trust in the sufficiency of revelation. McDermott, meanwhile, commends the more "enlightened" aspect of Edwards's thinking, namely, the tendency to embrace reason wherever it may be found, even outside of a specifically Christian context.

Jenson begins by charting the debility of eschatology in modern

---

5. Joseph A. Conforti, *Jonathan Edwards, Religious Tradition, and American Culture* (Chapel Hill: University of North Carolina Press, 1995), 47-48; and Michael J. Crawford, *Seasons of Grace: Colonial New England's Revival Tradition in Its British Context* (New York: Oxford University Press, 1991), 189.

theology, and he looks to Edwards for its rehabilitation. Eschatology has proven awkward for modern systematicians because of the persistent assumption, articulated during the eighteenth-century Age of Reason, that all things happen according to predictable laws of nature. In this scheme, any notion of a dramatic eschaton becomes suspect along with all other miracles. Theologians are therefore saddled with the conceptual burden of demythologizing biblical predictions of the end time. But, asks Jenson, what if the seemingly predictable laws of nature are in fact a "phantasm," a human construction failing to account for God's unpredictable, but ultimately harmonious, ordering of all things? This was Edwards's conclusion, which Jenson commends for contemporary theology. Jenson also endorses the specific content of Edwards's eschatological hope—a vision of the end as music, or the sweet harmony of the saints in heaven singing together. Standing behind this metaphor of harmony is the ultimate end of Edwards's eschatological hope: the love emanating from the Trinity itself.

McDermott's concern, meanwhile, is not the supreme harmony of the celestial city but the question of who, in Edwards's view, will inherit this heavenly reward. McDermott's careful examination of Edwards's corpus reveals a heretofore unrecognized openness to the possibility that some non-Christians will be saved. Edwards believed that nearly all humans receive divine revelation, even though it is often distorted by the superstitions and idolatries of non-Christian religions. Yet the ubiquity of revelation is not the determining factor in the salvation of non-Christians, who must, like their Christian brethren, be endowed with a holy disposition: a tendency to recognize their own wickedness and their complete dependence on God's mercy. This disposition is logically prior to faith itself, and can in theory occur in anyone, regardless of his or her exposure to the Christian message. Edwards thus appears surprisingly relevant to contemporary discussions of religious pluralism.

The nine essays in this volume are remarkable evidence of Edwards's ability to stimulate constructive reflection, even as we approach the three-hundredth anniversary of his birth. Yet any endorsement of Edwards for our time must also reckon with Edwards in his own time, as the essayists here show in various ways. The flier for the 1996 "Edwards in Our Time" conference represented this temporal disjunction with a picture of Edwards, clad in powdered wig and Geneva bands, superimposed upon a photograph of modern Philadelphia's glittering skyline. This surreal juxtaposition, the commentary of a clever graphic artist, is a salutary reminder of Edwards's foreignness to us—a foreignness that nevertheless fails to obscure his perennial relevance.

The Perennial Jonathan Edwards

JOHN E. SMITH

T he ideas of Jonathan Edwards continue to have an important bearing on religious and theological issues under discussion in our present situation. That this is so should come as no surprise; the enduring power of his thought is found in the incisive way he dealt with questions that have arisen ever and again in the long history of Christendom, questions arising for the most part at the intersection of religion and culture, questions that never seem to be permanently answered and hence must always be confronted anew. Edwards dared to see perennial problems in what was essentially a parochial situation; in order to understand and assess the awakenings of eighteenth-century New England he saw the need to rethink the meaning of God and the make-up of the human self, as he often put it, in the light of Scripture, experience, and reason; to rethink the meaning of freedom and of grace; to reflect on the sources of evil in the world; to consider divine Providence in the course of history; and, not least, to approach in a penetrating way the challenge of distinguishing true from false piety as expressed in the biblical injunction to "test the spirits."

In carrying out these reflections with the aid of his vast knowledge of the Bible, his own experience plus his philosophic understanding of the role of experience in religion, and his acute mind, Edwards showed his independence in expressing the many new and original ideas on which his reputation as one of America's foremost thinkers rightly rests. We must build on that originality and avoid trying to fit him into a convenient category of thought, just as we

1

should seek to emulate his independence of mind. When, for instance, I see Edwards simply classified as a "Calvinist" in a textbook, I find myself wanting to underline what he wrote in the Preface to *Freedom of the Will*, "I utterly disclaim a dependence on Calvin, or believing the doctrines which I hold, because he believed and taught them."[1] That is vintage Jonathan Edwards and it expresses an integrity and candor that help to account for the durability and significance of his thought. Recognition of this significance has been the chief motivation behind the scholarly effort that has been made to publish his works in an enduring form and to interpret them not only for the academy and the churches, but for a wider audience that stretches across American culture.

I propose here to consider three of Edwards's ideas, those I regard as his most illuminating and most powerful in the way of providing resources for dealing with recurrent problems in the world of religion as that world bears on the fabric of society. I cite, first, the concept of affections with, as I shall suggest, the ramifications that go beyond the role it played in his appraisal of the revivals; second, his philosophical realism and rejection of the nominalism according to which only individuals exist and corporate forms such as "mankind," the "church," the "nation" are merely fictions conjured up by the law or by language; and, third, his idea of the two methods employed by God in the order of history. I will not attempt to direct attention to all that could be said about these ideas and I shall devote proportionally more of this chapter to the first, since it is the most complex and is relevant to consideration of several issues.

The idea of affections has, of course, its initial application in the sphere of religion where Edwards used it as a way of understanding the biblical "fruits of the Spirit" in the experience of individual believers. I now believe that it has a further use in providing the basis for a much needed objectivism in the judgments we make about what is of value and importance. The idea is also of direct relevance for overcoming the unfortunate consequences of setting the "heart" and the "head" in opposition in matters of religion; these consequences were felt in Edwards's time and have come back to vex us in our own. In addition, Edwards saw in the connection between affections and his idea

---

1. *The Works of Jonathan Edwards*, 1, *Freedom of the Will*, ed. Paul Ramsey (New Haven: Yale University Press, 1957), p. 131.

of a spiritual understanding the means of correcting the view that those alone should be appointed ministers who are presumed to have been touched by the Spirit as opposed to candidates who supposedly have no credentials other than an academic degree and certification by an ecclesiastical authority.

The more I think about Edwards's idea of affections the more convinced I am that it is an original insight and that, accordingly, it must be understood in its own terms and not in terms which seem to us to be more familiar, such as "feeling" or "emotion" or, especially, "commotion"! An affection — love, joy, hope — is first of all an inclination of will, a *response, not a reaction*, made by the whole person to a reality — God, Scripture, neighbor — whose nature and "excellency" have been properly *understood* by that person through the Bible, reason, and experience, or what he called a "spiritual understanding." Edwards made this basic point in *Religious Affections* as part of his description and defense of true religion. I now find, however, that he gave a much clearer account of this idea in a sermon, "The Importance and Advantage of a Thorough Knowledge of Divine Truth," based on a text from Hebrews 5:12. After distinguishing between *speculative* and *practical* knowledge, the former being a "notional" understanding and the latter a "sense" or experience, he claims that both are essential because, while the speculative without the practical is in vain, without the speculative there is no practical knowledge. "All teaching," he says, "is in vain without learning" and this is so because "God deals with man as with a rational creature, and when faith is in exercise, it is not about something he knows not what."[2]

Edwards develops this thought in his usual serial form. There can be no love without knowledge, for it is contrary to the nature of the soul to love an object entirely unknown. Nor can the heart be fixed on an object of which there is no idea in the understanding. "The reasons," he writes, "which induce the soul to love, must first be understood, before they can have a reasonable influence on the heart . . . nothing can come at the heart but through the door of the understanding," and it is for this reason that, for Edwards, there can be no spiritual (i.e., "practical") knowledge of that of which there is not first a ra-

---

2. Sermon, "The Importance and Advantage of a Thorough Knowledge of Divine Truth," Hebrews 5:12. *The Works of President Edwards*, 4 vols. (New York, 1843), vol. 4, p. 5. This edition is also known as Worcester Revised Edition.

tional knowledge.[3] As he goes on to point out, the knowledge in question is knowledge of divinity, of "the things that pertain to the end of our being, and for the great business for which we are made." The crucial point is that the reasons that induce the soul, that is, the person and not a faculty, to love, or in his other language, to have the affection of love "raised," must be understood before they can affect the heart.

This analysis of experience seems to me profoundly correct and in my view it nullifies any attempt to set "head" and "heart" in opposition to each other, as if either alone could be sufficient. The antagonism often supposed to exist between them stems either from some disproportion in emphasis or from conceiving each in total abstraction from its essential relation to the other. As an example of the first case, I think of some efforts in what we now call the '60s to introduce popular music, dance, and other forms of contemporary expression into worship services. I now see that as a protest in the name of the heart against an over-emphasis on the cerebral in religion. If a personal anecdote be permitted here, I recall after many years the spirited comment of President Henry Sloane Coffin to a number of us in the senior class at the Union Theological Seminary who were planning careers teaching in what has come to be called the field of Religious Studies. He began by reminding us that the Christmas angel had said, "Behold, I bring you glad tidings of great joy" and, he continued, "that angel did *not* say, 'Behold, I bring you a topic for discussion'"! The imbalance can as easily go in the other direction, as indeed happened in Edwards's time in the form of the excesses in the revivals which he rejected as "no certain signs" of anything spiritual, but merely as tares among the wheat. It happens again in our time when would-be defenders of "real" religion declare that something vaguely called "having the Spirit" is superior to the knowledge of divinity that Edwards thought so important. This religious mindlessness, unfortunately, fits in too well with the current anti-intellectual spirit abroad in this country.

The second case — conceiving understanding and affection in abstraction from their relation to each other — gives me an opportunity to set forth briefly why Edwards's theory of the affections and its synthesis of understanding and will can provide us with the basis for overcoming the skepticism and subjectivism that pervade virtually all

3. Ibid.

of our current thinking about judgments of value and importance. For some decades our thinking has been dominated by the belief that there exists, under the name of "nature," a world of bare fact that is as such valueless and purposeless until there appears on the scene a feeling self who adds to this bare fact in the form of a totally external addition all of the importance, value, and significance we know from familiar experience. As Whitehead, however, pointed out in this century, the so-called world of brute fact is a massive abstraction which, though it serves a scientific purpose, is not the world in which human beings actually live.[4] And indeed the idea that our valuational responses, our appreciation of the moral, aesthetic, and religious virtues of persons, events, and things, are merely subjective additions with no roots in reality stems precisely from our having already reduced that reality to a valley of dry bones from which all value has been excluded. Edwards, through his conception of affections, was making the same point in his time. Our affections, on his view, as expressions of inclinations — to love or to hate, to be just or unjust, to be merciful or hard-hearted — are *not* purely arbitrary and subjective increments to an otherwise valueless reality, but are based on our understanding of the essential nature, often called by him the "excellency," of what we are responding to in being thus affected. It was on this account that he could insist that our love for God, for example, is authentic only if it has been induced or "raised" by a spiritual understanding of the divine nature, beauty, and excellency.

Unfortunately, what has stood, and still stands, in the way of our grasping this point is the simple dichotomy — a legacy of the Enlightenment — supposed to exist between "reason" and "emotion." The former is to stand for knowledge of things, while the latter is taken as an arbitrary expression of feeling totally disconnected from this knowledge. Edwards's theory of the affections was a victim of the same error at the time of the revivals; his critics mistook affections for emotions divorced from ideas, and thus failed to see the central importance of understanding in every affectional response. The other frequent mistake, reinforced by revivalist excesses, was the identification of affections with passions, despite the fact that Edwards made a point

---

4. Alfred North Whitehead, *Science and the Modern World* (New York: Macmillan, 1941), pp. 25-26; *Modes of Thought* (New York: Macmillan, 1938), pp. 9ff., and cf. p. 25.

JOHN E. SMITH

of distinguishing the two. The difference is clear: passions are such that the person is overwhelmed or obsessed by them and thus becomes a "patient," whereas affections are *active* responses of the whole person, marked by self-control.

Another contribution made by Edwards's conception of the understanding and its role in religion is found in his insistence that the Spirit enlightens the mind to understand what is already contained in Scripture without any new revelation beyond what has already been revealed. He supplemented this idea with the corresponding claim that the Spirit's enlightening and enhancing the exercise of already existing human faculties is to be distinguished from the introduction of new faculties. Both ideas have a continuing value for coping with problems such as private and supposedly "inspired" interpretation especially of the prophecy in the Bible, pride in the assurance of being "converted" and in declaring others to be hypocrites, hankering after new revelations — all of which goes under the name of "enthusiasm."

In *The Distinguishing Marks* Edwards commented on St. Paul's "putting away childish things" and said that when he speaks of prophecies, tongues, and revelations ceasing in the church he means that what was necessary for the church in its infancy will vanish when maturity is reached, at which time faith, hope, and charity will remain. He declared further that he does not expect the return of these miraculous gifts in the future and that he would gladly enjoy the sweet influences of the Spirit for a quarter of an hour than to have prophetical visions and revelations for a whole year.[5] He spoke in a similar vein when he attacked immediate inspiration, "impulses and impressions" in the use of Scripture. Why can't we be contented, he asked, with the divine oracles "since the canon of Scripture is completed" and why should we want to have anything added to them "by impulses from above"?[6]

Edwards also had much of continuing relevance to say about understanding and learning in relation to theological education and preparation for the ministry. There is no need to rehearse what he wrote about the issue debated in his time over the perils of an unconverted ministry; it is enough to remember his repeated insistence that

5. "The Distinguishing Marks," in *The Works of Jonathan Edwards*, 4, *The Great Awakening*, ed. C. C. Goen (New Haven: Yale University Press, 1972), pp. 280-81.
6. "Some Thoughts Concerning the Revival," *Works*, 4, p. 434.

6

no one should judge the sincerity of another and that his signs of gracious affections are for self-examination alone. More timely is his defense of education and his warning against following those who belittle it and claim instead to have extraordinary experiences as their chief qualification. Those who say that human learning is of little or no use in the work of the ministry, he wrote, "do not consider what they say, for if they did, they would not say it."[7] To solidify his point, he explained that by "human learning" he means "improvement of that common knowledge which men have by human and outward means." God, he continued, "made great use of human learning in the Apostle Paul, as he also did in Moses and Solomon." Speaking by implication against those who denigrate human learning and substitute for it inspiration and the claim to speak with a special authority, Edwards chose to make a humble appeal to his own experience — I do not pretend, he stated, to have received the skill that fits me to be a pastor or shepherd in the church "by immediate inspiration, but by education," human learning, and instructions "by ordinary means." Those, he continued, who despise study and premeditation in preparing for the pulpit and hope for the coming of "inspiration" instead, are guilty of presumption because they do not see that the work of the Spirit is not in such "inspiration" but rather in "assisting natural principles," such as reason, memory, and conscience, to perform their respective tasks.[8]

The second of the three ideas put forth by Edwards which I would like to highlight is his conception of humanity as a unity and the use he made of that conception in his treatment of the doctrine of original sin. Perry Miller, in his classic book about Edwards, chose as a motto for the chapter on sin a passage from Charles S. Peirce which expresses the same point Edwards was making more than a century earlier.[9] "Though the question of realism and nominalism," Peirce wrote, "has its roots in the technicalities of logic, its branches reach about our life. The question whether the *genus homo* has any existence except as individuals, is the question whether there is anything of any more dignity, worth and importance than individual happiness, individual aspirations, and individual life. Whether men really have anything in com-

7. "The Distinguishing Marks," *Works*, 4, p. 282.
8. "Some Thoughts Concerning the Revival," *Works*, 4, pp. 434, 438.
9. Perry Miller, *Jonathan Edwards* (New York: William Sloane Associates, 1949), p. 264.

mon, so that the community is to be considered as an end in itself. . . ."[10] Nominalists are sense-bound atomists not simply in their belief that only individuals and particulars are real, but in their view of human behavior as a series of particular acts with no place for habit, tendency, and propensity all of which we often combine under the name of "disposition." Realists, by contrast, insist on the reality of real kinds, of the unities that connect individuals, of the communities that express a common heritage and endure though individuals come and go, and, finally, of habit and disposition that mark an individual as having this or that enduring *character*.[11] Edwards adopted this realism as a philosophical position, but he had as well the science of Newton on his side. A law of nature, said Edwards, is "something in the permanent state of things," a tendency to behave in a consistent way. It would be ridiculous, he wrote, to say that "although it often happened that water quenched fire, yet there was no tendency in it to such an effect."[12]

Edwards used the foregoing ideas to express his original conception of how Adam is related to his posterity. For Edwards, Adam is not a legal representative of the race with whom God enters into a contract; he is instead one with his posterity through the continuous creation of God. The one who treats the roots of the tree treats every branch because they are at one with the root. In this way mankind is constituted as a unity wherein God treats everyone, rich and poor, proud and humble, strong and weak, as one. There is indeed a meaning to mankind above individual happiness and it is found in the community of transgression in which all participate.

There were, in addition, other important consequences of Edwards's anti-nominalist view of things. First, he could point out with good reason that there is far more evil and corruption in the world than can be accounted for by trying to combine the particular transgressions of individuals. Second, the idea that I alone can corrupt my nature — the essential claim of John Taylor — is contradicted by the course of experience. Miller put the point succinctly: "Edwards's *Orig-*

10. *Collected Works of Charles Sanders Peirce*, ed. Arthur W. Burks (Cambridge: Harvard University Press, 1958), 8:38.

11. For a discussion of the importance of disposition in Edwards's view of reality, see Sang Hyun Lee, *The Philosophical Theology of Jonathan Edwards* (Princeton: Princeton University Press, 1988).

12. Miller, *Jonathan Edwards*, p. 268.

inal Sin declares on the contrary that an observable propensity extending over the ages cannot adequately be explained as a discontinuous
series of private decisions."[13] In challenging those who deny this propensity, Edwards asked with sly humor how it happens that millions
of people in successive generations "all agree, *without consultation*, to
exercise their freedom in favor of evil." Third, the notion of tendency
in human conduct makes it possible to make clear the distinction between sin as the state of separation from God and sins as particular
wrongdoings that flow from that state. The distinction is important because it enables us to overcome the error in identifying sin as such
with some particular sphere of human experience such as sexuality.
Finally, evil and corruption are not confined to individuals alone but
infect institutions and all the relations that make up society. It is for
this reason that overcoming the ills of a social order cannot be accom-
plished merely by the transformation of individuals one at a time.

I turn now to the last of the three ideas to be highlighted — Edwards's conception of history and especially what he calls God's two
methods or modes of activity in the historical order. For this aspect of
his thought we must, of course, turn to that remarkable document, *The
History of Redemption*, a work that surely sets a record for the length of
its commentary on one biblical text. We should begin by reminding
ourselves that, while history as both event and record is as familiar to
us as anything can be, it was otherwise in Edwards's day. Our recognized idea of history as a dynamic, sometimes creative, sometimes destructive, order of events fraught with human significance was not
born until the middle of the nineteenth century. It is no accident that
this took place when life and organic development, the concerns of the
rapidly growing biological sciences, were thrust into the foreground
and the world of Newtonian physics was no longer thought to be the
only reality. Edwards, however, living in the middle of the previous
century, did not have the advantage of this change in the climate of
opinion and was thus left to his own resources. Miller has captured
Edwards's response very nicely: "For a mind imbued with Newto-
nianism," he writes, "to break away from the reigning conception of
space toward an appreciation of time, to subordinate the idea of an
eternal and immutable, or at least a cyclical, pattern of the past to a vision of a dynamic process of realization within temporal existence —

13. Ibid., p. 278.

9

this was such a metaphysical excursion as his contemporaries could not begin to comprehend."[14]

Much of the attention hitherto paid to the *Redemption* has been concentrated on Edwards's interpretation of the millennium and its implications for the new world in general and America in particular. Important as this has been, I would like to focus instead on a few points that have not received the notice they merit. The simple and un-suspecting way Edwards approaches biblical narrative may lead one to overlook his sophistication in thinking about history. He distin-guished, for example, between the "fabulous age" which is unreliable and the "historical age," the latter being the "beginning of 'authentic profane history,'" which, as he says, was designed by God to serve as a reliable basis for judging prophecy. God, moreover, is said to have had a further hand in this historiography by taking care that events of an historical period not much covered in Scripture history would be pre-served in profane history.[15] Hence, on Edwards's view, profane history is not to be disparaged or taken lightly.

One of my favorite examples of Edwards's historical interpreta-tion is his account of the importance of the Septuagint, or the Greek translation of the Jewish Bible. Referring to the establishment of the "Grecian empire," he took note of the making of the Greek language *common* in the world and declared that this development did remark-ably promote the work of redemption. The Septuagint was the instru-ment whereby the texts could now be understood by Gentiles because they were no longer locked up in Hebrew, in his own words, "a lan-guage understood by no other nation."[16] The apostles, Edwards says, could then use the Old Testament writings, especially the prophecies about Christ, in their preaching to the Gentiles. If you consult the cur-rent edition of the *Oxford Classical Dictionary* under the entry "Septua-gint" you will find there the same interpretation Edwards gave more than two centuries ago.

Central to the sustained line of thought in the *Redemption* is the distinction drawn between a "limited" and a "broad" sense in which the work of redemption is to be understood. The limited sense refers to

14. Ibid., p. 311.
15. *The Works of Jonathan Edwards,* 9, *A History of the Work of Redemption,* ed. John F. Wilson (New Haven: Yale University Press, 1989), p. 243.
16. Ibid., p. 273.

the work performed by Christ from birth to resurrection, and, by comparison with what is yet to come, this work, says Edwards, "was not so long a-doing." The broad sense has to do with the important fact that, although salvation was gained, "the work itself and all that appertained to it was *virtually* done and finished but not *actually*," which means that the completion of God's grand design is yet to take place as the work of the Spirit in a real historical order.[17] It is in connection with this distinction that Edwards introduced his idea of the two methods employed by God in history. In the first case, the redemption of individuals, God works by "repeating after continually working the same work over again, though in different persons . . . ," and the process is the same age after age. With respect to the grand design which extends beyond individuals to include the church, the nations, and their social, cultural, and political institutions, God, says Edwards, "works in a different manner." It is not by repeating the same effect on different subjects in every age that the design is realized, "but by many successive works and dispensations . . . all tending to one great aim and effect."[18] In a summary statement comparing the two methods, Edwards set forth his version of the dynamic conception of history which was not to receive its fullest expression until much later. The grand design, he wrote, "is carried on not only by what is common to all ages [but] by successive works wrought in different ages, all parts of one whole or one great scheme whereby one work is brought about by various steps, one step in each age and another in another."[19]

Our continuing efforts to study and interpret Edwards's thought should always be motivated by a concern for those resources to be found in his ideas which help us to deal with the recurrent problems facing religion on the contemporary scene. Ours should be no antiquarian concern aimed at preserving the past, but a creative application in the present of the insights bequeathed to us by so monumental a thinker.

17. Ibid., p. 117.
18. Ibid., p. 121.
19. Ibid., p. 122.

PART I

GOD, BEING, AND NATURE

Edwards on God and Nature: Resources for Contemporary Theology

SANG HYUN LEE

E dwards's personal closeness to the physical environment is well-known throughout his accounts of spiritual experiences in nature — the most prominent of such accounts being his "Personal Narrative." His references to things in nature as the "images" or "shadows" of divine things are ubiquitous in his writings. Scholars since Perry Miller have duly noted Edwards's extension of the doctrine of typology from a methodology of discovering the prefigurements of Christ in the Old Testament to a theology of apprehending the divine images in nature as well as in biblical and secular history.[1] All the indications are that nature or the physical environment occupied a place of central importance in the fabric of Edwards's thought.

But the interpretation of Edwards's theology of nature and its place in the overall framework of his thought has not been a simple task. Neo-platonic readings of Edwards's metaphysics have led some scholars to

---

1. I wish to note that this essay draws some of its materials from my earlier article, "Jonathan Edwards on Nature," *Faithful Imagining: Essays in Honor of Richard R. Niebuhr*, ed. Sang Hyun Lee, Wayne Proudfoot, and Albert Blackwell (Atlanta: Scholars Press, 1995), pp. 39-59. See "Personal Narrative," *Jonathan Edwards: Representative Selections*, ed. Clarence H. Faust and Thomas H. Johnson (New York: Hill and Wang, 1962), pp. 57-72; Perry Miller, "Introduction," Jonathan Edwards, *Images or Shadows of Divine Things*, ed. Perry Miller (New Haven: Yale University Press, 1948), pp. 27-30.

wonder how such a worldview could be consistent with Edwards's obvious high valuation of nature. Edwards's so-called idealism has also made unclear the exact nature of the ontological status of the physical universe as distinct from God's consciousness as well as from the minds of human beings.[2]

Moreover, interpreters of Edwards have been concerned about the basic question of what it is in Edwards's theological mind that could so boldly put nature on the same level with history and even with Scripture. What drives Edwards to see rivers and rocks as well as the sacred events in biblical history as the types of divine things? What led Edwards, who so consistently insisted upon the eternal sovereignty of the Divine Being, to appreciate the significance, not only to humanity but even to God, of the temporal and spatial factuality of the earthly images of divine things?[3]

I intend in this essay to argue that it is in the light of Edwards's highly innovative dispositional reconception of the nature of God and God's relation to the world that the meaning of Edwards's appreciation of nature can be properly understood. My particular concern will be to suggest ways in which Edwards's doctrines of God and of nature provide us with helpful insights for the theological concerns that are important to us in our own time.

My discussion will center around six main points. I will argue: (1) that Edwards worked out, with the help of his dispositional ontology, an innovative reconception of the nature of God as at once actual and

2. See, for example, Clyde A. Holbrook, *Jonathan Edwards, The Valley and Nature: An Interpretative Essay* (Lewisburg, PA: Bucknell University Press, 1987), pp. 71-72, 88-93. For other important studies of Edwards on nature, see Paula M. Cooey, *Jonathan Edwards on Nature and Destiny: A Systematic Analysis* (Lewiston, NY: The Edwin Mellen Press, 1985); Conrad Cherry, *Nature and Religious Imagination: From Edwards to Bushnell* (Philadelphia: Fortress Press, 1980), pp. 13-64.

3. See, for instance, Janice Knight, "Learning the Language of God: Jonathan Edwards and the Typology of Nature," *William and Mary Quarterly*, 3rd ser. 48 (1991), pp. 531-51; Wallace E. Anderson, "Editor's Introduction" to "Images of Divine Things" and "Types," and Mason I. Lowance with David H. Watters, "Editor's Introduction" to "Types of Messiah," *The Works of Jonathan Edwards*, 11, *Typological Writings* (New Haven: Yale University Press, 1993), pp. 3-33, 157-82; John F. Wilson, "Editor's Introduction," *The Works of Jonathan Edwards*, 9, *A History of the Work of Redemption* (New Haven: Yale University Press, 1989), pp. 40-61; Stephen H. Daniel, *The Philosophy of Jonathan Edwards: A Study in Divine Semiotics* (Bloomington and Indianapolis: Indiana University Press, 1994).

also eternally disposed for self-communication and self-enlargement; (2) that such a dynamic understanding of God involved the conception of God's creation of the world as the everlasting process of God's repetition of God's prior actuality now in time and space, thus making the created realm internally related to God's own life; (3) that Edwards uses his dispositional ontology to articulate the ontological status of the physical dimension of the created realm as having a reality of its own, distinguishable from either God or humanity; (4) that, in Edwards's conception, there is a mutuality as well as distinctiveness between nature and humanity; (5) that Edwards's extension of typology to include nature can be best understood in the light of his theocentric understanding of the entire created realm as God's repetition of God's own glory; and (6) that the strong ecological motif present in Edwards's theology can be illustrated through his conceptions of both the sensible knowledge of the regenerate and the Christian's hope for the new heaven and new earth.

1. Dispositional Ontology and Edwards's Reconception of the Divine Being

Edwards makes a new beginning in Christian theology by conceiving the nature of God as at once fully actual and also dispositional. God is perfect in actuality and also inherently disposed to further actualizations — that is, to repetitions of the prior actuality.

The philosophical renovation utilized in Edwards's theological reconstruction is the replacement of the age-old notion of substance with the idea of disposition or habit.[4] The Aristotelian concepts of substance and form with which the West did its thinking about the nature of reality for a long time had become problematic. Newtonian science suggested motion and force as the more basic categories, while the empiricistic spirit of the seventeenth and eighteenth century was increasingly putting in doubt the utility of the notion of the inexperienced and unknowable substance. Already in his early philosophical notes, Edwards began to think about reality in terms not of substance

4. For a fuller discussion of Edwards's dispositional ontology, see my *The Philosophical Theology of Jonathan Edwards* (Princeton: Princeton University Press, 1988), pp. 34-114.

and form but — utilizing a new language — in terms of dispositional forces.

What made this fundamental metaphysical reformulation possible for Edwards was his realist, as opposed to nominalist, idea of habits and dispositions. "In memory, in mental principles, habits, and inclinations, there is something really abiding in the mind when there are no acts or exercises of them," writes Edwards.[5] A habit or disposition, in other words, has a mode of reality apart from its manifestations in actual events and actions. A habit as an abiding principle is also "lawlike," for Edwards, in that it actively and prescriptively governs the occurrence and character of actual events. "All habits," writes Edwards, "[are] a law that God has fixed, that such actions upon such occasions *should* be exerted."[6] When there is a habit or disposition, it functions like a prescriptive law that certain events will, not only may, occur whenever certain circumstances prevail. Habits or dispositions, in short, are ontologically real and causally active law-like powers.

Redefining the Aristotelian metaphysics, Edwards declares in a remarkable sentence in "Subjects to Be Handled in the Treatise on the Mind": "it is the laws that constitute all permanent being in created things, both corporeal and spiritual."[7] A human being is no longer a substance or form. "[The soul's] essence consists in powers and habits."[8] Reality, in short, is a system of law-like dispositions and habits.

The being of God, for Edwards, is also essentially a disposition. God's essence, Edwards tells us, is a "disposition to communicate Himself."[9] But, unlike created reality, God's being is not only a disposition but also a full actuality — that is, an infinitely perfect exercise of the divine dispositional essence. And the internal exercises of the divine dispositional essence constitute the inner-trinitarian actuality of the Divine Being.

Edwards articulates the inner-trinitarian exercise of the divine dispositional essence with the help of the analogy of the human self as

5. "The Mind," no. 69, *The Works of Jonathan Edwards*, 6, *Scientific and Philosophical Writings*, ed. Wallace E. Anderson (New Haven: Yale University Press, 1980), p. 385.

6. "Miscellanies," no. 241, *The Works of Jonathan Edwards*, 13, *The "Miscellanies," a-500*, ed. Thomas Schafer (New Haven: Yale University Press, 1994), p. 358.

7. "Subjects to Be Handled in the Treatise on the Mind," *Works*, 6, p. 391.

8. "Miscellanies," no. 241, *Works*, 13, p. 358.

9. "Miscellanies," no. 107, *Works*, 13, pp. 277-78.

knowing and loving as well as the Lockean notion of the self's reflexive knowledge of its internal acts.[10] So the first person of the Trinity, for Edwards, is "the deity in its direct existence" — that is, the first and primordial exercise of the divine dispositional essence in knowing and loving.[11] But the first person is and remains the divine disposition because God's essence, for Edwards, is disposition. The Father, in other words, is the eternal actuality of the divine knowing and loving *and* the disposition to repeat or communicate this divine actuality. In God, in other words, actuality and disposition coincide, although it is legitimate to make a distinction between them.[12]

The second person of the Trinity is the Father's reflexive knowing of his own knowing and loving, and the third person, the Father's reflexive loving of his reflexive knowing and loving. So the full exertion of the divine disposition constitutes "God, the idea of God, and the love of God."[13]

So, to say that for Edwards God is a dynamic being means at least two things. First, God in God's own being, for Edwards, is actuality *and* its repetition or self-communication. "In the Son the deity, the whole deity and glory of the Father, is as it were repeated or duplicated," thereby representing "an eternal, adequate, and infinite exercise" of the Father's divine dispositional essence. In a similar manner, the third person repeats the deity — this time, affectionally.[14] God's be-

---

10. John Locke, *An Essay concerning Human Understanding,* ed. John W. Yolton (London: J. M. Dent and Sons, 1961), bk. 2, ch. 1, nos. 1-5; "An Essay on the Trinity," *Representative Selections,* pp. 375-81.

11. Ibid., p. 379.

12. God's perfection would imply, according to Edwards, that "there is no distinction to be made in God between Power or habit and act." But Edwards immediately adds: "But the divine Perfection will not Infer [i.e., imply] that his understanding is not by Idea and that there is not Indeed such a thing as Inclination & Love in God." Ibid., pp. 375-76. And Edwards freely makes a distinction between the divine disposition and its exercise throughout his writings. God's essence, for Edwards, is a disposition; but this disposition has to be seen as fully in exercise because otherwise the eternal actuality of God would be compromised. But then God's essence remains a disposition. In short, the coincidence of the divine disposition and the divine actuality is the only way the depth of the divine reality can be described in human words.

13. "Miscellanies," no. 308, *Works,* 13, p. 393.

14. "An Essay on the Trinity," *Representative Selections,* pp. 377-80.

ing is indeed also becoming — a becoming without being incomplete or fully actual.

God in God's own inner-trinitarian being is dynamic also in the sense that God remains eternally a disposition to repeat or communicate himself, although the inner-trinitarian exercise of the divine disposition is "an eternal, adequate, and infinite exercise" of that divine disposition. This can only be so because disposition is God's essence. So, again, however paradoxically it may be, we have to say that God, for Edwards, is at once a dynamic trinitarian actuality *and* the eternal disposition to repeat that actuality. This second point, of course, leads us to the question of the end for which God created the world.

2. The End for Which God Created the World

God is internally fully actual. But God's essence, for Edwards, remains a disposition to communicate his actuality. So, Edwards's answer to the question of the why of creation points to God's dispositional essence. God's dispositional essence is fully exercised *ad intra*, but God, "who delights in the exercise of His perfection, delights in all kinds of its exercise." So "the same disposition" that is fully exercised internally is exercised now *ad extra*.[15] God's end in creation, in other words, is to communicate or repeat God's internal dynamic fullness now in time and space. Intelligent beings are created so that they can know and love God's beauty, thereby repeating in time and space God's inner-trinitarian knowing and loving of beauty. "In the creature's knowing, esteeming, loving, and rejoicing in, and praising God, the glory of God is both exhibited and acknowledged; his fullness is received and returned." The result is "an increase, repetition, or multiplication" of the divine fullness.[16] The physical universe is also created for the same end and thus has the same destiny as humanity — namely, to repeat God's internal glory in time and space. "Outward things are ordered as they do to that end, that they might be images of spiritual things."

15. "Miscellanies," no. 553, *The Philosophy of Jonathan Edwards from His Private Notebooks*, ed. Harvey G. Townsend (Eugene: University of Oregon Press, 1955), p. 136.

16. Jonathan Edwards, *The Works of Jonathan Edwards*, 8, "Dissertation concerning the End for Which God Created the World," in *Ethical Writings*, ed. Paul Ramsey (New Haven: Yale University Press, 1989), p. 433.

"The beauties of nature are really emanations or shadows of the excellencies of the eternal Son of God."[17] In Edwards's conception of God's relation to the world, humanity and nature are equal partners in their common destiny to serve God's own end in creation. We shall return to this point later.

What I want to highlight here is that this conception of God as at once fully actual and dispositional enables Edwards to see God as internally related to the world and also independent of the world in God's prior actuality. God's creation of the world is not for self-realization of God as God. It is rather for the repetition of God who already is God. This self-communication of God *ad extra* is an act of God's self-realization to the extent that it is a further exercise of God's dispositional essence. But it is an act of self-realization in a peculiar sense — namely, as a self-extension or repetition of what is already fully actual. So the world is meant to be "an increase, repetition or multiplication" of God's internal fullness.[18]

The notion of repetition has a dual function here: it protects God's prior actuality (because repetition requires something *already* there), and also sees God's life as dynamic (because repetition is the coming to be of something that is not numerically identical with that which is repeated). God's actuality that is primordially already there is now repeated in time and space. The world is intended to be God "enlarged" or "existing *ad extra*."[19] The world however, will never completely be God enlarged but always in a process of becoming that, since the spacio-temporal repetition of the Infinite Being would require an "infinite duration."[20] In this way, for Edwards, the God-world distinction never disappears.

In short, the world does not enlarge or add anything to God, since God as God *ad intra* is infinitely perfect. But the world does enlarge and add to God in the sense that the world is God's own life repeated *ad extra* in time and space as the exercises of God's dispositional essence *ad extra*. So "God's glory and happiness [which] are in and of himself, [and] are infinite . . . cannot be added to." "And yet, in some sense it can be truly said that God has more delight and pleasure for

17. "Images of Divine Things," no. 95, *Works,* 11, p. 88; "Covenant of Redemption: 'Excellency of Christ,'" *Representative Selections*, p. 373.

18. See note 16.

19. "End in Creation," *Works,* 8, p. 527.

20. Ibid., p. 534.

the holiness and happiness of his creatures."[21] And the special sense in which God takes "more delight and pleasure" is the sense of "a pleasure in diffusing and communicating to the creature, [rather] than in receiving from the creature."[22] The ethical implication of this discussion, of course, is that human beings ought to consider what happens in nature and history as having an ultimate significance. So God "really loves being honored by [creatures], as all try to be well thought of by those they love. Therefore, we are to seek the glory of God as that which is a thing really pleasing to Him."[23]

Edwards's perspective on the ultimate reality here outlined is certainly to be distinguished from that of Neoplatonism, although certain Neoplatonic elements do exist in Edwards's thought. One difference is that in Neoplatonism the world is emanated out of the fullness of the transcendent One without there being any telos for the existence of the world. The One is perfect in such a way that it cannot possibly be inclined to aim at anything. The creation of the world, for Edwards, however, is for the purpose of the external exercises of God's dispositional essence. Therefore, the creation for Edwards is at once an emanation (an extension of God's being) and a purposeful activity (the exercise of God's disposition). Thus, he freely mixes emanationistic with teleological metaphors in his discussion of the creation.[24]

Underlying Edwards's emanationistic and teleological language is his dynamic reconception of the Divine Being. Lovejoy has argued that the thought system of the great chain of being in the West contains a contradictory idea of God that juxtaposes the idea of the Good as the eternal and immutable principle behind all things, on the one hand, and the idea of Goodness as the creative source of all things, on the other.[25] Edwards's dispositional reconception of God represents a synthesis of these two ideas. For Edwards God is at once the eternal and perfect actuality and also an eternal disposition to self-enlargement. Thus, his dynamic conception of God implies a telos for the creation, thereby giving the creation a God-given ultimate meaning.

Another basic difference between Edwards's thought and the per-

21. Ibid., p. 447.
22. Ibid., p. 448.
23. "Miscellanies," no. 208, *Works*, 13, p. 342.
24. See, for instance, "End in Creation," *Works*, 8, pp. 460, 528, 530-34.
25. Arthur Lovejoy, *The Great Chain of Being: A Study of the History of an Idea* (New York: Harper and Row, 1936), pp. 43-50.

spective of the great chain of being involves a further elaboration of the point just made — namely, the ultimate significance of the material universe. The Neoplatonic nature of the great chain of being entailed that the material aspects of entities are really undesirable containers of the emanations of the spiritual reality, the various grades of which make up the hierarchy of being. The material universe as such, therefore, does not have any inherent ultimate meaning or reality of its own. The salvation of the spiritual aspect of being is its deliverance away from the material world and not a fulfillment in and through it.

Edwards also posits a hierarchy of beings with various grades of the embodiment of the spiritual within the material. He maintains that the closer to the spiritual reality an entity is, the higher in the hierarchy that entity is located. To this extent, Edwards is influenced by Neoplatonism. However, there is a fundamental difference. In contrast to Neoplatonism, Edwards holds that spiritual realities, at whatever level of the hierarchy of being, are embodied in the material dimension of actual entities. That is, the material dimension of particular beings embodies in a physical way the ultimate spiritual reality. Every entity in the world is somehow intended to be a spatio-temporal repetition of God's glory at whatever level that entity may be.[26] All levels of the hierarchy do not just contain but embody a relation to the ultimate reality. In this sense, Edwards's hierarchy of being has a horizontal or egalitarian meaning. The spiritual dimension of a finite entity, therefore, cannot be separated from the material dimension since the former does not exist except in and through the latter. In short, the material universe as such, for Edwards, has a God-given telos and, therefore, is of an ultimate and lasting significance.

Before moving on to a discussion of Edwards's concept of nature in the light of his dispositional reconception of God, I want to pause and note the way in which that reconception of God provides us with a compelling alternative to our contemporary discussions. The theological issue of how to include both being and becoming in the conception of God has been peculiarly urgent in contemporary theology. Also associated with this time-honored problem is the concern to see God as related to the world not just externally but internally. There is a yearning to see temporality and history as ultimately significant — signifi-

26. See, for example, "Covenant of Redemption: 'Excellency of Christ,'" *Representative Selections*, p. 373.

cant even to God's own life. If the incarnation of God in Jesus is really God in flesh, would not God have to be seen as somehow involved in temporality — in all of its tragedies as well as in its joys? Would not God have to be seen as being affected by what happens in temporality? But, then, how can God be seen as completely perfect and transcendent, as the historic Christian tradition holds, and at the same time be conceived as involved in history, in the flux of becoming?

It is beyond the purview of this essay to review the discussions of these questions in contemporary theology. It suffices to note that process theology has presented a most profound challenge to traditional Christian theology's tendency to overemphasize God's transcendence and perfection at the expense of God's dynamic involvement in the world. But process theology has gone, in my opinion, to the other extreme of tending to overemphasize God's involvement in time at the expense of God's prior actuality and self-sufficiency.

Edwards's reformulation of the doctrine of God and God's relation to the world suggests another possible option. Edwards's conceptual tools are his dispositional ontology, the *God ad intra/God ad extra* distinction, and the idea of God's creative activity as repetition. God's creation of the world, for Edwards, is the exercise of God's original dispositional essence. Therefore, the world does extend God's actuality, except that this extension is a repetition of a prior actuality.[27] In this

27. Karl Barth has used the idea of "reiteration," which is very similar to Edwards's "repetition," to conceive of God's incarnation in Christ as God's own presence in time and thus as a kind of "becoming" — a becoming which "reiterates" what God eternally already is in God's own dynamic "self-relatedness." In this way, Barth also attempted to see God as dynamic and creative without compromising God's eternal prior actuality. Barth, unlike Edwards, however, limits God's temporal "self-reiteration" within God's self-revelation in Christ rather than in the entire creation. But then to put it that way may be to speak from outside Barth's own framework of thought.

See Eberhard Jüngel, *The Doctrine of the Trinity: God's Being Is in Becoming* (Grand Rapids: Eerdmans, 1976), especially pp. 89-108; Hendrikus Berkhof, *Christian Faith: An Introduction to the Study of the Faith* (Grand Rapids: Eerdmans, 1979), pp. 152-53.

For other discussions of the being and becoming issue other than the writings of process theologians, see, for example, Keith Ward, *Rational Theology and the Creativity of God* (Oxford: Blackwell, 1982); Colin E. Gunton, *Becoming and Being: The Doctrine of God in Charles Hartshorne and Karl Barth* (Oxford: Oxford University Press, 1978); Royce G. Gruenler, *The Inexhaustible God: Biblical Faith and the Challenge of Process Theism* (Grand Rapids: Baker Book House, 1983).

way, God's prior actuality and thus transcendence are preserved. Furthermore, God's creative activity is carried out completely out of God's own resources without depending upon any other power. So, another traditional mark of God's perfection, namely God's self-sufficiency, is also reaffirmed. Unlike process theology, Edwards views God as identical with the principle of creativity.[28]

But, still, the created existence, for Edwards, is real and significant — even to God. The world does "add" and "enlarge" God's being although no such addition or enlargement is necessary for God to be God. And the world is a new venture for God to the extent that the world is where God is extending God's eternal glory in ever new ways and circumstances. And this new venture of God, in time and space, has its grounding in the inner-trinitarian dynamic life of God *ad intra*.

3. The Reality of Nature:
The Problem of Edwards's Idealism

Edwards's thought system, as outlined above, requires that beings within the spatio-temporal realm, including the physical universe, have a reality of their own, since the very end for which God created the world entails their being where they are and what they are. But exactly what sort of reality material beings have, and whether they have reality of their own in any way distinguishable from that of humanity and God, are the questions that must now be raised. A consideration of these questions is necessitated by Edwards's assertion that "corporeal things exist no otherwise than mentally," that is, "either in created or uncreated consciousness."[29]

A thorough discussion of the nature of Edwards's idealism is beyond the purview of this essay. I shall only outline a dispositional interpretation of Edwards's conception of the physical universe and indicate the implications of this interpretation for the reality and significance of nature in Edwards's thought.

As I indicated above, Edwards no longer thought about reality, in-

---

28. For a critique of process theology on this point, see Robert C. Neville, *Creativity and God: A Challenge to Process Theology* (New York: Seabury Press, 1980), pp. 21-47.

29. "The Mind," no. 10, *Works*, 6, p. 342.

cluding matter, in terms of substance and form. In his early writings, "Of Being" and "Of Atoms," Edwards critiqued the notion of material substance and reconceived matter as solidity or resisting — resisting annihilation. Edwards then quickly moved to see that this resisting which cannot be thwarted by any finite power must be the immediate activity of God himself. And it is the manner or pattern of this resisting that constitutes the quality and permanence of a material entity. In "Of Being," Edwards tells us that "all body is nothing but what immediately results from the exercise of divine power in such a particular manner." A body is "the Deity acting in that particular manner in those parts of space where He thinks fit."[30] The "particular manner" of resisting or God's acting in space is "established" and "fixed" by God and thus permanent.[31] Therefore, the "manner" or "laws of resistance" are "essential to the very being of nature." Extending this analysis to the nature of all beings, Edwards concluded: "It is laws that constitute all permanent being in created things, both corporeal and spiritual."[32]

A law of nature, as Edwards uses the term, is a dispositional force or a habit with a mode of reality apart from its exercises. Thus, when God causes resistance, God follows the law that God had fixed: that a particular sort of resisting occurs at a particular point in space at a particular time.[33] To put it differently, a body is essentially and abidingly a disposition — to have a particular kind of resisting caused by God to occur at a particular space and time.

If material entities are essentially law-like habits and dispositions in Edwards's realist sense of those terms, then they have a reality of their own which is distinguishable from that both of humans and also of God. Habits and dispositions have a mode of reality apart from their manifestations in actual events and actions. Here I am assuming that one can think of real-ness as a category broader than actuality. An entity as habit, in other words, is real in the sense of virtual though not in the sense of actual — the term "virtual," here, referring to the sort of real-ness that falls between full actuality and a mere potentiality.[34] Therefore, in whatever manner material entities may be dependent

30. "Of Atoms," *Works*, 6, p. 215.

31. "Miscellanies," no. 1263, Townsend, pp. 184-93.

32. "Subjects to Be Handled in the Treatise on the Mind," *Works*, 6, p. 391.

33. "Miscellanies," no. 1263, Townsend, pp. 184-88.

34. For a fuller discussion of this point, see my *The Philosophical Theology of Jonathan Edwards*, pp. 42-46, 106-14.

upon human consciousness for their actuality, those entities do have a mode of reality as habits and dispositions *before* human perception occurs. Perception does not exhaust the reality of material entities.

One of the problems Edwards wrestled with in connection with his idealism was the reality of unperceived objects; his treatment of this problem illustrates the point I am arguing. How do objects in a locked room that are not seen by any human being, for example, exist, asked Edwards. Earlier, in his notes on "The Mind," Edwards tried the answer that objects unperceived by humans exist by being in the consciousness of God, and also the answer that they exist by being "supposed" by God in God's other actions.[35] But at the every end of "The Mind," Edwards settles for a dispositional conception. Edwards writes in no. 69 of "The Mind":

> In memory, in mental principles, habits, and inclinations, there is something really abiding in the mind when there are no acts or exercises of them, much in the same manner as there is a chair in this room when no mortal perceives it. For when we say, there are chairs in this room when none perceives it, we mean that minds would perceive chairs here according to the laws of Nature in such circumstances.[36]

In order to explain the reality of unperceived objects, Edwards here turns to the "laws of nature in such circumstances," laws clearly having an ontological priority to the actual event of perception. In the corporeal universe, in other words, there is something abiding that is distinguishable from human perception. It is no wonder, then, that in a philosophical note written very late in his life, Edwards observed that "there may be more in material existence than man's perception, past, present or future."[37]

Wallace E. Anderson, in his "Editor's Introduction" to the Yale volume of Edwards's scientific and philosophical writings, makes essentially the same point I am making, although he does not make much systematic application of it. Anderson discusses Edwards's view in "The Mind" no. 27 that resistances themselves may be best thought of as mental or as "a mode of idea." For Edwards, Anderson observes, there is still something real about resistances, presumably including

---

35. "The Mind," nos. 13, 40, *Works,* 6, pp. 344-45, 356-59.
36. Ibid., p. 385.
37. "Notes on Knowledge and Existence," *Works,* 6, p. 398.

the resistances of material kinds, and their realness consists in the divinely established laws or "the determination of God that such and such ideas [of resistances] shall be raised in created minds upon such conditions."[38] As Anderson observes:

> Edwards holds that bodies have real natures independent of the ideas and beliefs we form concerning them. But he rejects Locke's view that these real natures are unperceived and unknowable properties of substances; instead he holds that they consist in the general laws that govern the order and regularity of the series of ideas that are "raised in our minds" in the course of sense experience. These general laws, Edwards asserts, are established by God.[39]

It should be noted here that material entities are a distinguishable reality not only from human minds but also from God as well. The laws and habits that make up the permanence of material beings are the manner or method of God's direct activity of causing resistances in space or of God's raising of resistances (ideas) to human minds. Whether resistances in space are mental or not, one thing remains the same: they are direct activities of God. And the laws and habits that govern them are "the proportion of God's acting."[40] These laws and habits, however, are created principles and cannot be identified with God's disposition or actuality. They are the laws of God's activity *ad extra* and have a reference to time and space.[41] They are created and thus dependent principles but do enjoy a God-given integrity as abiding realities. God, according to Edwards, is "subject in His acting to the same laws with inferior beings."[42] So Edwards's assertion that God "must comprehend in himself all being" cannot mean that the God-world distinction is abolished; it rather means that God is the one from whom "all are derived and from whom everything is given."[43] In this way, Edwards's dispositional ontology helps us understand the particular way in which nature, as all creation, has in Edwards's thought an abiding, though thoroughly dependent, reality of its own.

38. "The Mind," nos. 27 and 36, *Works*, 6, pp. 350-51, 355.
39. "Editor's Introduction," *Works*, 6, p. 97.
40. "The Mind," no. 34, *Works*, 6, p. 353.
41. This point is also made by Egbert C. Smyth in "Jonathan Edwards's Idealism," *American Journal of Theology* 1/4 (Oct., 1897), p. 959.
42. "Miscellanies," no. 1263, Townsend, p. 193.
43. "Miscellanies," no. 697, Townsend, p. 262.

4. Nature and Humanity:
Distinctiveness and Mutuality

I have thus far argued that in Edwards's theological system the world, including the physical universe, has its own reality that is ultimately important to the end for which God created it. I have also indicated that there are reasons for not thinking of Edwards's idealism as completely vitiating the objective reality of the physical universe. Building on these discussions, I can now enter into a consideration of nature's relation to humanity in Edwards's theology.

Partly due to the biblical tradition that human beings are created in the image of God, the theological tradition of the West has accorded humanity a uniqueness that sets it apart from the rest of creation. Edwards follows this tradition but also asserts a mutuality between nature and humanity — a mutuality that is undergirded by a theocentric perspective. The distinguishing mark of humanity, for Edwards, consists in its consciousness or perception. And Edwards sometimes puts this matter rather sharply. "Perceiving being only is properly being." "Spirits are much more properly beings and more substantial than bodies." Further: "The state of the inanimate, unperceiving part of the world is nothing regarded any otherwise than in a subserviency to the perceiving or intelligent parts."[44]

Here again is a Neoplatonic influence; the spiritual is higher than the material. However, this superiority of perceiving beings has to be put in its theological context. Perceiving beings are not higher in and of themselves but rather because their special role is necessary for a theocentric reason: namely, the repetition of God's glory in time and space. God's inner beauty is repeated whenever God is known and loved in time and space, and it is the perceiving beings that are capable of knowledge and love and thus capable of actively participating in God's own project.[45] Any Neoplatonic bias toward the spiritual over the material is, in Edwards, undercut and qualified by his theocentric emphasis. In fact, the higher capacity of intelligent beings, according to Edwards, can turn into a greater evil if that capac-

---

44. "The Mind," no. 45, *Works,* 6, p. 363; "Things to be considered an[d] Written fully about," no. 44, *Works,* 6, p. 238; "Miscellanies," no. 547, Townsend, p. 136.

45. "Miscellanies," no. 547, Townsend, p. 136.

ity is used in an inappropriate way.[46] Even when this capacity of intelligent beings is rightly used, their superiority over the material has meaning only because it serves God's purpose and not in and of itself. So, "intelligent beings are created to be the consciousness of the universe, that they may perceive what God is and does."[47] Edwards writes further:

> What could this vast universe of matter, placed in such excellent order and governed by such excellent law, be good for if there was no intelligence that could know anything of it? Wherefore, it necessarily follows that intelligent beings are the end of the creation, and that their end must be to behold and admire the doings of God and magnify Him for them, and to contemplate His glories in them.[48]

Intelligent beings are the "end of creation," but this end is qualified by a more ultimate end "to behold and admire the doings of God." And this ultimate end of perceiving beings is none other than the very end of the creation itself. The uniqueness or superiority of intelligent beings, therefore, does not give them any right to dominate over other parts of the universe. Any element of anthropocentrism in Edwards is thoroughly subordinated to his theocentric outlook. In their ultimate responsibility toward God, therefore, nature and humanity are equal partners.

Perceiving beings, according to Edwards, then, have a special role in God's scheme of things. And this special role consists of "actively promoting God's glory" by virtue of their ability to repeat in time God's internal acts of knowing and loving God's beauty.[49] Now, it is upon these perceiving beings that Edwards says non-perceiving beings depend for their existence. I argued in the previous section that material things as habits and laws have a virtual reality apart from human perception. So, material entities' dependence upon consciousness cannot be for their virtual reality. What exactly, then, is the nature of this dependence? Edwards's dispositional ontology, with its undergirding theocentric perspective — the interpretative guideline of my discussion thus far — affords us at least one possible reading of the

46. "The Mind," no. 62, *Works*, 6, p. 381.
47. "Miscellanies," no. 87, *Works*, 13, p. 252.
48. "Miscellanies," no. gg, *Works*, 13, p. 185.
49. "Miscellanies," no. 547, Townsend, p. 126.

meaning of nature's ontological dependence upon human perception in Edwards's thought.

Habits and laws that make up the permanence and the virtual reality of created beings, according to Edwards, are propensities to exist in a particular manner, a manner that is fittingly related to the Divine Being. Thus, humanity's "end is to behold and admire the doings of God." The end of nature or non-perceiving beings is no less theocentrically determined. "External things," Edwards tells us, "are intended to be images of things spiritual, moral, and divine."[50] Material entities possess what Edwards calls the "secondary beauty," the sort of harmony or regularity that does not involve the consent or love between perceiving beings or the "primary beauty." But the reason why "secondary beauty" is beautiful, according to Edwards, is its resemblance to consent between spiritual beings and ultimately its analogical relation to the beauty of God.[51] Thus, material entities with their secondary beauty are essentially dispositions to be images or shadows of divine things.

At this point, it is crucial to remember that for Edwards actions or relations and actual existence are identical.[52] The essence of a being is not a separate substance but the disposition to act and to be related in a certain manner. Therefore, created entities, perceiving or non-perceiving, would exist as actual beings only in and through those actual actions and relations to which they are essentially disposed. Entities actually are, in other words, only as they are related and engaged in action.

The meaning of this is two-fold: first, perceiving beings are fully actual — that is, moved from virtuality to actuality — only when their God-directed dispositional essence is exercised, when they know and love God; and, second, non-perceiving beings would be fully actual only when their own God-directed dispositional essence is exercised, that is, when their destiny to be images or shadows of divine things is somehow played out, so to speak.

In the case of perceiving beings, knowledge and existence are explicitly correlated with each other by Edwards throughout his writ-

---

50. "Images of Divine Things," no. 203, *Works*, 11, p. 125.

51. "The Nature of True Virtue," *Works*, 8, pp. 564-65.

52. For a fuller discussion of this point, see my *The Philosophical Theology of Jonathan Edwards*, pp. 77-95.

ings. "The increasing knowledge of God in all elect creatures to all eternity is an existence, a reality infinitely worthy to be in itself."[53] But, how can the dispositional essence of material entities with their God-directed destiny be exercised and thus made explicit and actual? How can the sun and the moon, hills and mountains, attain their end of being the images or shadows of divine things? Edwards does not explicitly state an answer to this question. But my thesis is that Edwards's conception of material entities as inherently disposed to exhibit a Godward relation at least suggests an answer: namely, that non-perceiving beings could achieve their actuality as images or shadows of divine things only through a power that can see material things in their relational meaning broader than what is immediately given. This power is the imagination of the regenerate person's mind, and the true actuality of material things could then be achieved only via the regenerate person's imaginative perception of them *as* images or shadows of divine things. In perceiving beings' knowledge and love of material entities *as* images of God's beauty, their essential relation to the divine would be made *explicit mentally*, thus existing actually in a mental way.

The interpretation offered here is consistent with what Edwards actually says about what goes in the regenerate's experience of nature. After having declared that "the beauties of nature are really emanations or shadows of the excellencies of the Son of God," Edwards continues:

> When we behold the fragrant rose and lily, we see [Christ's] love and purity. So the green trees, and fields, and singing of birds are the emanations of His infinite joy and benignity. The easiness and naturalness of trees and vines are shadows of His beauty and loveliness. The crystal rivers and murmuring streams are the footsteps of His favor, grace, and beauty. When we behold the light and brightness of the sun, the goldened edges of an evening cloud, or the beauteous bow, we behold the adumbrations of His glory and goodness.[54]

What is described here is not only an epistemic event but an ontological one. Through the regenerate person's apprehension of material things as images of God's beauty, such things are not just known but

---

53. "Miscellanies," no. 1225, Townsend, pp. 152-53.
54. "Covenant of Redemption: 'Excellency of Christ,'" *Representative Selections*, p. 373.

are actualized. As Edwards himself says, "the existence of the created universe consists as much in it as in any thing: yea, this knowledge is one of the highest, most real and substantial parts of all created existence, most remote from nonentity and defect."[55] Speaking of the world as "the expression" of God's being, Edwards writes: "The very being of the expression depends on the perception of created understandings. And so much the more as the expression is known, so much the more it is."[56]

The consistency of this interpretation with Edwards's thought can be seen also by restating the discussion above from the point of view of the purpose of the creation. As noted already, the purpose of the universe is the knowledge and love of God. And, as also noted above, Edwards correlates the creature's knowledge of God with the creature's being. How can the material universe, then, attain a knowledge of God so that it fulfills the purpose of the universe and also achieves existence? Here one reaches the same conclusion discussed earlier: material things could attain a knowledge of God only indirectly, that is, by being known as an image of the knowledge of God. So Edwards says that "intelligent beings are the consciousness of the creation."[57]

Thus, whether one starts from the God-directed dispositional nature of material entities themselves, or from the purpose that God had in mind in creating the universe, the being of material entities appears to be dependent upon their being known by perceiving beings. Wallace E. Anderson once noted that Edwards could have argued the material things' ontological dependence upon perceiving beings on the basis of the purpose of the creation. Anderson further noted that Edwards never explicitly uses this argument but rather seems to have thought of the material things' dependence upon perception as self-evident.[58] This much is clear from my discussion, however: the dispositional and theocentric metaphysics articulated by Edwards is consistent with, or even requires, that the true actualization of material things cannot occur apart from the perception of regenerate minds.

Thus, the responsibility of perceiving beings vis-à-vis nature, ac-

55. "End in Creation," *Works*, 8, p. 432.

56. "Miscellanies," no. 662, Townsend, pp. 137-38.

57. "Miscellanies," no. 3, *Works*, 13, p. 200.

58. Anderson, "Editor's Introduction," *Works*, 6, pp. 78-80; See also George Rupp, "The 'Idealism' of Jonathan Edwards," *Harvard Theological Review* 62 (1969), p. 225.

cording to Edwards, is weighty indeed. But fallen humanity, with the narrowness of its imagination, cannot fulfill this responsibility toward nature, according to Edwards. It takes nothing less than the indwelling of the Holy Spirit for human minds to apprehend the wider meanings of things. Only sanctified minds with their widened imagination are able to experience things "in their true relations and respects to other things, and to things in general."[59] Thus, to put it more accurately, it is God who works in and through the regenerate and does the creative work in time and space.

So, without such a widening of the imagination, human beings do not "consent to being" but fall into a narrow or deformed perspective on reality.[60] Such a narrowness of vision is none other than sin, according to Edwards. And sin has a serious effect on nature:

This visible world has now for many ages been subjected to sin, and made as it were a servant to it, through the abusive improvement that man, who has the dominion over the creatures, puts the creatures to. Thus the sun is a sort of servant to all manner of wickedness, as its light and other beneficial influences are abused by men, and made subservient to their lusts and sinful purposes. So the rain, and the fruits of the earth, and the brute animals, and all other parts of the visible creation . . . for the creature is abused in it, perverted to far meaner purposes than those for which the author of it made it, and to which he adapted it. . . . 'Tis a bondage the creature is subject to, from which it was partly delivered when Christ came and the gospel was promulgated in the world; and will be more fully delivered at the commencement of the glorious day we are speaking of; and perfectly at the day of judgment.[61]

Nature, or the physical universe, then, is dependent upon perceiving beings for the actualization of what it was ultimately intended to

59. "Miscellanies," no. 408, *Works*, 13, p. 470.

60. Edwards wrote: "A natural [man] may love others, but 'tis some way or other as appendages and appurtenances to himself; but a spiritual man loves others as of God, or in God, or some way related to Him." "Miscellanies," no. 821, Townsend, pp. 240-41. For a fuller discussion of the effect of the indwelling of the Holy Spirit upon the imagination, see my *The Philosophical Theology of Jonathan Edwards*, pp. 140-46.

61. "An Humble Attempt," *The Works of Jonathan Edwards*, 5, *Apocalyptic Writings*, ed. Stephen J. Stein (New Haven: Yale University Press, 1977), pp. 344-45.

be. At the same time, there is a sense in which perceiving beings are also dependent upon material entities. As was noted earlier, this mutuality is grounded in the common God-given destiny that both nature and humanity share together. The essence of human beings is to know and love God and thereby repeat God's beauty in time and space, just as nature's destiny is to be images or shadows of the same divine beauty. It would follow then that perceiving beings are truly actual only when they know and love God. And if the physical universe is in any way helpful to the perceiving beings' fulfillment, then to that extent perceiving beings would be dependent upon, or at least benefited by, nature.

For one thing, nature, for Edwards, is as much God's self-revelation as the Scripture. So there is "the book of nature" and the book of Scripture. The Scripture does have a kind of centrality:

> The book of Scripture is the interpreter of the book of nature two ways, viz., by declaring to us those spiritual mysteries that are indeed signified and typified in the constitution of the natural world; and secondly, by making application of the signs and types in nature as representations of spiritual mysteries, in instances.[62]

So the Scripture is a more direct way of God's speaking, and it interprets for human beings the meaning of God's communication in nature. However, nature in itself is also a communication of God.

> And as the system of nature and the system of revelation are both divine works, so both are in different senses a divine word, both are the voice of God to intelligent creatures, a manifestation and declaration of Himself to mankind.[63]

At the same time, the book of nature has certain advantages over the book of Scripture:

> If we look on these shadows of divine things as the voice of God purposely by them teaching us these and those spiritual and divine things, to show of what excellent advantages it will be, how agreeably and clearly it will tend to convey instruction to our minds, and to impress things on the mind and to affect the mind, by that we

62. "Images of Divine Things," no. 156, *Works*, 11, p. 106.
63. "Miscellanies," no. 1340, Townsend, p. 233.

may, as it were, have God speaking to us. Wherever we are, and whatever we are about, we may see divine things excellently represented and held forth. And it will abundantly tend to confirm the Scripture, for there is an excellent agreement between these things and the holy Scripture.[64]

So the concrete images and representations of the divine beauty in nature have a contribution to make by virtue of their being *physical*. Images in nature "agreeably and clearly will tend to convey instruction to our minds," and "impress things on the mind and affect the mind." Concrete physical images, therefore, facilitate God's communication to perceiving beings. But beyond their facilitating function, natural images as such *are* emanations, communications or embodiments of God's beauty and God's truth. Thus, when Christ makes use of material images of spiritual truth, "these things are not merely mentioned as illustrations of meaning, but as illustrations and evidences of the truth of what he says."[65] So, as communications of God in their own right, natural images "abundantly tend to confirm the Scripture."

In short, just as the physical universe depends upon perceiving beings for the actualization of their God-given destiny, perceiving beings are also helped by nature in the actualization of their own being. When the regenerate person knows and loves nature as an image of God's beauty, that person's own dispositional essence is exercised. That person becomes actually what a human being is intended to be, namely, "the image of God's own knowledge of himself."[66] The dependence of humanity upon nature could not be more fundamental. And the mutual dependence of nature and humanity is ultimately grounded in their common destiny of being the participants in God's own self-extension in time. To put it differently, the mutuality of nature and humanity is part of the mutuality God has with the world; and through this mutuality, God, nature, and humanity are united and thereby enlarged.

64. "Images of Divine Things," no. 70, *Works*, 11, p. 74.
65. Ibid., no. 26, p. 57.
66. "End in Creation," *Works*, 8, p. 441.

5. Edwards's Typology of Nature

In recent years, Edwards's theory of typology has received consider-able attention from scholars.[67] I wish to mention two aspects of that theory and suggest that they must be understood in the framework of Edwards's dynamic reconception of God and God's end in creation.

The first has to do with Edwards's extension of the use of typology to nature, which was first noted by Perry Miller in his intro-duction to *Images or Shadows of Divine Things*.[68] The strict practice of typological interpretation was to identify the prefigurations of the Christ event in the Old Testament history. But Edwards extended ty-pological interpretation beyond Scripture to history in general and to the physical universe. The sun, moon, stars, the flocking of birds, and indeed "the whole outward creation," according to Edwards, are im-ages or shadows, that is, types, of divine things.[69] The question has been: What in Edwards's fabric of thinking is moving him to typologize even nature?

Edwards's dynamic reconception of God and God's end in cre-ation is, I believe, fundamental to his typological practices. The basic direction of my interpretation has been already set forth by scholars such as Janice Knight and Mason Lowance. Janice Knight, identifying Edwards's doctrine of God as inherently self-communicating as the key to his extension of typology to nature, has written: "Simply stated, Edwards's theory of typology rested on a faith that the coming of the kingdom establishes God's glory on earth as it is in heaven."[70] After many years of studying Edwards's theory of typology, Mason Lowance has concluded that it is Edwards's christology coupled with his "awareness that God was actually speaking to his saints through the representative, symbolic, *typological* language of nature, that gave Jonathan Edwards's writings on typology a transforming authority over the rigid practices" of earlier periods.[71]

My own proposal pushes a bit further the identification by Knight and Lowance of Edwards's doctrine of God as the key to his typology. As we have seen, Edwards's dispositional reformulation of the doc-

---

67. See note 3.
68. Miller, "Introduction," *Images or Shadows of Divine Things*, pp. 27-37.
69. "Images of Divine Things," nos. 53 and 79, *Works*, 11, pp. 65-66, 81.
70. Knight, "Learning the Language of God," p. 533.
71. Lowance, "Editor's Introduction," *Works*, 11, p. 181.

trine of God leads to the view of creation in which God's end in creation is the repetition in time and space of God's internal glory. The everlasting span of human history, as well as the physical universe itself, in other words, are to be an extension of God's own life. It is no wonder, then, that nature receives the attention it does in Edwards's thought.

The second aspect of Edwards's typological theory that has received much scholarly attention is the importance which Edwards assigns to the this-worldly facticity or historicity *per se* of types, whether natural or historical. What scholars have noticed is that a type, for Edwards, points to its antitype not because a type is a mere reflection of some meaning that transcends the spatio-temporal world but rather because a type in its own earthly nature has within itself the intentionality for relations. In Stephen Daniel's words, a type has "its immanent demand for completion in an other."[72] Perry Miller, in his introduction to *Images or Shadows of Divine Things*, already noted that Edwards, influenced by Lockean empiricism, sought to find "in things an intelligibility not transcending them but immanent in them."[73] This is not to forget, however, that the ultimate meaning and reference of earthly types had a transcendent ground. Types were images or shadows of the things of God. The ultimate antitype, as Mason Lowance reminds us, "after all, was Christ, who was not to be restricted to temporal boundaries, but is eternal and atemporal."[74] How then do we explain Edwards's grounding of the ultimate meaning of all types in the transcendent God and Edwards's clear emphasis on the historicity and immanence of the earthly types' meaning within the types themselves?

The answer again, I submit, is Edwards's dynamic reconception of God and God's creation of the world. God *ad intra* is the eternally complete and perfect being who is the fountain of all creativity and the criterion of all meaning. But, as we have seen, the world is meant to be a repetition of God's own prior actuality in such a way that the world is an extension of God's own life. God is the disposition to repeat God's own life in time and space. The temporal and spatial types or images and shadows of the divine things, therefore, need to be temporal and

72. Daniel, *The Philosophy of Jonathan Edwards*, p. 50.
73. Miller, "Introduction," *Images or Shadows of Divine Things*, p. 29.
74. Lowance, "Editor's Introduction," *Works*, 11, p. 181.

spatial in the reality and meaning even from God's point of view. In this way, Edwards's insistence upon the immanence of the meaningfulness of types in types themselves is not inconsistent with his equally strong affirmation of God's own internal life as the earthly types' ultimate ground and meaning.

If the created system of being is to be a repetition of God's internal fullness, the world then would have to have a dependent and yet real integrity of its own. That is to say, the created existence would have to be a beautiful system or network of relations which repeats God's inner-trinitarian glory. The world in all of its spatio-temporal reality would have to repeat all the coherence, harmony, or excellence of God's own being. Seen in this light, Stephen Daniel's insistence that the reference and meaningfulness of the earthly types be found within the temporal network of relations is entirely understandable and is consistent with Edwards's perspective.[75] I have written elsewhere that

> a material entity's connection with the spiritual truths of God is not something that the human beholder imposes upon it; such a connection is something to which the law of that material entity itself tends — something that is itself an integral part of the total framework of created laws.[76]

This emphasis upon the immanence of relational meaning, however, would not entail an exclusion of the possibility of such meaning's ultimate grounding in a transcendent reference point as Daniel seems to believe it does.[77] Edwards's doctrine of the world as a repetition of God's own life, I believe, enables us to respect the integrity of the immanent harmony of the world without compromising the reality of the eternal God as the source and foundation of that immanent harmony.

6. The Ecological Promise of Edwards's Theology: Fecundity and the Migration to a Good Land

Now I would like briefly to draw a connection between Edwards's theology of nature and our contemporary ecological concerns. H. Paul

---

75. See Daniel, *The Philosophy of Jonathan Edwards*, for example pp. 20-40, 50-82.
76. *The Philosophical Theology of Jonathan Edwards*, p. 89.
77. Daniel, *The Philosophy of Jonathan Edwards*, for example pp. 67, 105.

Santmire, who has written extensively on the theology of ecology, has challenged the impression in the minds of some that Christian theological tradition in its roots is unhelpful to, or even uninterested in, the ecological concerns regarding the physical environment. In his historical survey of select Christian theologies, Santmire describes those theologies that are affirming of nature with the help of two metaphors: the metaphor of fecundity (over against ascent) and the metaphor of a migration to a good land.[78]

The metaphor of fecundity represents a world-affirming perspective in which one ascends toward the higher levels of being in order to achieve fulfillment, but does so not to leave the world behind but rather to appreciate it with a wider vision. Thus, with such a vision, one sees the fullness of being and beauty in all parts of the mundane world. This metaphor of fecundity, therefore, is contrasted to the metaphor of ascent that stresses the need to leave the world behind. The metaphor of a migration to a good land has to do with the place of the earthly and the bodily in the vision for the future. This metaphor contrasts with an other-worldly vision for the ultimate future; it carries with it a hope for the fulfillment of the earthly rather than its elimination.

Both of these metaphors are appropriate to Edwards's thought. First of all, there is ascent in Edwards's worldview, but it is for a fuller apprehension of the fecundity of the mundane rather than an eschewal of it. Here again Edwards's dynamic conception of God and God's relation to the world functions as the critical background. God's end in creating the world is that God's own life be extended and repeated *ad extra* in time and space. Thus, time and space have an ultimate significance in Edwards's perspective. And the fulfillment of the world has to be within the matrix of time and space and not outside of them.

Thus, the regenerate person's religious experience which constitutes the actualization of his or her own being and also of God's end in creation involves an ascent — an ascent, however, that has the purpose of returning. The ascent, in Edwards, is necessary because every created entity is to be a repetition or image of God's beauty, and one cannot repeat God's beauty without knowing and loving it. The knowl-

78. H. Paul Santmire, *The Travail of Nature: The Ambiguous Ecological Promise of Christian Theology* (Philadelphia: Fortress Press, 1985), pp. 13-29.

edge and love of God, for Edwards, is the first requirement for all ontological and epistemic fulfillment.

This movement of ascent-and-return-to-earth is dramatically illustrated in Edwards's account of his own experience of God. Edwards writes in his "Personal Narrative":

> Not long after I first began to experience these things, I gave an account to my father of something that had passed in my mind. I was pretty affected by the discourse we had together; and when the discourse was ended, I walked abroad alone, in a solitary place in my father's pasture, for contemplation. As I was walking there, and looking up on the sky and clouds, there came into my mind so sweet a sense of the glorious *majesty* and *grace* of God, that I know not how to express. I seemed to see them both in a sweet conjunction; majesty and meekness together; it was a sweet, and gentle, and holy majesty; and also a majestic meekness; an awful sweetness; a high, and great, and holy gentleness.[79]

Edwards's ascent to his inexpressible experience of God did not in any way remove him from the earth but rather brought him right back to it — but with a difference. He continues:

> After this my sense of divine things gradually increased, and became more and more lively, and had more of that inward sweetness. The appearance of every thing was altered; there seemed to be, as it were, a calm, sweet cast, or appearance of divine glory, in almost every thing. God's excellency, his wisdom, his purity and love, seemed to appear in every thing; in the sun, moon, and stars; in the clouds, and blue sky; in the grass, flowers, trees; in the water, and all nature; which used to fix my mind. I often used to sit and view the moon for continuance; and in the day, spent much time in viewing the clouds and sky, to behold the sweet glory of God in these things; in the mean time, singing forth, with a low voice my contemplations of the Creator and Redeemer.[80]

It is true that in the same "Personal Narrative," Edwards occasionally uses a few times the kind of expression that may make the reader suspect a world-denying way of thinking. In his experience

79. "Personal Narrative," *Representative Selections*, p. 60.
80. Ibid., pp. 60-61.

of God, Edwards felt "wrapt and swallowed up in God," involving "a calm, sweet abstraction of soul from all the concerns of this world."[81] Such traces of Neoplatonism are scarce in the "Personal Narrative," however. The document is, rather, overwhelmingly full of references to concrete natural objects, such as the sun and the moon, trees and grass, which, in their being what they are, embody and manifest the divine glory. The end for which God created the world needs material objects. Time and space are not left behind in Edwards's view of the religious imagination; they rather make up the very stuff of it.

The other metaphor for nature-affirming theology, "the migration to a good land," also finds an affinity to Edwards's thought. Nature or the physical reality has a positive role in Edwards's vision for the ultimate future of the creation. As was noted already, the accomplishment of God's end in creation, according to Edwards, is going to take an "infinite duration" since the end, befitting God, is "an infinite end."[82] What has to be repeated in time is none other than the infinite glory of God, and thus this project can never come to a temporal completion. The eschaton represents the finishing of God's redemption of the fallen creation that puts it on track again, so to speak, for the accomplishing of God's end in creation. So redemption comes to a terminus. But God's end in creation does not. So God's end in creation has to go on in a process of an unending progress. Thus, there needs to be time and space in some form for an unending duration. The spatio-temporal realm after the end of the present one is the "new heaven and new earth" in which physical reality, in a new form, will have a positive role.[83]

At the eschaton, God will put an end to the world as we know it now "as a machine is taken down when it has answered the workman's end." He will not leave it "to a gradual decay."[84] So there is an end to this creation but the creation does not end. As promised in Revelation 21:1, there will be "a new heaven and new earth." Noting how this new world contains a "new earth," Edwards comments:

'Tis probable 'tis called by the name of the new earth, because 'tis the place of the habitation of bodies as well as souls, a place wherein their

81. Ibid., pp. 60, 59.
82. "Miscellanies," no. 1006, Townsend, p. 196.
83. *Works, 9, A History of the Work of Redemption,* pp. 348-50, 508-10.
84. "Miscellanies," no. 1263, Townsend, p. 189.

bodily senses shall be exercised. There shall be that whereon they shall tread with their feet, and an expanse over their heads.[85]

So there is a continuity between the bodily reality of this world and that of the new world. But there is also a discontinuity. Edwards does not see just a restoration of the old fallen world but a radical new construction, that is, a restoration without sin and corruptibility, and a restoration with new perfection. It will be "vastly, immensely more glorious than it was before the fall . . . a new one materially as well as in form."[86] The new quality of the physical universe is described by Edwards, as follows:

> How ravishing are the proportions of the reflections of rays of light, and the proportions of the vibrations of the air! And without doubt, God can contrive matter so that there shall be other sort of proportions, that may be quite of a different kind, and may raise another sort of pleasure in a sense, and in a manner to us inconceivable, that shall be vastly more ravishing and exquisite . . . there shall be external beauties and harmonies altogether of another kind from what we perceive here, and probably those beauties will appear chiefly on the bodies of the man Christ Jesus and of the saints.[87]

And the saints will see "a divine person [the man Christ Jesus] with bodily eyes in the same manner as we see one another."[88]

In conclusion: Nature or the physical universe has an important and positive place in Edwards's framework of thought. For that reason, Edwards belongs to the list of theologians who are helpful in the contemporary search for an ecologically responsible theology of nature. His dispositional ontology secures nature a reality of its own apart from perception although nature's ultimate destiny requires perception for its actualization.

The contemporary helpfulness of Edwards's theology of nature, however, is properly understood only within the framework of Edwards's highly innovative reconception of God and God's relation to the world. For Edwards, God creates the world because God's inher-

---

85. "Apocalypse Series," no. 41, *Works,* 5, p. 141.
86. Ibid., no. 40, p. 141.
87. "Miscellanies," no. 182, *Works,* 13, p. 328.
88. "Miscellanies," no. 678, quoted from *Works,* 8, pp. 723-24.

ent disposition moves him to extend or repeat his eternal reality into the realm of time and space, thereby making time and space ultimately significant.

Postmodern Concepts of God and Edwards's Trinitarian Ontology

STEPHEN H. DANIEL

F or some people, the mere mention of postmodern theology is reason enough to suspend the niceties of civil discussion. In their
minds, *postmodern* is associated with the denial of reality, disbelief in
God, epistemological skepticism, and moral relativism. Any attempt
to discern a theology in postmodern beliefs must certainly be a waste
of time or an occasion, perhaps, for derision if not outright condemnation.[1] For if certain tenets of postmodern thought are taken seriously,
that would mean the end of much of what passes as theological reflection.

It is definitely not my purpose here to develop a definition of
postmodernity that would respond to the concerns of those who see it
as the road to perdition. But since postmodern themes pop up with relative frequency these days in discussions about God, it is useful to examine just what is identified as postmodern theology and to determine the extent to which its ideas can clarify issues about doctrines
that are as problematic today as they were for Edwards.

My raising Edwards's name within a discussion of postmodernity

---

1. See Bruce L. McCormack, "Graham Ward's *Barth, Derrida and the Language of
Theology,*" *Scottish Journal of Theology* 49 (1996), pp. 97, 109; and Ronald F.
Thiemann, "Response to George Lindbeck's 'Barth and Textuality,'" *Theology Today*
43 (1986), pp. 377-82.

might strike some as anachronistic and even perverse. Certainly, talk of the death of God, concrescing actual entities, or pan-textuality is so remote from his concerns that it would require an act of faith to see any connection between him and some of our contemporaries. Nevertheless, I am going to suggest that Edwards's treatments of (1) God as the space of intelligibility and (2) the Trinity as a communication hint at ideas that have become focal in postmodern discussions. I am also going to suggest that recognizing such a parallel helps us understand why Karl Barth links revelation necessarily to the Trinity. For if (as Barth notes) the nature of revelation itself requires us to think of God in trinitarian terms, then many of the problems traditionally associated with trying to understand the status and relations of the persons of the Trinity can be replaced by an analysis of the discursive character of existence.

As postmodern theorists indicate, in such an analysis existence is a function of discourse and is not simply presumed by discourse. By treating God no longer as a substance or subject but as the communicative matrix in terms of which everything is meaningful, this shift in focus shares, with Barth, the Heideggerian turn from the study of beings to the study of how Being is revealed. In its terms, revelation becomes the key for understanding the nature of God as the principle of intelligibility, and it identifies God as inherently intentional and discursive. To say (as Edwards does) that God is communicative would mean, then, that God and the persons of the Trinity are defined in terms of communication, and that the rationale for God's triune nature is based on the nature of discourse.

Insofar as this reorientation toward communication suspends the assumption that God is like a Cartesian-Lockean substance or subject, it reorients how we understand Edwards's doctrines in two ways. First, it identifies God as communication itself, about which no transcendental claim can be made (except in a derivative sense, as when we speak of human communication), since there is nothing other than the discursive space in which such claims can be communicated. This notion of God is not of some being who transcends all discourse; rather, it is the notion of the discourse in terms of which talk of being and transcendence is itself intelligible. Second, since all claims about God are ultimately claims about discourse, the key for speaking about God would consist in focusing on features that characterize meaning, significance, or intelligibility. That is what Edwards does through his doctrines of God's *ad intra* communication (the Trinity) and God's *ad extra* communication (creation).[2] Rather than describing some fact about the nature of God or the relation of God to the world, those doctrines display how God and world become meaningful within a discursive process or matrix. Since the notions of God, being, or cause are intelligible only in virtue of this discourse, God cannot be presupposed as the being who accounts for the discourse (other than in a derivative sense). In order to avoid the conclusion that God is derivative, Edwards portrays God as the communicative process or matrix of intelligibility itself. In terms of that discourse, God can subsequently be understood as internally intelligible (viz., as a Trinity) and as externally intelligible (viz., as the rationale of the world).

When associated with Barth's doctrines and those of postmodern theology, Edwards's model of divine communication provides a radical alternative to the classical-modern way in which the problematic of God and the persons of the Trinity is typically formulated. For example, discussions of Edwards's treatments of the Trinity and God's creative activity often correctly point out that divine communication is based on God's inherent disposition, and that such a disposition is essential to what God is.[3] But to say that God has a disposition to communicate in virtue of who he is merely describes *how* God's actions are based on his nature without explaining *why* God has such a disposition in the first place. So even if it is true that Edwards describes being in terms of a dispositional ontology, the more important question would have to do with why he *has to* adopt such an ontology or what is gained by his doing so.

Of course, someone might claim (as Edwards himself does) that God communicates as a result of his fullness or glory, and that the internal glory of God as the Trinity explains the external glory of creation.[4] The question then becomes what it means to say that God has a

2. See Stephen H. Daniel, *The Philosophy of Jonathan Edwards: A Study in Divine Semiotics* (Indianapolis: Indiana University Press, 1994), pp. 114-28.

3. See Sang Hyun Lee, *The Philosophical Theology of Jonathan Edwards* (Princeton: Princeton University Press, 1988), pp. 196-210; and Anri Morimoto, *Jonathan Edwards and the Catholic Vision of Salvation* (University Park: Pennsylvania State University Press, 1995), pp. 99-101, 148-50.

4. See Jonathan Edwards, "Dissertation concerning the End for which God Created the World," in *The Works of Jonathan Edwards*, 8, *Ethical Writings*, ed. Paul Ramsey (New Haven: Yale University Press, 1989), pp. 439-40, 452.

disposition to communicate himself in virtue of his fullness or glory. For Edwards, that is like asking what it means to mean something, and to that question he responds by pointing repeatedly to the Trinity as the model for cognitive and affective integration. Since that same question is at the heart of the postmodern agenda, it is likely that the key to Edwards's doctrine of the Trinity lies in appreciating just how much his ideas subvert classical-modern assumptions.

Accordingly, I will argue (1) that ideas that are implicit in Edwards and Barth become more thematically accessible by considering how postmodern theology focuses on the meaning of intelligibility; (2) that one of those ideas is that significance or intelligibility is necessarily creative, communicative, revelatory, *and thus trinitarian;* and (3) that this explains in part why the doctrine of the Trinity is now such a hot topic in theological circles — especially where postmodern themes (such as the rejection of humanistic subjectivity) have drawn significant attention.

I. The Space of God

By associating Edwards and Barth with postmodernity, I don't mean to imply that they are proto-postmoderns, for they obviously do not adopt the strategies typically identified as postmodern. But they do draw on doctrines that, according to postmodern critiques, are ignored or subverted in the Platonic-Aristotelian metaphysics of substances and in the representationalist epistemologies of Descartes and Locke. In particular, they insist on the primacy of revelation as that in which *the beginning* was truly *the Word* — expressive creativity — not some transcendental subject who uttered the Word. This, in turn, requires that we acknowledge that existence is a function of revelation and that discourse precedes and identifies the parties of communication.

This same emphasis on the immanent process by which intelligibility or signification is established is what guides much of postmodern theology. It appears in the postmodern dismissal of attempts to describe ultimate principles of existence in grand transcendental narratives.[5] It also appears in the postmodern insistence that binary

5. See A. T. Nuyen, "Postmodern Theology and Postmodern Philosophy," *International Journal for the Philosophy of Religion* 30 (1991), pp. 65-67.

oppositions like God and world, or self and other, are functions of a discursive activity that is itself intelligible only in the derivative terms it inscribes. Because the change to a postmodern mentality requires that we consider all intelligible existence as inherently communicative, it is a way of thinking that is difficult for classical-modern critics of process theology, semiotics, and deconstruction to imagine.

. Just how difficult such a change of mind can be is apparent in Augustine's fruitless efforts to make sense of such ideas when he encounters them in the Cappadocian view of the Trinity. Since Edwards's doctrine of *ad intra* communication among the persons of the Trinity and Barth's insistence that the nature of the Trinity is revealed in revelation draw on similar presuppositions, they likewise continue to confound readers.

The fact that some postmodern ideas have been around for some time should come as little surprise to those who recall how the early Stoics challenge the attempt to speak of world, self, or God as if they were things about which we can predicate attributes.[6] For the Stoics, the primacy of *Logos* is expressed most obviously by subordinating the logic of predication to the semantics of propositions. Subjects and predicates (they argue) have meaning in virtue of their places in practical activity and exchange, since only through discursive alignments are things identified as things at all. So in the Stoic mentality, any attempt to deduce the conditions for thought apart from a communicative matrix is unintelligible.

But postmodern theory does not merely reinstate an earlier, alternative way of thinking. Rather, it engages in a critique of thinking itself, inasmuch as it questions the transcendental possibility of relating an unmediated world to a transparent self. For postmoderns, the effort to interpret experience in order to discern some reality behind it inevitably fails, not because of human inabilities but because both world and self are functions of the discursive processes in terms of which any purported interpretation would have to be couched. The justification for hermeneutics is thus undermined simply by recognizing how all

6. See Gilles Deleuze, *The Logic of Sense*, trans. Mark Lester and Charles Stivale; ed. Constantin V. Boundas (New York: Columbia University Press, 1990), pp. 4-9, 19, 132-33; Benson Mates, *Stoic Logic* (Berkeley: University of California Press, 1961), pp. 2, 11-13; and A. A. Long, *Hellenistic Philosophy: Stoics, Epicureans, Sceptics* (New York: Charles Scribner's Sons, 1974), pp. 121-24, 142-43.

strategies of interpretation are conditioned by the presuppositions that allow those strategies to be employed.

Instead of interpreting God's revelation, postmodern theology describes how God and his creation are originally discernible as functions of revelation. This reorientation in mentality is so radical that it amounts, in Edwards's account, to the kind of difference that distinguishes the elect from the rest of fallen humanity.[7] Unlike those who are stained with the original sin of Cartesian-Lockean subjectivity, the elect recognize that all things are significant in terms of the divine discourse in which they are embedded. In that discourse, the mind of the saint designates the complexes of meaning in which things are related; and bodies are seen as functions of solidity, resistance, gravity, and motion.[8] Neither minds nor bodies, therefore, are substances to which meaning or significance is attached; they are rather various expressions or meanings themselves. What they are is what they mean, and what they mean always consists in pointing to something other than themselves.

Since personality or intention is a function of this discursive matrix, all references to God as a subject or a person must thus be understood as derivative. In line with Heidegger's critique of ontotheology, this means that instead of thinking about God as if he were *a* being or being *itself*, we must first presuppose the context or "clearing" in which the distinction of self and other is made intelligible.[9] But since that context or discursive matrix is what identifies even God's subjectivity and existence, it cannot be said to exist nor can it be alluded to (via negative theology) in transcendental terms. It is unrepresentable and can only be displayed, as Barth remarks, as "the hiddenness of the revealed," the *mysterium* in which God "cannot unveil Himself to us in any other way than by veiling Himself."[10] God is revealed not as a subject behind the text of the revelation; rather, God is revealed *as* the text of revelation.

---

7. See Daniel, *Philosophy of Edwards*, p. 131.

8. See Edwards, "Of Atoms"; and "The Mind," no. 21(a), no. 27, no. 29, no. 36, in *The Works of Jonathan Edwards*, 6, *Scientific and Philosophical Writings*, ed. Wallace E. Anderson (New Haven: Yale University Press, 1980), pp. 215-16, 345-46, 351-52, 355; and Daniel, *Philosophy of Edwards*, pp. 95-100.

9. See Robert Scharlemann, ed., *Theology at the End of the Century: A Dialogue on the Postmodern* (Charlottesville: University of Virginia Press, 1990), pp. 2-6.

10. Karl Barth, *Church Dogmatics*, trans. G. T. Thomson, 2nd ed. (Edinburgh: T. & T. Clark, 1960), I.1, 188, 371.

For classical-modernists, such pronouncements merely add to the unintelligible jargon and syntactic flights of fancy they ascribe to postmodern theorizing. So instead of trying to make sense of this different approach, philosophers and theologians continue to rely on presuppositions of subjectivity and substantialist ontology that force them to refer to God and the Persons of the Trinity in inevitably unsatisfactory ways. Their unfortunate situation is often written off simply as a limitation of human language or intelligence. But postmodern theology attributes the ongoing confusion less to the inherent complexity of the topics than to an inability to appreciate how those topics require a thoroughly different methodology.

Spelling out what that other methodology might entail is at the heart of process, semiotic, and deconstructive theologies. Though feminist and liberation theologies also have postmodern features, their ontological reassessments of the divine body or abject "matrix" of "a God in the feminine" have focused thus far only indirectly on the presuppositions of intelligibility.[11] By contrast, process, semiotic, and deconstructive theologies thematize God's intelligibility as a *product* of creative expression. They do not ascribe the creation of meaning to God as some self-thinking subject, but instead emphasize how in the beginning was *the Word*, the aboriginal discursive activity which embodies the split or divided subjectivity in terms of which intelligibility is originally possible.

This focus rejects classical-modern interpretations of Whitehead's creativity, Peirce's semiosis, and Derrida's *différence* as activities engaged in by a self, because in postmodern views, subjectivity or identity (including God's subjectivity or identity) is intelligible only in terms of such notions. Postmodernity thus extols distinctly anti-humanistic and anti-relativistic views in that it does not privilege the individual subject as a source of meaning. This displacement of divine subjectivity signals, as Paul Tillich puts it, the "God above God," the God who is a symbol for the absolute, transcendent, and humanistic subject of modernity.[12] In such terms, creativity is not some super-

---

11. Cf. *The Postmodern Bible,* ed. George Aichele et al. (New Haven: Yale University Press, 1995), pp. 214-22; and Philippa Berry, "Woman and Space According to Kristeva and Irigarary," in *Shadow of Spirit: Postmodernism and Religion,* ed. Philippa Berry and Andrew Wernick (New York: Routledge, 1992), pp. 254-55.

12. See Paul Tillich, *The Courage to Be* (New Haven: Yale University Press, 1952), pp. 182-90; and Paul Tillich, *The Dynamics of Faith* (New York: Harper Torchbooks, 1958), p. 46. Cf. Max A. Myers, "Toward What Is Religious Thinking

transcendent Being who includes God and the world, nor can it be an object of predication. Rather, it is that in virtue of which everything else has an identity. Even it can be said to have *an* identity only in derivative terms.

Barth recognizes that this means that, properly speaking, God is "Himself Space," the discursive space in which all else comes to have an identity.[13] Edwards makes the same point, noting that to attempt to think of God as something that could be placed in a binary relation is already to assume that which has no counterpart. As Edwards puts it:

> Space is this necessary, eternal, infinite and omnipresent being. We find that we can with ease conceive how all other beings should not be. We can remove them out of our minds, and place some other in the room of them; but space is the very thing that we can never remove and conceive of its not being. . . . But I had as good speak plain: I have already said as much as that space is God.[14]

Not only is God, for Edwards, not just another being; he is also not Being *itself*. Since the space of God is not in dialectical opposition to Non-being, it is (as the postmoderns say) the Other to otherness.[15] And because there is no other in relation to which God is intelligible, he cannot be understood aboriginally in the personalist or subject-object terms that normally characterize discussions about God as creator and the Trinity.

Underway?" in Thomas J. J. Altizer et al., *Deconstruction and Theology* (New York: Crossroad, 1982), pp. 137-38; Charles E. Winquist, "The Silence of *The Real:* Theology at the End of the Century," in *Theology at the End of the Century,* p. 36; and Gary A. Phillips, "Exegesis as Critical Praxis: Reclaiming History and Text from a Postmodern Perspective," in *Poststructural Criticism and the Bible: Text/History/Discourse,* ed. Gary A. Phillips (Atlanta: Scholars Press, 1990), pp. 24-25.

13. See Barth, *Church Dogmatics,* II.1, 470; and Colin E. Gunton, "Barth, the Trinity, and Human Freedom," *Theology Today* 43 (1986), p. 317.

14. Edwards, "Of Being," in *Works,* 6, *Scientific and Philosophical Writings,* pp. 203, 207. Cf. "Editor's Introduction," *Works,* 6, pp. 24, 57-58, 74; and Stephen H. Daniel, "Toland's Semantic Pantheism," in *John Toland's "Christianity Not Mysterious,"* ed. Philip McGuinness (Dublin: Lilliput Press, 1997). Also see Daniel, *Philosophy of Edwards,* pp. 84-88.

15. See D. G. Leahy, "The New Beginning: Beyond the Post-Modern Nothingness," *Journal of the American Academy of Religion* 62 (1994), pp. 408-12, 429-31.

II. The Persons of the Trinity as Functions of Revelation

This shift in theological strategies results, of course, in the death of a certain kind of God — the kind of God who is a subject or substance, and about whom the doctrine of three persons in one nature has been, to say the least, problematic. It is here, though, that postmodern concepts can be most helpful in refocusing current trinitarian theology away from the substantialist model of God as a self-conscious subject to the model of God as the discursive space of intelligibility. Using that latter model, it is much easier to avoid concluding that the three "persons" of the Trinity are either three Gods or three modes of an individual self.

Commentators as astute as Jürgen Moltmann and Wolfhart Pannenberg claim that, in order to skirt such conclusions, Barth and Rahner adapt a Hegelian philosophy of spirit in which the Father's self-identity is established by positing the Son as his other.[16] But this is to read Barth and Rahner as if they endorse the substantialist ontology that dominates many trinitarian discussions. To think of the Father as an aboriginal subject would merely internalize substantialist relations rather than replace substantialist thinking altogether. So Barth and (perhaps less explicitly) Rahner appeal instead to the discursive and propositional space of revelation. That space cannot be reinscribed in the derivative terms of substantialist ontology and subjectivity, because to do so would mean appealing to yet another discursive space in terms of which *it* is understood as some thing, thus generating an infinite regress. So Barth concludes that attempts to model trinitarian personhood on human social relations (such as those proposed later by Moltmann, Pannenberg, and Eberhard Jüngel) must be rejected.[17]

---

16. Cf. David Brown, *Continental Philosophy and Modern Theology* (Oxford: Basil Blackwell, 1987), pp. 63, 141, 145; John L. Gresham, Jr., "The Social Model of the Trinity and Its Critics," *Scottish Journal of Theology* 46 (1993), p. 329; Ronald J. Feenstra and Cornelius Plantinga, Jr., eds., *Trinity, Incarnation, and Atonement: Philosophical and Theological Essays* (Notre Dame: University of Notre Dame Press, 1989), pp. 4-7; Roger E. Olson, "Wolfhart Pannenberg's Doctrine of the Trinity," *Scottish Journal of Theology* 43 (1990), pp. 184-85; and Anselm K. Min, "The Trinity and the Incarnation: Hegel and Classical Approaches," *The Journal of Religion* 66 (1986), pp. 184-86.

17. See Paul D. Molnar, "The Function of the Immanent Trinity in the Theology of Karl Barth: Implications for Today," *Scottish Journal of Theology* 42 (1989), pp. 369, 381-98. Cf. Jürgen Moltmann, *The Trinity and the Kingdom* (Minneapolis: Fortress

Since Barth and Edwards often sound as if they agree with these "social trinitarians," it is important to be clear about how they differ from them. Though social trinitarians do not assume that the three persons of the Trinity are distinct substances or subjects, some think that the Father, Son, and Holy Spirit are distinct centers of consciousness that are related in their mutual recognition and love of one another.[18] This idea of the Trinity as a community is certainly more person-oriented than Augustine's psychological portrait of divine memory, understanding, and will. But it hardly explains how to think of them as *self-conscious* individuals except by appealing to an analogy of human relationships.[19] And that is precisely the kind of subject-based ontology that is typically denied for trinitarian relations. So even if the persons of the Trinity are conscious without being self-conscious, or are self-conscious only in acknowledging the transcendence of their individuality in the unity of the Godhead, it is still difficult to see what is gained by invoking the vocabulary of personhood.[20]

The Cappadocian solution to this problem (especially as developed by Gregory of Nyssa) is the one that Edwards appropriates.[21] According to it, the communion of the Trinity *ad intra* is not a communication among persons who exist apart from the communication. Rather, it is the communication itself that defines the three divine per-

---

Press, 1993); Wolfhart Pannenberg, *Systematic Theology* (Edinburgh: T. & T. Clark, 1991-94); and Eberhard Jüngel, *God as the Mystery of the World* (Grand Rapids: Eerdmans, 1983). By contrast, see Robert W. Jenson, "What Is the Point of Trinitarian Theology?" in *Trinitarian Theology Today: Essays on Divine Being and Act*, ed. Christoph Schwöbel (Edinburgh: T. &. T. Clark, 1995), pp. 32-33.

18. See Cornelius Plantinga, Jr., "Social Trinity and Tritheism," in Feenstra and Plantinga, *Trinity*, p. 22; Colin E. Gunton, *The Promise of Trinitarian Theology* (Edinburgh: T. & T. Clark, 1991), pp. 10, 156; Todd H. Speidell, "A Trinitarian Ontology of Persons in Society," *Scottish Journal of Theology* 47 (1994), p. 285; Joseph A. Bracken, *The Triune Symbol: Persons, Process, and Community* (Lanham, MD: University Press of America, 1985), p. 29; and T. W. Bartel, "Could There Be More Than One Almighty?" *Religious Studies* 29 (1993), p. 466.

19. See Brown, *Continental Philosophy*, pp. 69-72; and Bracken, *Triune Symbol*, pp. 17, 27.

20. Cf. David Brown, "Trinitarian Personhood and Individuality," in Feenstra and Plantinga, *Trinity*, pp. 49-54, 69.

21. See Robert W. Jenson, *America's Theologian: A Recommendation of Jonathan Edwards* (New York: Oxford University Press, 1988), p. 93; and Michael Jinkins, "'The Being of Beings': Jonathan Edwards's Understanding of God as Reflected in His Final Treatises," *Scottish Journal of Theology* 46 (1993), p. 183n.

sons as functions of the communication.[22] The three persons are thus not modes of being of a logically prior substance or substratum but are rather (as Barth notes) subsistences or modes of existing. That is, they are the characteristics of divine communicability itself.[23] God is not a substance underlying the communication; he is *the substance of* communication or, as Edwards concludes, the only true substance.[24]

Barth puts it this way: The doctrine of the Trinity explicates the *subject* of revelation by showing how the activity of revelation is something that God *is* rather than something that God *does.* In the Bible God is portrayed as a concrete authority and agent — specifically, a revealer — in order to draw attention to the nature of revelation as that which authorizes all things (including human existence). Revelation is thus the self-interpretation or "self-unveiling" of God as his Word, the communication in virtue of which God becomes a self or person.[25]

There is no God behind this manifest God, no entity discernible apart from the veil of communication. Insofar as he has an intelligible identity (what Edwards calls "excellence"), God (like everything else) means something: that is, he is intentional and significatory. In himself, he is meaningful only as a Trinity, and the triune God is intelligible as a person only through the communication of his Word to his creation. The persons of the Trinity are thus requirements for God's internal identity, and the communication of himself to others is a requirement for God's external identity, because signification requires three functions: signifier, signified, and that which differentiates and associates signifier and signified.

This displacement of humanistic subjectivity by communication is crucial in the effort to dissolve difficulties created by speaking in humanistic and subjectivist ways about God and the persons of the Trin-

22. See Colin Gunton, "Augustine, the Trinity, and the Theological Crisis of the West," *Scottish Journal of Theology* 43 (1990), pp. 42-45, 56-57. Cf. Cornelius Plantinga, Jr., "Gregory of Nyssa and the Social Analogy of the Trinity," *The Thomist* 50 (1986), pp. 341, 351; and Christoph Schwöbel, "Christology and Trinitarian Thought," in *Trinitarian Theology Today*, pp. 132-33. In *The Triune Identity* (Philadelphia: Fortress Press, 1982), Robert W. Jenson suggests that love constitutes persons.

23. Barth, *Church Dogmatics*, I.1, 407, 418.

24. See Edwards, "Of Atoms," in *Works*, 6, p. 215. Cf. Daniel, *Philosophy of Edwards*, pp. 91-93, 97; and Jenson, *America's Theologian*, pp. 25-26, 121.

25. Barth, *Church Dogmatics*, I.1, 362; also pp. 157, 199-200, 340-43, 349-51, 358-59, 436-39.

ity. To think of God as if he were yet another being engaged in discourse would overlook how his very existence is unintelligible apart from that discourse. As Barth insists, God is his Word and "cannot be an entity which we could delimit from all other entities and thereby make into an object," because to identify such an object would suppose the very discursive matrix it needs to make the delimitation.[26]

That matrix is the language of God or Book of Nature in which subjectivity or personhood is simply a function or place (a *topos*) and not the transcendental guarantor of the intelligibility of discourse. That is why Edwards says that God's existence can be meaningful (i.e., "excellent") only in terms of the discursive exchange constituted by a plurality of persons.[27] Since discourse requires the displacement of a topic by another in order that both can be identified and associated in a meaningful relation, God himself cannot be intelligible unless he is a Trinity.

Barth extends this analysis to human identity as well, noting that each human being has a determinate essence in virtue of having been called into being through God's Word.[28] Edwards makes the same point when he describes God's relation to his creatures in terms of the mutually defining moments in communicative exchange. For as Edwards remarks, God's disposition to communicate himself requires the existence of creation in order for God's existence itself to be meaningful:

> If God be in himself disposed to communicate himself, he is therein disposed to make the creatures to communicate himself to; because he can't do what he is in himself disposed to, without it. . . . I observe that there is some impropriety in saying that a disposition in God to communicate himself *to the creature,* moved him to create the world . . . because an inclination in God to communicate himself to an object, seems to presuppose the existence of the object, at least in idea. But the diffusive disposition that excited God to give creatures existence was rather a communicative disposition in general.[29]

26. Barth, *Church Dogmatics,* I.1, 186; also see pp. 343, 349.

27. See Edwards, "Miscellanies," no. 182, in *Works,* 13, *"The Miscellanies": Entries a-z, aa-zz, 1-500,* ed. Thomas A. Schafer (New Haven: Yale University Press, 1994), pp. 328-29; and Edwards, "The Mind," no. 62, in *Works,* 6, p. 381. Cf. Daniel, *Philosophy of Edwards,* pp. 183-85.

28. See Barth, *Church Dogmatics,* I.1, 183-84.

29. Edwards, "Miscellanies," no. 445, in *Works,* 13, p. 494; and Edwards, "Dissertation concerning the End," in *Works,* 8, p. 434. Cf. Daniel, *Philosophy of Edwards,* pp. 121-28.

God's "disposition" to communicate himself to others cannot begin with the assumption that God and others are intelligible apart from one another, for that would require some more fundamental principle in virtue of which they could be considered different. To say that that principle "exists" as the *a priori* condition for such intelligibility would already presume it as that which makes such a claim intelligible. So God cannot be said to exist prior to his communication, and his disposition to communicate cannot be described merely as a characteristic or property that he has, since it is in virtue of communication that he is.

This focus on the essentially communicative nature of God has a number of implications. First, unlike attempts to model trinitarian relations on a community of human persons who exist mysteriously as the termini of those relations, it equates community with communication. Accordingly, the necessarily trinitarian character of intelligible expressivity serves as the divine exemplar for all other persons. Second, as Edwards, Barth, and Rahner insist, God's communication or revelation is essential to what God is. This means that the reality of the Trinity is revealed not in scattered texts but through the very nature of revelation.[30] And third, in order to wean ourselves away from the view that revelation is a communication from one subject (God) to other subjects (us), we have to think of subjectivity as itself a function of discourse. By providing us with tools to retrieve this sensitivity to communicative discourse, process, semiotic, and deconstructive strategies reinstate the centrality and indispensability of revelation.

This is not to say that all versions of process, semiotic, or deconstructive thought can be used to develop a postmodern trinitarian theology. Some process theologians think that by saying that God is a relational being, we mean that he, like everything else, becomes what he is through his historical relation to the world.[31] But this still treats God as if he were a subject whose history grows with the passing of every state of the universe. It also treats the Trinity as a commu-

---

30. See Barth, *Church Dogmatics*, I.1, 349-62, 436-39. Cf. John Thompson, "Modern Trinitarian Perspectives," *Scottish Journal of Theology* 44 (1991), p. 353; and Colin E. Gunton, *Becoming and Being: The Doctrine of God in Charles Hartshorne and Karl Barth* (Oxford: Oxford University Press, 1978), pp. 129-31.

31. See David Ray Griffin, *God and Religion in the Postmodern World: Essays in Postmodern Theology* (Albany: State University of New York Press, 1989), pp. 4-10. Cf. Nuyen, "Postmodern Theology," pp. 65, 76.

nity of persons about whom one can predicate characteristics and activities.[32] What *postmodern* process theology requires, however, is a rejection of the logic of substantialist predication itself. When process theology begins with *creativity* (what Edwards calls God's glory)[33] and portrays trinitarian features of God (e.g., Whitehead's primordial, consequent, and superject natures) as aspects of communication rather than as subjects, it properly takes on postmodern features.[34]

Proponents of postmodern semiotics and deconstruction are more explicit in describing the communicational character of God. They propose that, instead of thinking of God as a subject who communicates himself through revelation, we should understand God as signification itself. Theological semiotics thus replaces the question of personhood in intra-trinitarian relations with an explication of the nature of divine communication. Not unlike Edwards, Peirce thinks of God not as some transcendental signified, but as the ultimate sign, the ultimate trinitarian model of intelligibility.[35] When Barth concludes that the Word made flesh constitutes "the first, original and controlling sign of all signs," he likewise indicates how signification itself is central in understanding revelation as revelation.[36]

This focus on revelation as the communication of intelligibility or significance opens up the prospects for a *deconstructive* theology. For by explaining how divine communication identifies the members of the Trinity as intelligible, it also retrieves the possibility that the world can be saved from meaninglessness through the subordination of sub-

32. See Charles Hartshorne, *A Natural Theology for Our Time* (LaSalle, IL: Open Court, 1967), p. 105.

33. See Daniel, *Philosophy of Edwards*, pp. 120-29.

34. See Bracken, *Triune Symbol*, pp. 20-28; Joseph A. Bracken, "Process Philosophy and Trinitarian Theology — II," *Process Studies* 11 (1981), pp. 85-86; Joseph A. Bracken, "Subsistent Relations: Mediating Concept for a New Synthesis," *Journal of Religion* 64 (1984), pp. 194-96; and Leahy, "New Beginning," p. 422.

35. See Charles S. Peirce, "A Neglected Argument for the Reality of God," in *Peirce on Signs*, ed. James Hoopes (Chapel Hill: University of North Carolina Press, 1991), pp. 260-67; and John Deely, *New Beginnings: Early Modern Philosophy and Postmodern Thought* (Toronto: University of Toronto, 1994), pp. 179, 247. On Edwards and Peirce, see James Hoopes, *Consciousness in New England: From Puritanism and Ideas to Psychoanalysis and Semiotic* (Baltimore: Johns Hopkins University Press, 1989), pp. 198-205, 282-86; and Daniel, *Philosophy of Edwards*, pp. 30-32.

36. Barth, *Church Dogmatics*, II.1, 199. Cf. Graham Ward, *Barth, Derrida, and the Language of Theology* (Cambridge: Cambridge University Press, 1995), pp. 28-31, 235.

jectivity. For Edwards and Barth this means that communicants are functions of the discursive web of signs in terms of which a person or speaker is intelligible or discernible. This aboriginal net of constantly self-displacing sign-relations identifies what it means for something to be thinkable in the first place because it defines the grammar and syntax of thought. Since consciousness itself is the communicative web of signs in virtue of which anything is intelligible, all existence (as Nietzsche claims) must therefore be a function of consciousness (though not, of course, the consciousness *of a subject*).[37] So Edwards concludes that God's glory consists in communicative (i.e., conscious, intelligible) existence.[38]

In deconstructive theology, this communicative matrix is the Word of God, the text that does not refer to anything beyond itself because "beyond" is intelligible only in terms laid down by and in the text. It is the gratuitous expression (or "act of grace") that meaningfully differentiates God, self, and world.[39] It is the positing of all things as intelligibly identifiable. It is a necessarily trinitarian revelation, inasmuch as the positing is different from that which is posited, and both are different from the contrast that identifies them as the signifier-signified components of an intelligible sign. It is Edwards's space of discourse, in terms of which even *nothingness* is something determinate and meaningful.[40] Instead of being *a* text or *a* language, it is the textuality of texts, the linguisticality of languages.

Some critics reject this appeal to sign systems and texts as nothing less than an attempt to portray everything, including God and the Trinity, as functions of *human* discourse.[41] They treat Edwards's pervasive allusions to God's communication *ad intra* and *ad extra* as metaphors for Neoplatonic emanationism, and they assume that Barth's fo-

---

37. See Friedrich Nietzsche, *The Gay Science,* trans. Walter Kaufmann (New York: Random House, 1974), p. 299. Cf. Carl A. Raschke, "The Deconstruction of God," in *Deconstruction and Theology,* p. 6.

38. See Edwards, "Miscellanies," no. 247, *Works,* 13, p. 360; and Edwards, "Notes on Knowledge and Existence," in *Works,* 8, p. 398.

39. See Winquist, "Silence," pp. 37-39; Myers, "Religious Thinking Underway," p. 139; and Charles E. Winquist, "Body, Text, and Imagination," in *Deconstruction and Theology,* pp. 48, 54.

40. See Edwards, "Of Being," *Works,* 6, pp. 202, 207; and Edwards, "Miscellanies," no. 650, *The Philosophy of Jonathan Edwards,* ed. Harvey G. Townsend (Eugene: University of Oregon Press, 1955), p. 82. Cf. Daniel, *Philosophy of Edwards,* pp. 83-85.

41. See Thiemann, "Response to Lindbeck," pp. 377-78.

cus on revelation emphasizes God's intimate involvement in human history, not his inherent textuality.[42]

But in saying that "God is a communicative being," Edwards understands revelation in a way similar to Barth. When Barth comments that God "cannot be unveiled," he does not mean that God is somehow intelligible behind his revelation and it just happens he is inaccessible to us.[43] Rather, he means that God's intelligibility is inherent in his revelation: there is no other, more substantial text than the veil of revelation. As that which provides the grammar and syntax by means of which all other texts are interpreted, revelation is neither regulated by dialectical reason nor constrained by the natural (personalist) theology of social trinitarianism. Revelation certainly does not depend on human discursive strategies for interpretation, for it is the discourse in terms of which all other discourses are originally intelligible. That is why, for Barth, revelation is free and cannot be bound to any historical economy of salvation, especially one that promises a key to interpret (and thus mediate) revelation.[44]

Rather than thinking of communication or textuality as functions of human discourse played out by individual subjects, Edwards and Barth invite us therefore to address the intra-trinitarian relations of the divine persons and the relation of God to creation in an entirely new way. But as Edwards observes, our language of subjects and predicates is inadequate for the task because it grants legitimacy to a fallen mentality.[45] To get around this linguistic difficulty, Whitehead, Peirce, and Derrida fashion their own arcane vocabularies and strategies. Edwards and Barth, however, simply immerse themselves in the foreign-enough sounding environment of Scripture in hopes of discerning the patterns of thought that guide the elect.

42. See *Works,* 8, p. 433n; Gunton, *Becoming and Being,* pp. 135-36; and McCormack, "Ward's Barth," p. 110. Cf. Daniel, *Philosophy of Edwards,* pp. 104-5, 120-22.

43. Edwards, "Miscellanies," no. 332, *Works,* 13, p. 410; and Barth, *Church Dogmatics,* I.1, 362. Cf. Daniel, *Philosophy of Edwards,* pp. 22, 127; and Gunton, *Becoming and Being,* p. 132.

44. See Barth, *Church Dogmatics,* I.1, 163, 358-62, 383-99. Cf. Molnar, "Immanent Trinity," pp. 370, 378; and George Lindbeck, "Barth and Textuality," *Theology Today* 43 (1986), pp. 361, 374.

45. Edwards, "Miscellanies," no. 1066, in Townsend, *Philosophy of Edwards,* p. 139; and Edwards, "Dissertation concerning the End," *Works,* 8, pp. 434-35.

Not surprisingly, those patterns are revealed in and as the relations of the divine persons. In Edwards's account, the Son is the idea (i.e., the signifier) of the Father (i.e., the signified), and the Holy Spirit is the association of signifier and signified that constitutes God's identity and intelligibility. The Son is the idea of the Father, the means by which "the Deity is begotten," the means by which the Father is meaningfully identified as that which has been "supposed" or displaced by the idea of it.[46] No one comes to the Father except through the Son, since the Son is the idea by means of which the Father has an identity.[47] But the Father and the Son cannot be merely distinct; they must be differentiated as mutually related realities. That association and differentiation is the function of the Holy Spirit.

This account of the Trinity does not assume that supposition is an activity engaged in by some ontologically prior subject. For when Edwards says that the Father is supposed by the Son, he again does not mean that the Son *does* something but rather that the Son *is* something, namely, the structural displacement of a topic by means of which the topic can be designated as fit or proper. In this sense, the displacement of the Father by his image, the Son, is a necessary requirement of significance itself. Accordingly, the propriety of the Father consists in his being intentionally related to the Son as the fulfillment of meaning for both of them. They both become intelligible in being supposed (i.e., displaced) by the Holy Spirit as the designation of their communicative functions.

The Holy Spirit is thus the designation of the intelligibility of the Father in virtue of the possibility of his being imaged as the Son. The Son is the image of the Father but is not *in* the image of the Father, since that would imply that the Son has an identity distinct from the Father, as if the Son were a copy or simulation of the Father. Instead, in Edwards's terms, the Son is the "perfect idea" of the Father, the simulacrum of the Father by means of which the Father is identified.[48] The Father does not exist as a determinate substance *(substantia)* prior to

46. Edwards, "Miscellanies," no. 94, *Works*, 13, p. 258. Cf. Jonathan Edwards, *An Unpublished Essay of Edwards on the Trinity*, ed. George P. Fisher (New York: Charles Scribner's Sons, 1903), pp. 84-86; and Daniel, *Philosophy of Edwards*, pp. 114-19.

47. See Edwards, "Miscellanies," no. 777, Beinecke Library, Yale University.

48. See Daniel, *Philosophy of Edwards*, pp. 47-48, 115-17, 141, 198-99. Cf. Jean Baudrillard, "Simulacra and Simulations," in *Jean Baudrillard: Selected Writings*, ed. Mark Poster (Stanford: Stanford University Press, 1988), p. 169.

his designation as that of which his image (the Son) is an image. So apart from the Holy Spirit's identification of the Father as that about which there is an associated idea, there is no Father. The Son is not another substance who "proceeds" from the Father, but is rather (as Barth says) a "mode of existence of one who exists" *(subsistentia).*[49]

This way of setting up the problematic of the Trinity indicates how Edwards and Barth side with the Eastern Church in the *filioque* controversy, insofar as they think of each member of the Trinity not as an independent person (or *prosopon*) but as a function of intelligible being (a *hypostasis*). For them, the Holy Spirit cannot proceed from the Father *and* the Son, since that would imply that the Son has an identity independent of the Father. But since everything has an identity in virtue of that which delineates or signifies it (viz., its idea), any self-identity that the Son would have would require that there be an idea of the Son — which itself would require a further idea to delineate it, thus creating an infinite regress of ideas (and persons) in the Trinity. So, as the Eastern Church Fathers maintain, the Son can be considered an equal to the Father and the Holy Spirit only by assuming that all three "persons" are aspects of what constitute the meaning or intelligibility of God.

In saying that the members of the Trinity are intelligent, spiritual persons, Edwards does not therefore mean that they *are* minds or *have* minds. Rather, together they constitute intelligibility, and individually they embody the inherently intentional characteristics of mentality in that they point beyond themselves for their meaning. The Father cannot have an identity without being signified by the Son; the Son is nothing other than the signifier of the Father; and the Holy Spirit is the identification of that relation as a relation of significance. Insofar as the persons of the Trinity are significant precisely in virtue of their self-effacing *dis*-positions relative to one another, they are a model for all existence.

This communicative (and necessarily trinitarian) strategy for understanding intelligibility not only redirects questions of divine personhood but also identifies how the world can be considered intelligible. If the world is to have a meaning, it must participate in the same kind of trinitarian relations that identify the divine persons. That is, the world must be understood as the supposition or displacement of

49. Barth, *Church Dogmatics,* I.1, 413.

the Trinity, a signifier pointing beyond itself to God as its fulfillment and salvation. The recognition of that displacement as something that has meaning is the recognition of the world as "the creation of God" (in both senses of that phrase). That is, in saying that the world is God's creation, we identify it *along with God* as a function of the same discursive matrix.

The world at large and all things in the world must thus be understood as signs whose meaning consists in being completed in an other. To the extent that the world and the things in the world do not display their inherently communicative character and seem only to draw attention to their ability to be meaningful in themselves, they lack excellence. They can be said to exist only in a derivative and truncated sense, because they lack the significance that is identified (in and through the Holy Spirit) as the intentionality or mentality of effective expression. Such a transformation of the world — from lacking significance to being inherently significant — is exactly what Rahner highlights in linking the economy of salvation with intra-trinitarian relations.[50]

Edwards and Barth, however, are not satisfied with simply saying that the dynamic of salvation is bound up with the activity of the Trinity. They want to show how this observation is justified by grounding the link between the economy of salvation and the economy of the Trinity in the communicative nature of revelation. In their accounts, the Scriptures narrate the history of the Sign, first, by recounting the displacement of the world as signifier (in the Fall); second, by indicating how the world can be saved from isolated meaninglessness through the prophetic (typological) promise of reconciliation with God; and third, by emphasizing the continuing completion of significance in the Spirit's association of creation (through Christ) with divinity.

For Edwards and Barth, revelation and divine communication thus become central as the semantic conditions for salvation. This is the feature of their thought that is made explicit in process, semiotic, and deconstructive strategies that focus on how the ontological identity of anything (including God) depends on its function within a discursive matrix. But it is Edwards, in particular, who insists that this re-

---

50. See Karl Rahner, *The Trinity* (New York: Seabury Press, 1974), p. 22; and Ingolf U. Dalferth, "The Eschatological Roots of the Doctrine of the Trinity," in *Trinitarian Theology Today*, pp. 167-68.

quires us to think of references to God's communicative activity and the Book of Nature not as mere metaphors that are modeled on human language and that are intended to reinstate Neoplatonic emanation theory. Rather, his invocations of the vocabulary of divine expression and revelation are challenges to the classical-modern, Aristotelian-Cartesian-Lockean assumption that the distinction of things, ideas, and words is intelligible apart from a matrix of discursive practices. And it is in virtue of this feature that his philosophy has a distinctive postmodern character.

PART II

ETHICS

Religious Ethics Today: Jonathan Edwards, H. Richard Niebuhr, and Beyond

ROLAND A. DELATTRE

One way of asking about the contribution Jonathan Edwards might make to contemporary religious ethics is to ask: In whose company would he feel most himself? Among contemporary figures I think of most readily are, of course, H. Richard Niebuhr and James Gustafson, but also Jim Wallis, Abraham Joshua Heschel, and Martin Luther King, Jr. What makes Edwards kin to all of them is a commitment to radically reconceptualizing the nature and the dynamics of the moral and spiritual life in response to his own experience of the divine presence and power, in ways that offer an alternative to the dominant and received options. All those I have mentioned share qualities of mind and heart nicely suggested by the title given by Susannah Heschel to her recent collection of her father's writings: *Moral Grandeur and Spiritual Audacity*.[1]

In 1960 Niebuhr wrote that old phrases and traditional terms had become worn out clichés "by means of which we can neither grasp nor communicate the reality of our existence before God." Retranslation would not be enough. What he looked for was "a resymbolization . . . in pregnant word and in symbolic deeds . . . of the mes-

---

1. Abraham Joshua Heschel, *Moral Grandeur and Spiritual Audacity*, ed. Susannah Heschel (New York: Farrar, Straus, Giroux, 1996).

sage and the life of faith in the One God."[2] Niebuhr also expressed late in his life an intention to go even further than Edwards had in exploring what Niebuhr called "the land of the emotions."[3] I intend to suggest here that if we explore an even broader region charted by the Edwardsean themes I will foreground, we will have the resources to advance Niebuhr's aim and, more particularly, to consolidate his effort to develop a relational ethics of responsibility as a full-blown alternative to the still-dominant deontological and teleological approaches to ethics.

Edwardsean theology and ethics are quite often adventurous and daring; I cannot help but think that the reason must be a need deeply felt on Edwards's part to explore both reality and language for ways to express more adequately and render persuasive to others what he himself found to be actual in his own experience. This is an essential mark of genuine piety or reverence and, therefore, also of truly religious ethics. For, although there may be ethics without piety or reverence for being, there can be no genuinely *religious* ethics that is not grounded in piety or reverence for being. Religious ethics should be driven by a passion — like the one so evident in Edwards — to seek out further evidence of the divine presence and power active in the world, and a like passion to conform the rhythm and pattern of one's life to the rhythm and pattern discerned in the creative and transformative presence and power of divinity.

Notice that my topic is *religious* ethics, not just *Christian* ethics today. Although Edwards was a decidedly Christian theologian, and his ethics is framed as a guide to living a Christian life as he understood it, his central convictions are — or can be — fairly expressed, without sacrificing anything of their distinctively Christian features, in language addressed to a wider circle of religious believers and spiritual seekers. Such a broad potential relevance and appeal across as well as within confessional boundaries is likely to be of increasing importance in a time such as ours when such boundaries are of diminishing importance to many who take issues of faith seriously. Of particular importance here are two volumes of the Yale Edition of Edwards's works:

2. In H. E. Fey, ed., *How My Mind Has Changed* (New York: Meridian, 1961), pp. 79-80.

3. H. Richard Niebuhr, *Theology, History, and Culture: Major Unpublished Writings,* ed. William Stacy Johnson (New Haven: Yale University Press, 1996), p. 48.

the *Religious Affections*[4] and the *Ethical Writings*.[5] The latter volume contains the fifteen 1738 sermons on "Charity and Its Fruits" and the posthumously published pair of essays on "The End for Which God Created the World" and "The Nature of True Virtue." In these works especially, Edwards offers a model of ethics and morality which, though appropriate to his very Christian piety, are formulated in images and symbols that are in no way prisoner to that specific piety. Indeed, as expressed with particular force in these works, the very distinctive Edwardsean aesthetic, relational, and processual resymbolization of language about God, God's relation to the world, and the pattern of human life appropriate to and required by an appreciation of that vision, makes his work peculiarly relevant to the broader questions of religious ethics in our time.

There are three formative ideas in Edwards's writings that I want to draw upon and make central to my interpretation of the contribution he can make to contemporary religious ethics:

1. The centrality of beauty in his understanding of God and of the nature and dynamics of the spiritual and moral life;

2. The idea that the very creation of the world results from the joyful overflowing into the world of the fullness of being and beauty in the divine life;

3. The idea that the Christian life is a life made new by participation in the life of God.

Taken together, the meaning of these ideas for contemporary religious ethics can be expressed as follows: the religious life (or the Christian life) is a life made new by cordial consent to the being and beauty of the divine life and by enthusiastic participation in the beauty and beautifying activity of the divine life overflowing into the world. I believe that this is a fair statement of Edwards's thought. And quite apart from that, I believe it is a true statement, and that none of its truth is lost if it is said not just of a Christian life but of any authentically religious life.

An alternative expression of these convictions might be: Beauty is the home of being if being ever has a home; and beauty is our home if ever we have a home.

---

4. Jonathan Edwards, *The Works of Jonathan Edwards, 2, Religious Affections*, ed. John E. Smith (New Haven: Yale University Press, 1959).

5. Jonathan Edwards, *The Works of Jonathan Edwards, 8, Ethical Writings*, ed. Paul Ramsey (New Haven: Yale University Press, 1989).

Beauty

Beauty is for Edwards that "wherein the truest idea of divinity does consist."[6] It is our central clue to the nature of God and to the nature and dynamics of the moral and spiritual life. Beauty is for Edwards the first principle of being, the inner, structural, creative principle of Being-itself by virtue of which all things that are have their being, and according to which the universal system of being is articulated. Beauty consists most generally in the consent of being to being, as opposed to discord and dissent among beings. Edwards distinguishes between the natural or secondary beauty of proportion and harmony and the primary or spiritual beauty of cordial heart-felt consent in which the will, disposition, or affection of the heart are involved. Beauty enlarges and enhances being; dissent and deformity diminish and constrict being. Everything is to be loved in proportion to its being and beauty, i.e., according to its relationship to God.

Beauty is objective rather than subjective for Edwards because it is constituted by objective relations of consent and dissent among beings, the beauty of which is defined by conformity to God (consent to being in general) rather than by degree of subjective pleasure. So beauty is a structural concept, its nearest synonym being excellence rather than pleasantness. Moreover, beauty is more properly and fully exhibited in creative spiritual relations of consent than in created material (or even moral) relations of proportion. Beauty is a formative principle of being more than a principle of well-formed being; it is more fully exhibited in bestowing beauty than in receiving it. So God is most beautiful, for God is the effulgent fountain of all being and beauty, the beautifying one, the bestower of all beauty.

There arises from a sense of spiritual beauty "all true experimental knowledge of religion; . . . [and] he that sees not the beauty of holiness . . . in effect is ignorant of the whole spiritual world."[7] Edwards even adds: "take away all the moral beauty and sweetness in the Word, and the Bible is left wholly a dead letter, a dry, lifeless, tasteless thing."[8] Beauty is not the only word about being and God, but it is the first word, such that everything about the system of being and the life of

6. *Works,* 2, p. 298.
7. Ibid., p. 275.
8. Ibid., p. 274.

God reflects the priority of beauty. Beauty is the home of being if ever being has a home.

The beauty of spiritual beings, divine or human, is the cordiality of their consent to being, the heartiness of their love for all that has being, the enthusiasm with which they embrace the gift of their own being and cordially participate in the beautifying activity of the divine presence and power. Every other form of beauty, such as proportion or harmony, is an image or shadow of such spiritual beauty, and when appreciated for its beauty is transparent to and manifests the beautifying power of divine presence.[9] Beauty is our home if ever we have a home.

Of course, not every claim to beauty can withstand examination. In our own culture, so given to the assignment of value on the basis of appearances, we are surrounded by claims to beauty. But many of those claims are narrowly and superficially based, and could not measure up to the standards offered by Edwards.

Creation: Divine Life Overflowing

The beauty Edwards finds in God does not consist in being beautiful but in creating or bestowing beauty; not in being passively beautiful, but in joyful, beautifying activity. It is not by force but by the creative and attractive power of beauty that the power of God is at work in the world.

It was Edwards's view that fullness of being and beauty is what most distinguishes God from everything and everyone else, and that the beauty of God consists in the fullness of God's love and joy, or holiness and delight. For Edwards, love and joy are always partners in the divine life. Together with knowledge and love, joy is represented by him as one of the three formative perfections of God — and of humanity wherever that same knowledge, love, and joy are communicated by God to the creature. It is a distinctive mark of Edwards's theology that joy is represented by him as one of the formative perfections of God — not just one of the attributes of God, but a formative attribute or per-

---

9. For fuller analysis of Edwards on beauty see my *Beauty and Sensibility in the Thought of Jonathan Edwards* (New Haven: Yale University Press, 1968) and "Beauty and Theology: A Reappraisal of Jonathan Edwards," *Soundings: A Journal of Interdisciplinary Studies* 51/1 (Spring 1968), 60-79.

fection, one that is ontologically constitutive of God. In his view it joins knowledge and love in displacing a whole list of classical perfections — omnipotence, omniscience, etc. — which Edwards (I think rightly) dismisses as what he calls merely natural rather than moral perfections in his vision of God.

The very creation of the world has its origin in the joyful fullness of being and beauty in the divine life itself, a fullness that could not be contained even by God, but overflows into the world, creating and sustaining the world as an enlargement of its own life, an extension of its own being and beauty in continuing creation. For Edwards, God's end in the creation of the world is "the emanation of God's glory; or the excellent brightness and fullness of the divinity diffused, overflowing, and as it were enlarged; or in one word, *existing ad extra*."[10] The very existence of the world is an outgrowth of the divine life. It exists, for Edwards, only by virtue of a disposition in God to a fullness of life that spills over *ad extra*, beginning in the work of creation — not *ex nihilo*, but out of the fullness of God's own being, enlarged and communicated outward like streams from a fountain — a flowing forth that is a process of continuing creation, every moment and every thing existing only by virtue of the immediate communication of God's presence, and not by virtue of any preceding cause or condition; that is, not by virtue of something communicated *from* God but something communicated *of* God.

Edwards is not a pantheist, but he can fairly be called a panentheist — though for different reasons than contemporary process theologians. The creation does not exist apart from or separate from or exterior to the continuing life of God, but has its existence within the fullness of God's life overflowing *ad extra*. That is the setting in which life is given to the creature, and the measure of the spiritual and moral quality of the human creature's life is the extent of cordial consent to or of dissent from that condition or setting.

Of the several terms or images Edwards employs to describe God's continuing creation — emanation, communication, flowing forth, diffusion, enlargement, increase, repetition, and multiplication — perhaps the most striking is enlargement, or creation by God's self-enlargement. He employs the term in a way that leads directly to the

10. Edwards, "Dissertation concerning the End for Which God Created the World," in *Works*, 8, p. 527.

creature's participation in the life of God. For example, God "from his goodness, as it were enlarges himself . . . by communicating and diffusing himself; and so instead of finding, making objects of his benevolence: . . . by flowing forth, and expressing himself in them, and making them to partake of him, and rejoicing in himself expressed in them, and communicated to them."[11] Thus God's self-enlargement makes the creatures to partake of himself, makes them participants in the life of God — a life that is enlarged by their creation and by the communication and diffusion and flowing forth to them of God's fullness.

The appropriate response to such an overflowing of love for the world and joy in the world's being and well-being is to participate wholeheartedly in God's love for the world and delight in the world's being and well-being. The world is an enlargement of the divine life, the setting in which we are called upon and enabled to participate in the beautifying activity and presence of God. The appropriate human response to the divine self-enlargement will be a corresponding enlargement of soul toward the world, toward "benevolence to being in general," i.e. an enlargement of what in the world counts as among the interests of the self or of a community. William James observes that a person's "religion involves both moods of contraction and moods of expansion of the person's being."[12] I would add that nothing expands the soul so much as the experience of beauty and of participating in beautifying deeds. And nothing contracts or constricts the soul of humanity, individually or collectively, so much as the absence of beauty in their lives and the world they experience.

Love for the world will consist primarily in attending to its beautification, enlarging its beauty where possible, and rejoicing in the beauty of the divine presence and power. Richard R. Niebuhr discerns the importance of this theme as he concludes his 1980 Kyoto lecture on Edwards by indicating the ultimate direction of Edwards's religious thinking and vision, namely, that the meaning of cordial consent "is to take part in the enlargement of being in general and so in the enlargement of the divine life itself."[13] Beauty, holiness, love, and virtue en-

11. Ibid., pp. 461f.
12. William James, *The Varieties of Religious Experience* (1902; New York: Penguin Books, 1982), p. 75.
13. Richard R. Niebuhr, *Streams of Grace: Studies of Jonathan Edwards, Samuel Taylor Coleridge, and William James* (Kyoto, Japan: Doshisha University Press, 1983), p. 35.

large and expand whatever they touch in the direction of fullness of being. Deformity and dissent from being, diminish and contract whatever they touch in the direction of emptiness and nothingness. Only the continuous creative presence of God's life in the life of the world maintains the world in being and keeps it from collapsing into nothing at all. In beauty the world is created; in beauty will God's end in creation be fulfilled.

Christians find the divine beauty overflowing into the world — the beauty of holiness — most powerfully and attractively present in the figure of Jesus of Nazareth, and we represent the experience of participating in the divine life as one of participating in the presence and power of the Holy Spirit. And so it is for me. Yet I have no doubt that the God from whom comes the whole of creation (including all of humanity) seeks to and does draw persons into cordial participation in the divine life by the attractive power of divine beauty otherwise manifest than to the culturally tuned sensibilities given to me in my particular stream of time and place. The sons and daughters of Abraham — whether Jewish, Christian, or Muslim — are not the only children of God. Beyond that, the human drama is not the center of the cosmic drama. Accordingly, the center of gravity for the Christian life should be divinity rather than humanity. Its orientation should be responsive to God rather than to humanity as the center and measure of value, and to the living presence of God's beauty in everything that has being. Beauty is the home of being if ever being has a home; beauty is our home if ever we have a home.

Participation

The Christian life is a life made new by participation in the life of God and, more generally, the religious life is a life made new by participation in the divine life.

Such a life is, first of all, a life made new, transformed by a sense of the beauty of God and of the divine life overflowing into the world, for it is only that perception that has the transformative power to make our lives new and keep renewing them. It has its beginning in piety or reverence, by which I mean an affective response to the experience of divine presence and power — an affective response called forth by a felt need to make sense of that experience and to align the pattern of one's own life with the perceived manner of being and pattern of activity on the part of that divine presence and power. There follows from this perception of beautifying presence and power an engagement of the self to seek further evidence of the actuality of that divine being and activity, and to respond in cordial and active consent by participating in the beautifying activity of that living presence and power to the extent of one's capacities and conditions. The Christian life begins, as H. Richard Niebuhr also observed, with the experience of life beginning to be made new.

The language of participation in the divine life is evident across the range of Edwards's published and unpublished writings, and it is woven together with the other formative themes of his thought. In the *Religious Affections*, for example, the saints are represented as partaking of God's beauty and Christ's joy and as participating in the Holy Spirit. The "Spirit of God," Edwards says, dwells in the heart of the saint "as a seed or spring of life, . . . making the soul a partaker of God's beauty and Christ's joy" even as it is "having the communion or participation of the Holy Ghost."[14] Edwards cautions that in this world it is the life and nature of God and not the essence of God in which the saints participate: "Not that the saints are made partakers of the essence of God, and so 'Godded' with God, and 'Christed' with Christ, . . . but they are made partakers of God's fullness (Eph. 3:17-19; John 1:16), that is, of God's spiritual beauty and happiness, according to the capacity of a creature."[15] Only in his description of heaven does Edwards represent the saints as participating in "the very essence of God," as in a passage from *Charity* Sermon Fifteen, "Heaven Is a World of Love," that, in its ecstatic language, anticipates the famous "emanation and remanation" passage from "End of Creation": "There [in heaven] dwell God the Father, and so the Son. . . . There is [also] the Holy Spirit, the spirit of divine love, in whom the very essence of God, as it were, all flows out or is breathed forth in love . . . , there the fountain overflows in streams and rivers of love and delight, enough for all to drink at, and to swim in, yea, so as to overflow the world as it were with a deluge of love."[16] In Edwards's view, when the Spirit of God imparts itself, communicates its own nature in the ordinary gifts of Christian love, the saints enjoy a participa-

---

14. *Works*, 2, p. 201.
15. Ibid., p. 203.
16. "Charity and Its Fruits," in *Works*, 8, p. 370.

tion in God's own knowledge of himself, as also of God's own love and joy. Thus do the saints participate in the life of God by way of love and joy as well as knowledge — a participation which takes them to the very center of the divine life.[17]

I can well imagine Edwards raising his voice with contemporary Congregationalists in singing Hymn #476 in the *New Century Hymnal*, a hymn that joyfully celebrates themes central to the piety upon which rests the theology and the ethics developed by Edwards:

> My life flows on in endless song; above earth's lamentations,
> I hear the sweet, though far-off hymn that hails a new creation.
> Through all the tumult and the strife, I hear the music ringing;
> It finds an echo in my soul — How can I keep from singing?[18]

Homeward toward Beauty

The import for religious ethics in our time of the three ideas I have examined (centrality of beauty, divine life overflowing into the world, and participation), can be expressed as follows: the religious life (or the Christian life) is a life made new by cordial consent to the being and beauty of the divine life and by enthusiastic participation in the beauty and beautifying activity of the divine life overflowing into the world. Beauty is our home if ever we have a home.

If beauty is our home, then we do well to turn ourselves homeward — which is not somewhere else, but a different way of being right here, where we are — appreciating and enjoying the beauty by which our lives are gifted and enhancing the beauty of whatever we touch, cordially participating in the beautifying life of God overflowing into the world. We are to be responsive to the presence and absence of beauty in the full range of the interdependent system of being — in the natural world, in the relations among forms of life, and in the fabric of consenting and dissenting relations among human beings. These all impinge upon one another. For instance, we enhance

17. For a fuller development of participation in the divine life overflowing into the world as a formative theme in Edwards's ethics, see my "The Theological Ethics of Jonathan Edwards," *Journal of Religious Ethics* 19/2 (Fall 1991), pp. 71-102.

18. "My Life Flows On in Endless Song," *The New Century Hymnal* (Cleveland: The Pilgrim Press, 1995), Hymn #476.

the beauty of our own souls as we beautify the material and artifactual world, just as we certainly diminish and impoverish our souls by the aesthetic ugliness and brutality of so much of the urban landscape. The beauty and aesthetic quality of our artifactual world has an enormous impact upon the moral quality of our social fabric and human relations, especially because the artifactual world we construct often stands between our urban populations and the beauties of the natural environment.

A homeward turn toward beauty is a journey of discovery, an awakening and sharpening of my appreciative powers, the discovery of realities that may have been at best marginal to my consciousness, but that come in some fashion to shift toward the center of gravity of my consciousness. Or, to express myself the other way around, a homeward turn toward beauty begins with the discovery of myself as attracted and drawn into the ambit of a divine presence and beautifying power experienced as having the character of ultimacy. The appropriate response to such an experience is quite literally one of appreciative and grateful enthusiasm, of being drawn *en-theos*, into the life of God. It is an experience of our life beginning to be made new. Such a discovery is the refreshing and transformative recognition that it is within the divine life that we live and move and have our being. This is what I understand to be the meaning and inner logic of the classical proposition that the first end of humanity is to glorify God and enjoy God forever.

The journey of discovery and transformation that begins in the homeward turn toward beauty is a social as well as a personal journey. It is the witness of Scripture and of Christian faith that the life of God is social and relational. That is one reason most Christians find it necessary to speak of God in trinitarian terms, however much trouble they may have with the doctrinal formulations of the Trinity. Participation in the divine life is therefore also a social and relational life. Indeed I doubt that it can be sustained without the spiritual nourishment made possible by a worshipping and celebrating community. The give and take, the challenge and support, the mutual nourishment in the ways of love and justice among differing but kindred minds, the reverence expressed and nourished in corporate worship as well as the ways of prayer and meditation — this fabric of corporate piety and celebration is an indispensable condition of a Christian life.

I am reminded of another hymn (#399) in the *New Century Hymnal*.

It has a sort of Gilbert-and-Sullivan lilt to it, though it is more serious of purpose:

> When minds and bodies meet as one, and find their true affinity,
> we join the dance in God begun, and move within the Trinity,
> so praise the good that's seen and done in loving, giving unity,
> revealing God, forever One, whose nature is Community.
>
> In Christ we come to break and bless the bread of new society,
> created for togetherness from infinite variety,
> so praise the good that's seen and done in Spirit given unity,
> revealing God, forever One, whose nature is Community.[19]

Otherwise expressed: we find our true humanity as we are drawn into joining the dance in God begun, moving within the divine life itself, manifesting by our participation the world-embracing nature of the divine life, the life of God. It is a beautifying dance of "unity within variety" not unlike the "cosmic dance" described by Thomas Merton in the closing paragraphs of his *New Seeds of Contemplation*. For Merton, "the world and time are the dance of the Lord"; he concludes the book by announcing that "we are invited to forget ourselves on purpose, cast our awful solemnity to the winds and join in the general dance."[20]

If beauty is our home, we are not yet home, but only on a homeward journey of discovery until we are living surrounded by beauty — the beauty of cordial consent among spiritual beings and all the private or particular systems of beauty that contribute to peace and justice among people and between humanity and the wider system of being. We are enabled to participate in the divine life, but we imagine only dimly its transformative intention and power. So we may properly share a conviction Diane Yeager recently attributed to H. Richard Niebuhr, that "our deepest religious responsibility is to love creation and hallow it — in order that it may be changed."[21]

19. "When Minds and Bodies Meet as One," *The New Century Hymnal*, Hymn #399.

20. Thomas Merton, *New Seeds of Contemplation* (New York: New Directions, 1962), p. 297.

21. D. M. Yeager, "The Social Self in the Pilgrim Church," ch. 2 in Glen H. Stassen, D. M. Yeager, and John Howard Yoder, *Authentic Transformation: A New Vision of Christ and Culture* (Nashville: Abingdon Press, 1996), p. 126.

Religious Ethics Today

Further development of these ideas and their implications along Edwardsean lines offers a distinctive and timely contribution to religious ethics today. A religious ethic informed by an Edwardsean orientation toward beauty and a sense of our lives as empowered to participate in the divine life overflowing into the world offers a way of articulating a systematic account of the moral life that recognizes its grounding in reverence for a divine presence transcendent in beauty and power yet immediately active and available rather than distantly demanding and awesome. Such an ethic will be clearly religious, grounded in religious experience — not offering religious endorsement for moral action and ethical reflection grounded elsewhere.

We need to give at least as important a place to beauty in our lives as we do to goodness and truth. I have a bumper sticker on my car that reads: "Practice Random Kindness and Senseless Acts of Beauty." By individual and collective acts of beauty we are enabled to participate in the life of God — especially if our acts of beauty are senseless, done for the sheer joy of performance, out of overflowing enthusiasm for the gift of life and out of pleasure in the exercise of our human capacities for wonderfully useless, beautiful acts. It may be by creative and even senseless acts of beauty, as much as by very sensible social policies — even those aimed at peace and justice — that we are enabled to participate in God's redemption of the world. William Schultz, Executive Director of Amnesty International USA, recently quoted E. B. White's observation, "Every morning I awake torn between a desire to save the world and an inclination to savor it. This makes it hard to plan the day." Schultz adds, "but if we forget to savor the world, what possible reason do we have for saving it? In a way, the savoring must come first." It may be essential to the restoration of shattered communities and ravaged urban landscapes that we respect and find ways to satisfy the hunger for beauty in every person.

A recent experience offers a modest illustration of my point. An attorney of my acquaintance told me of his experience as a volunteer tutor with boys and girls in a juvenile detention facility. On one occasion he was assigned a group of six young girls. He loved poetry, so thought to tutor them in poetry. At their first meeting the girls acknowledged knowing what poetry is, but none would join in reading any with him; they listened as though not listening as he read. At a second meeting, he drew them into joining him in reading lines of poetry by turn. At a later meeting he told them they were not going to read any more poetry; they were going to create poetry. He drew them into doing that by turning and putting a simple couplet on the blackboard and asking them if they could continue the poem with another line or couplet. "Sure, I can do that," said the toughest one who seemed also to be the leader of the group. The others followed. When the attorney arrived for the next session he found that they had each written a poem of their own. Their hunger for beauty of some kind in their lives had drawn them into taking a small but awesomely moving step out of the confining narrowness and spiritual poverty of their lives.

Beautiful acts need not be senseless. They may be a thoughtful response to the knowledge that there is a deep hunger for beauty in every person, however seemingly overwhelmed by discord and darkness they may appear. The attorney tutoring those youthful prisoners might have seen his time with them as an opportunity to give them lessons in goodness or truth by which to mend their ways, but he had the imagination to do much more for them: to appreciate the hunger for beauty in them and to offer them gifts of beauty and of beautifying activity.

The presence of beauty is essential to spiritual well-being; its absence is powerfully destructive. To be in the presence of beauty is spiritually nourishing as only the divine presence can nourish. To be drawn into beautifying activity or senseless acts of beauty is even more nourishing, for it is to participate in the life of God overflowing into the world. As Frederick Turner recently wrote, beauty "is central to all meaningful human life and achievement, it gives access to the objective reality of the universe. . . . Its absence in the family, in schools, and in public life is a direct cause of the worst of our social problems and a contributing cause of all others, and its restoration to the center of our culture will bring real improvements to the lives of all citizens."[22] I agree with the apostle Paul regarding the spiritual trinity of faith, hope, and love: they are all important, but the greatest of them is love. I am inclined to say regarding that other great moral trinity of goodness, truth, and beauty: they are all essential, but the greatest of these is beauty. What difference would it make if we were to imagine

22. Frederick Turner, *Beauty: The Value of Values* (Charlottesville and London: University Press of Virginia, 1991), pp. 15f.

virtue and love, as Edwards did, as forms of beauty rather than as forms of goodness?

A major contribution these Edwardsean themes can make to contemporary religious ethics is to help us reclaim the intimate and essential relation between aesthetics and ethics. We make our way through the world largely in terms of a generally inarticulate but aesthetically powerful *sense* of how things are out there and a corresponding *sense* of how it is to be appropriately human. That sense of reality and sense of humanity is always culturally informed, and at our best we struggle with less than complete success to render it more adequate. Edwards understands how the transformation of the moral life begins with the actualization of a new sense of reality no less than a new "sense of the heart." The formation and the transformation of the moral life is a matter of sensibility as well as of the affections.

As Edwards shows so clearly, the relation between the affections and their objects provides the dynamic of the moral and spiritual life. Most especially is it important for ethics to attend to the cultivation of the affirmative affections as distinguished from the negative ones. For the moral and spiritual life is better guided by what we are moved to affirm than it is by what we reject and deny, even if it is true that we have a more reliable sense of what constitutes injustice than we do of what makes for justice. Recall how the affirmative affections of joy and delight are for Edwards partner to virtue and love as ingredient in the life of God, and how he calls the will the enjoying faculty.

Our appreciative capacities or powers provide a further means of specifying the senses and affections as they figure in the moral and spiritual life. Enthusiastic appreciation is what I read in Diane Yeager's characterization of H. Richard Niebuhr's sense of what is "our deepest religious responsibility": "to love the world and hallow it."[23] And James Gustafson has made discernment and a whole range of senses or sensibilities — all of them modes of appreciation — central to his *Ethics from a Theocentric Perspective,* a landmark contribution to contemporary religious ethics, and one in which the idea of participation also plays a formative role.[24] Our appreciative capacities are morally important for another reason made much of by both Niebuhr and

23. See note 21 above.
24. James M. Gustafson, *Ethics from a Theocentric Perspective,* 2 vols. (Chicago: University of Chicago Press, 1981; 1984).

Gustafson: humanity comes upon the scene with action already well under way, and the action will continue after we depart; our personal lives, and even the wider human drama, are not the center of the cosmic drama. We need to cultivate our capacities to appreciate and cordially consent to a much wider system of being that comes to us with the overflowing divine life.[25]

Among other things, religious ethics needs to appreciate and attend to the place of suffering as well as flourishing, of patience as well as agency, of undergoing as well as doing and accomplishing in human experience. Such an ethics would be heavy with descriptive attention to how things are in the world, appreciative of our limited capacities as well as our possibilities, and responsive primarily to the divine presence and beautifying activity rather than to the agencies and forces in dissenting rebellion. We need to cultivate our capacities to appreciate and cordially consent to whatever can be discerned of the wider system of being and beauty that comes to us with the overflowing divine life.

H. Richard Niebuhr's ethics of responsibility is powerfully influenced by Edwards; it acknowledges the intimate relation between aesthetics and ethics and recognizes the morally and spiritually formative role of our appreciative powers and of the affirmative affections and, above all, of the necessity of responding primarily to the divine presence and activity rather than to the agencies and forces in dissenting rebellion.[26] Niebuhr shares with Edwards a relational understanding of reality and of an essentially aesthetic/affectional self, and he ex-

---

25. This and closely related ideas are given contemporary expression in a variety of distinctive and constructive voices. See, e.g., Donald Evans, *Spirituality and Human Nature* (Albany, NY: State University of New York Press, 1993); Sallie McFague, *Models of God* (Minneapolis: Fortress Press, 1987); Matthew Fox, *A Spirituality Named Compassion* (San Francisco: Harper & Row, 1979) and *Original Blessing* (Santa Fe: Bear & Company, 1983); and Sharon Salzberg, *Lovingkindness* (Boston: Shambala, 1995). For a splendid discussion of developments closer to Edwards and to H. Richard Niebuhr, see William C. Spohn and Thomas A. Byrnes, "Knowledge of Self and Knowledge of God: A Reconstructed Empiricist Interpretation," in *Christian Ethics: Problems and Prospects*, ed. Lisa Sowle Cahill and James F. Childress (Cleveland: The Pilgrim Press, 1996), ch. 7, pp. 119-33.

26. H. Richard Niebuhr, *The Responsible Self* (New York: Harper & Row, 1963). The most important contribution to the continuing discussion of an ethics of responsibility is William Schweiker, *Responsibility and Christian Ethics* (Cambridge, England: Cambridge University Press, 1995).

pressed late in his life an intention to follow Edwards even further in exploring what Niebuhr called "the land of the emotions." Niebuhr concluded the third of his Cole Lectures, entitled "Toward the Recovery of Feeling," with an Edwardsean reminder that "'true religion, in great part' — and true life in great part — 'consists in the affections.'"[27] I would only press the Niebuhrian ethic further along lines suggested by the Edwardsean themes I have foregrounded, for I think they provide the resources to advance and consolidate Niebuhr's effort to develop an ethics of responsibility as a full-blown alternative to the still-dominant deontological and teleological approaches to ethics.

I imagine the next step in that direction to be what might be called an aesthetics of responsibility, showing how an ethics of responsibility has a different beginning and different dynamics than either deontological or teleological ethics. The *aesthetics* of responsibility has to do precisely with the beginning and the dynamics of the moral life. Edwards laid the foundations for such a development with the ideas foregrounded in this essay. The appropriate beginning is to be attentive and responsive to the way things are in their actuality. I call Edwards an actualist — neither idealist nor realist are quite the right word. He sought always to know and to engage himself with how things are in their actuality. Crucial to the experience of the actuality of God and of the divine life, as Edwards understood it, was a perception of the divine beauty. He was convinced that the actuality of something could not be properly understood until perceived in relation to God, and that no life could be fulfilled apart from enjoying and cordially participating in the beautifying life of God overflowing into the world. So he both preached and wrote with the aim of bringing others to share and experience as living actuality what was actual for himself.

A religious ethics that shares these convictions will also recognize the essential role of celebration in nourishing and sustaining the energy and vitality of persons drawn into participating in the divine life. This is not a subject to which religious ethics has usually paid much attention, but it is one to which the religious ethics I have described will want to give careful attention. Concerning this aspect of Edwards's thought H. Richard Niebuhr wrote appreciatively:

27. H. Richard Niebuhr, "The Cole Lectures," in *Theology, History, and Culture,* p. 49.

What Edwards knew, what he believed in his heart and with his mind, was that man was made to stand in the presence of eternal, unending absolute glory, to participate in the celebration of cosmic deliverance from everything putrid, destructive, defiling, to rejoice in the service of the stupendous artist who flung universes of stars on his canvas, sculptured the forms of angelic powers, etched with loving care miniature worlds within worlds.[28]

Several Edwardsean themes are evident in this passage: participation, celebration, rejoicing, and (implicitly) the overwhelming beauty of God's artistry in the creation. I am reminded of the Introit with which the choir in my church often opens the service:

Come, ye that love the Lord, and let your love be known;
Join in a song of sweet accord and thus surround the throne.
The sorrows of the mind be banished from this place;
Religion never was designed to make our pleasures less.
Let those refuse to sing who never knew our God;
But favorites of the heav'nly one may speak their joys abroad.
(arr. Alice Parker)

I believe Edwards would stand today with Abraham Joshua Heschel in representing our appreciative and celebrative capacities as foundational to the spiritual and moral life.[29]

Finally, I want to suggest that an ethics articulated in Edwardsean terms, foregrounding beauty and the aesthetic dimensions of reality and of human experience, will provide timely resources to movements concerned with the transformation of public life. As Jim Wallis wrote recently in *The Soul of Politics*, "new politics and new spirituality can only emerge together."[30] An ethics grounded in the perception of divine beauty and cordial participation in the beautifying activity of God over-

28. H. Richard Niebuhr, "The Anachronism of Jonathan Edwards," in *Theology, History, and Culture*, p. 128. The title of this address is deliberately ironic, presented as it was at an occasion in 1958 honoring the memory of Edwards on the two-hundredth anniversary of his death, for it was Niebuhr's view that in our own time "We will concede perhaps that man is as wicked as Edwards said. What we do not know — or do not yet know — is that God is as holy as Edwards knew him to be" (p. 132).

29. See especially the opening and closing sections of Heschel, *Moral Grandeur and Spiritual Audacity*.

30. Jim Wallis, *The Soul of Politics* (New York: The New Press and Orbis Books, 1994), p. 47.

flowing into the world may well be more accurate and persuasive than any alternative approach in identifying as essentially spiritual issues those which are commonly treated as primarily social. Captivated by the spiritual beauty manifest in the divine life, persons and communities would be drawn into maximizing the visibility of the image of divine beauty in all creatures to whom that image properly belongs and would commit themselves to overcoming everything that breeds deformity among creatures or in the wider system of being.

The Return of the Will: Jonathan Edwards and the Possibilities of Free Will

ALLEN C. GUELZO

1

If certain national cultures seem to own certain great problems of the mind, then freedom of the will seems to be the American problem. This is not just because of the sheer stupifying bulk of what Americans have written on this problem over the past 300 years, from Benjamin Franklin to Daniel Dennett, from Quaker prophetesses in Vermont to prairie lawyers in Illinois. In the most fundamental sense, freedom of the will has been an American possession because it forms a cognate philosophical discourse to that most fundamental of all American ideas, that of political and civil liberty. To speak of liberty in the public sphere is, necessarily, to make a judgment about the capacity of people for choice in the most highly personal sense as well; the extent of those capacities for choice is, in philosophical terms, what a discussion of freedom of the will is all about.

But free will has possessed American imaginations for more mundane reasons as well: one of these is its simple strategic position at the intersection of precisely those intellectual disciplines which have had the longest innings in American thought, for free will is a question which links theology and metaphysics with ethics, with psychology, and with epistemology, all of which are easily recognizable as major American intellectual industries. But whatever the reasons, it stands plain before our faces that the passage of time and argument have done nothing to dim the intensity with which Americans summon each other to battle over free will. If anything, after more than a generation of seeming quiescence in American thought, our current cultural crises have kicked new life back into the American preoccupation with free will. A full-page ad in the New York *Times* in September, 1994, disgustedly recited a litany of popular "abuse excuses" and declared, "It's as though we've never heard of free will" (the implication being, that of course we have and it's time to start behaving accordingly); a nationally-syndicated Los Angeles talk show host aggressively scolds her listeners against "victimization" and complains that "Nobody is acknowledged to have free will or responsibility anymore"; a nationally-known Harvard Law School professor wails that unless we "reassert responsibility for our choices and actions" and "regain control over our destiny," we have nothing to look forward to but "lawlessness and then tyranny."[1] Even one of America's most popular public philosophers admits that "Over the years I have spent more time thinking about the problem of free will — it felt like banging my head against it — than about any other philosophical topic except perhaps the foundations of ethics."[2]

But ultimately, the peculiarly American hold on free will lies not just in the tenacity of our grip on it, but in the peculiar way we have held it, and the particular ways we have had of arguing about it. For us, free will has been predominately a fiercely theological and metaphysical problem, and more ink has been spilled from these bottles, probably, than all the others combined; it has also taken the shape of a problem about experience and the value of individuals and their choices in the unpredictable and unstable history of American society. But it has just as often been a question about science and mechanism and the discovery of order which we both crave and fear. For Americans, free will is not just a point of discussion; it is our national gargoyle, our favorite intellectual device for keeping conscience in the rocking chair.

Jonathan Edwards stands at the head of the intellectual history of freedom of the will in America, not only because of the direct influence

1. Laura Schlessinger, *How Could You Do That? The Abdication of Character, Courage, and Conscience* (New York: Little, Brown, 1996), p. 8; Alan M. Dershowitz, *The Abuse Excuse: And Other Cop-Outs, Sob Stories, and Evasions of Responsibility* (Boston: Little, Brown, 1994), p. 42.

2. Robert Nozick, *Philosophical Explanations* (Cambridge, MA: Harvard University Press, 1981), p. 293.

he exerted over a century of America debate on free will, but also because his great treatise of 1754, *A Careful and Strict Enquiry into the modern prevailing Notions of the Freedom of Will, which is supposed to be essential to Moral Agency, Vertue and Vice, Reward and Punishment, Praise and Blame*, accepted and stated the broadened parameters of the free will debate just at the moment when it was emerging from an almost exclusively theological concern into an enlarged debate about ethics and psychology in the first great age of modern philosophy. *Freedom of the Will* is, make no mistake, still fundamentally a theological work: its stated premise, after all, is to contradict "the Arminian notion of freedom of the will, and the supposed necessity of it in order to moral agency" rather than to undertake a general investigation of the question on the order of Hobbes's *Of Liberty and Necessity*, Anthony Collins's *A Philosophical Inquiry Concerning Human Liberty*, or the chapters "Of Power" in the successive editions of Locke's *Essay*. And of course the stated aim of the book is the "clearing up and establishing the Calvinistic doctrine in this point," so that a purely disinterested, much less purely philosophical, inquiry is never actually on offer.[3] To that end, Edwards has only two real goals in view: (a) to demolish any suggestion that the human will is "self-determined" or possessing within itself its own autonomous power of deliberating, choosing, hesitating, or balking, and (b) to prove that necessity — the determination of the human will by considerations extrinsic to the process of volition itself — is not inconsistent with a reasonable concept of freedom or moral accountability.[4]

All the same, Edwards was conscious, as many of his theological contemporaries were not, that no consideration of free will in eighteenth-century Anglo-America could stop at being theological alone. It also had to deal with frightening models of human behavior — of human choice as a pure response to pleasure or pain, of the human being as what de la Mettrie would call a "man-machine" — being tossed into popular discussion by the unholy English empiricist trinity of Hobbes, Locke, and Hume, not to mention the frightening accommodations made to these notions by New England divines like Charles Chauncy,

3. *The Works of Jonathan Edwards*, 1, *Freedom of the Will*, ed. Paul Ramsey (New Haven: Yale University Press, 1957), pp. 171, 431; Arthur Murphy, "Jonathan Edwards on Free Will and Moral Agency," *Philosophical Review* 68 (1959), pp. 181-82.

4. John E. Smith, *Jonathan Edwards: Puritan, Preacher, Philosopher* (Notre Dame: University of Notre Dame Press, 1992), p. 63.

who laid it down as early as 1739 that "Men . . . can't be *religious* but with the *free Consent of their Wills;* and this can be gain'd in no Way but that of *Reason* and *Persuasion.*"[5] And so Edwards looked for materials with which to make his two arguments in *Freedom of the Will* far beyond the kind of perfunctory anti-Arminianism one gets in John Gill or Peter Clark, where the chief task amounted to little more than rolling the boulder of standard Calvinistic scriptural citations on divine election and predestination back up the mountain one more time. Although the conclusions to which Edwards directed *Freedom of the Will* remained theological ones, his arguments would be predicated on a risky series of analytic propositions about the terms and processes of human volition.

It is for this reason, however, that *Freedom of the Will* perplexed a good many of its readers, friends as well as enemies; *Freedom of the Will* even today fuddles Calvinist divines who go to it expecting to find a straightforward reservoir of exegetical ammunition for their sermons. At least in structural terms, Edwards opens *Freedom of the Will* with what could be taken as an abandonment of the theological stance altogether, because the first of the four "parts" of *Freedom of the Will* is devoted to a highly detailed construction of the four key terms central to Edwards's task: will, motive, necessity, and liberty. The human will he slices off in the first two paragraphs: "the will (without any metaphysical refining) is plainly, that by which the mind chooses anything," so that "an act of the will is the same as an act of choosing or choice."[6]

This was a marvelous opening move, since with his first stroke Edwards forbade any separation of the act of choosing from the will itself: the will could not be said to choose, or to deliberate, or to resist while making up its mind, since the will was nothing but "an act of choosing or choice." Any notion of "self-determination," Arminian or otherwise, which thought of the will as an entity which performed a variety of review functions prior to the actual choice, was suddenly dashed out of the hand of Edwards's invisible opposition. However, if the will could only *choose*, then that raised the question of what determined the choosing, if not the will itself: Edwards's answer was *motive*, or rather "that motive, which, as it stands in the view of the mind,

---

5. Charles Chauncy, *The Only Compulsion Proper to be Made Use of in the Affairs of Conscience and Religion* (Boston: J. Draper, 1739), p. 10.

6. Edwards, *Works*, 1, p. 137.

is the strongest. . . ."[7] A motive was a catch-all concept for Edwards, since it covered "the whole of that which moves, excites or invites the mind to volition." And, concerned as he was to close off any opportunities for "Arminians" to smuggle "self-determination" back into the process of willing, Edwards makes such a close connection between the perception of the strongest motive and the act of choosing that they become welded into virtual identity with each other. "And therefore it must be true, in some sense, that the will always is as the greatest apparent good is."

This allowed Edwards to turn to the highly-charged term *necessity* with a freer hand: Arminians, he conceded, would be right to claim that necessity and free will are incompatibles *provided* that the only concept of necessity available were something on the lines of forced entry. But necessity also comes in other forms, such as logical or moral necessity, where the connections between terms are "full and fixed" without any application of physical force. Given the ease with which he has just defined how motives have precisely this "full and fixed" connection to willing, Edwards dismisses Arminian fears that "necessity" is the enemy of a free and unobstructed operation of the will. *Liberty*, in that case, is simply "being free from hindrance and impediment in the way of doing," so that "let the person come by his volition or choice how he will" — and he will always come to it by way of motive, since the will by definition does not will its own willings — "yet, if he is able, and there is nothing in the way to hinder his pursuing and executing his will, the man is fully and perfectly free, according to the primary and common notion of freedom."[8]

Having crisscrossed the terrain with the wires of these definitions, Edwards devotes the second part of *Freedom of the Will* to a ballet of errors, in which the reader is treated to the spectacle of Arminians tripping and blundering over Edwards's traps. Does the Arminian persist in believing that the will is "an agent that has a will" which it determines itself? Edwards leads them across the wire of infinite regress: "if the will determines all its own free acts, then every free act of choice is determined by a preceding act of choice, choosing that act . . . which brings us directly to a contradiction: for it supposes an act of the will preceding the first act in the whole train, directing and determining

7. Ibid., p. 141.
8. Ibid., pp. 163, 164.

the rest; or a free act of the will, before the first free act of the will."[9] Does an Arminian believe that somehow a first free act in this chain can materialize on its own? Only if "we begin to maintain, that things may come into existence, and begin to be, which heretofore have not been, of themselves, without any cause." But to abandon causality in order to get freedom will not get freedom; instead, it will jeopardize every rational argument for the existence of God from the being of the world and render every act of will uncaused and rudderless.[10] The free willer who finds necessity a hard mistress will find chaos, indifference, and contingency an ever harder one. There is, in sum, no refuge for the Arminian, because the notion of a self-determined will is analytically contradictory: if the will governs itself, it falls into the trap of infinite regress; if the will is governed by reason and the understanding, then it cannot be self-determined; if it is governed by nothing, it falls prey to accident and randomness; and if it is governed by God's foreknowledge — in that case, the Arminian has ceased to be an Arminian and become a Calvinist.

A good deal of the force of Edwards's logic depends on accepting two premises: that "motives" possess or acquire strength from some source which has no bearing on the mechanics of willing, and that the presentation of these motives in all future moments has already been fixed. Edwards was content to assume that motives have the force they have on willing because of individual human "dispositions": to a sinner (who by definition possesses "sinful dispositions"), sinful motives always have the strongest appeal, while to the saint, holy motives always appear strongest. Edwards raised no question in *Freedom of the Will* about how these dispositions were acquired in the first place — he would do that over the four years following the composition of *Freedom of the Will* in the treatise that became *Original Sin* — and he was inclined very much to dismiss the issue as unimportant to the immediate analysis of volition. But this omission would, in fact, become the Achilles' heel of Edwardseanism, as the subsequent history of the Edwardsean New Divinity demonstrated.

Edwards was similarly confident that he could rely on a general Protestant consensus about the eternality of God and futurity to close off any possible escape route Arminians might seek in a Boethian ap-

9. Ibid., p. 172.
10. Ibid., p. 183.

peal to "eternal timelessness," an Ockhamist appeal to "accidental necessity," or the Molinist formula of "middle knowledge." He allowed, for instance, no distinction to open up between God's foreknowledge and divine foreordination of all events, since for Edwards the eternality of God guarantees that what is foreknown by God can only be thus foreknown because it has already been foreordained. Otherwise, promises, covenants, prophecies, and even the protoevangelium in Genesis are reduced to the level of guesses, an image which Edwards clearly found personally as well as theologically repugnant: "It will appear to follow from it, that God, after he had made the world, was liable to be *wholly frustrated of his end* in the creation of it; and so has been in like manner liable to be frustrated of his end in all the great works he hath wrought."[11] But, Edwards could ask, "how do these things consist with reason, or with the Word of God?", and in 1754, he could feel fairly sure that such a question could only be followed by silence.

That confidence led Edwards in parts three and four to his ultimate questions: Is self-determination necessary to moral accountability? Obviously not: God is necessarily and eternally good, but nonetheless praiseworthy for it; even in human beings, the possession of an "evil inclination" is precisely what makes the evil volitions which emerge from it all the more damning, whereas by the Arminian logic of self-determination in the will, any evil action arising from an evil disposition ought to be excused.[12] Is necessity incompatible with liberty? Not if we understand the terms *liberty* and *necessity* correctly: if

> his will is guided by the dictates or views of his understanding; and in that, his will is guided by the dictates of views of his understanding; and in that his external actions and behavior, and in many respect also his thoughts, and the exercises of his mind, are subject to his will; so that he has liberty to act according to his choice, and do what he pleases; and by means of these things, is capable of moral habits and moral acts, such inclinations and actions as according to the common sense of mankind, are worthy of praise, esteem, love and reward; or on the contrary, of disesteem, detestation, indignation and punishment.[13]

11. Ibid., p. 255; Smith, *Jonathan Edwards*, p. 74.
12. Edwards, *Works*, 1, p. 309.
13. Ibid., p. 370.

Edwards was thus, in technical terms, a compatibilist: free will *and* necessity can work together — but it was a compatibilism in which divine determinism clearly had the upper hand, and in which a great deal depended on an acceptance of Edwards's claim to define *liberty* and *necessity*. And if this still looked to the Arminian too much like making human beings into machines, then better to be a machine than an Arminian. Machines, at least, "are guided by an understanding cause, by the skilful hand of the workman or owner," whereas by Arminian logic, "the will of man is left to the guidance of nothing, but absolute blind contingence."[14]

Curiously, it is not until the brief pages of the conclusion that Edwards reverts to being a non-stop theologian. Even his ontological assumptions about God's eternality appear only incidentally to his specific argument about the will, and only in certain sections of parts two and three. If anything, he is at pains to insist that he is really not being metaphysical at all. We must wait for the conclusion for Edwards to announce that, beyond justifying his answer to the questions about self-determination and necessity, he has also simultaneously made a "glorious argument" on behalf of confessional five-point Calvinism as the king's cure: not only is it a better theology for agreeing with what Edwards says about free will, but it is also better prepared for dealing with the host of non-theistic and mechanistic alternatives which hovered just over the American horizon in 1754.

Of course, it was not lost on suspicious critics like James Dana that Edwards's initial definition of the will was lifted without much apology from Hobbes (a fact which Edwards was sufficiently self-conscious of that he included a preemptive dismissal of his similarities to Hobbes in part four).[15] It was also bothersome that Edwards had offered no very specific definition of what he meant by *motives,* and that he had assumed a strikingly naive and monolithic notion of human personality, in that he had allowed no middle ground for people of mixed dispositions, and how those mixed dispositions might create precisely the sorts of struggle within the process of volition which he denied could take place. Never mind, though: beleaguered New England Calvinists seized on Edwards's argument as a godsend. Before *Freedom of the Will,* wrote Jonathan Edwards the Younger (with some pardonable familial

14. Ibid., p. 371.
15. Ibid., pp. 372-74.

prejudice), "The Calvinists began to be ashamed of their own cause and to give it up, so far at least as relates to liberty and necessity. . . . But Mr. Edwards put an end to this seeming triumph."[16] Over the century after Edwards's death, *Freedom of the Will* became almost a cultural synonym for Calvinism: Herman Melville's narrator in "Bartleby" looks into "Edwards on the Will" for direction on how to deal with the will-less scrivener; Longfellow's Killingworth parson does not need to be called a Calvinist for us to know what he is when we find out what he reads:

> . . . a man austere
> The instinct of whose nature was to kill;
> The wrath of God he preached from year to year,
> And read, with fervor, Edwards on the will. . . .

Even Abraham Lincoln, a sort of Calvinistic deist who all of his life described himself as a "fatalist," at the end of his life "hoped to get at President Edwards on the Will" as a solution to the terrible dilemma of a civil war in which Providence rather than human designs seemed to have a mysterious upper hand.[17]

And yet, it is possible to be too much taken with Edwards's dominance of the free will debate. Both Melville and Longfellow have already begun to treat Edwards as an emblem of dismissal, not respect, and "Edwards on the Will" was challenged from the 1760s onwards by those who feared that it gave too much of the game away to Hobbes, and by those who were framing a very different argument about free will based on an appeal to intuition and introspection rather than the "full and fixed connection" of terms. Scottish "common sense" realism, which became something of the American national philosophy in the nineteenth century, had very little use for *Freedom of the Will* as a text, and even Calvinists in the Scottish tradition, like Archibald Alexander and Francis Wayland, made their argument for the compatibility of divine sovereignty and free will on the mutual non-deniability of

16. Edwards the Younger, "Remarks on the Improvements Made in Theology by his father, President Edwards," in *The Works of Jonathan Edwards, D.D.* (Boston: Doctrinal Tract and Book Society, 1850), 1:482.

17. Noah Brooks, "Personal Recollections of Abraham Lincoln," *Lincoln Observed: Civil War Dispatches of Noah Brooks*, ed. Michael Burlingame (Baltimore: Johns Hopkins University Press, 1998), p. 219.

the authority of the Scriptures and the internal experience of moral freedom, without attempting an analytic resolution of any sort. But a far greater challenge to Edwards's argument for the compatibility of necessity and free will came from the rising tide of scientific mechanism in the nineteenth century. Laplace offered the classic statement of scientific necessity in his *Philosophical Essay on Probabilities* when he wrote, "All events, even those which on account of their insignificance do not seem to follow the great law of nature, are a result of it just as necessarily as the revolutions of the sun," and every turn toward scientizing Anglo-American intellectual disciplines — whether evolutionary biology, economics, sociology, or criminology — sprouted a crop of determinists who had no use for free will. "It is a matter of faith with me," wrote William Graham Sumner as a sociologist, that "there is a scientific substratum . . . principles and laws which are inevitable and perfect in their operation — which underlie all the social sciences." Evolution, wrote Chauncey Wright as a naturalist, had rendered the vocabulary of freedom "metaphorical."[18] Charles Sanders Peirce, who insisted in 1869 that both the mechanists and the statisticians were working from defective definitions of determinism and freedom, escaped mechanism only by suggesting, in his eccentric doctrine of "tychism," that the universe was only gradually becoming entirely deterministic.[19] Simply put (in the words of Steven Pinker), "Science is guaranteed to appear to eat away at the will, *regardless* of what it finds, because the scientific mode of explanation cannot accommodate the mysterious notion of uncaused causation that underlies the will."[20]

But social and natural science could also be a two-edged sword

18. Ian Hacking, *The Taming of Chance* (Cambridge: Cambridge University Press, 1990), p. 12; Sumner, in Dorothy Ross, *The Origins of American Social Science* (Cambridge: Cambridge University Press, 1991), p. 60; Edward H. Madden, *Chauncey Wright* (New York: Washington Square Press, 1964), p. 42.

19. Charles Sanders Peirce, "Grounds of Validity of the Laws of Logic: Further Consequences of Four Incapacities," *Peirce on Signs: Writings on Semiotic by Charles Sanders Peirce,* ed. James Hoopes (Chapel Hill: University of North Carolina Press, 1991), pp. 103-5; Peirce, "Evolutionary Love," *Collected Papers of Charles Sanders Peirce,* ed. C. Hartshorne and P. Weiss (Cambridge, MA: Harvard University Press, 1931-35), 6:287-90, 293-95, 302-17; Max H. Fisch, "Peirce's Arisbe: The Greek Influence in His Later Philosophy," *Peirce, Semiotic and Pragmatism,* ed. K. L. Ketner and C. J. W. Hoesel (Bloomington: Indiana University Press, 1986), pp. 238-39.

20. Steven Pinker, *How the Mind Works* (New York: Norton, 1997), p. 54.

when it came to determinism. The variability within social statistical aggregates led many of the pioneers of nineteenth-century sociology to insist that the uncertainty of individual events negated any possibility of predictability on the individual level.[21] But the most effective reply to mechanism was a solution nearly as ingenious on its own terms as Edwards's, and that was William James's formulation of the free will problem in the 1907 Lowell Lectures on *Pragmatism*. One of the central features of any James biography is the struggle the young James had prior to 1870 with the enervating spectre of scientific determinism. His solution was simply to assert his *own* will as proof of the freedom of *the* will; but he was clearheaded enough in looking back on this achievement to realize that this was an action which had been guided by his own need for psychological balance. Granted that psychological balance and not dogmatic truth was thus the *desideratum*, this might not be the best prescription in all cases. So, when James addressed the free will problem in 1907 as an example of how pragmatism could resolve the interminable epistemological debates of modern philosophy, he announced that "Free-will . . . has no meaning unless it be a doctrine of *relief*." Which view, in other words — free will or determinism — will most likely yield "*novelties in the world*, the right to expect that in its deepest elements as well as in its surface phenomena, the future may not identically repeat and imitate the past"? Had James posed that question to Edwards, Edwards might have replied that security, not novelty, was what people wanted, and that only divine determinism guaranteed security in an insecure world, and gave glory to a God who deserved it. But in 1907, the world was substantially less insecure to Americans than in 1754, and in the self-made world of industrial capitalism, God seemed more remote, and obviousness now veered over toward applauding free will — not because it possessed any ontological verity, but because it seemed to ratify an open and democratic society.

It is one measure of the popularity of pragmatism as the second American national philosophy that it was precisely this formula which dominated most discussion of the free will problem for a half-century after James. James's Harvard colleagues, Josiah Royce and

---

21. P. J. Croce, "From History of Science to Intellectual History: The Probabilistic Revolution and the Chance-Filled Universe of William James," *Intellectual History Newsletter* 13 (1991), pp. 23-24.

George Herbert Palmer, both preached free will on pragmatic grounds, and Palmer used his own Lowell Lectures in 1909 to affirm that necessity "under the prompting of Hume and Jonathan Edwards . . . is a spectre of the past."[22] This triumph of pragmatism over mechanism was fed by the discovery of "uncertainty" in mechanics, in the form of Werner Heisenberg's "uncertainty principle," which Arthur Compton seized on in 1931 as proof-positive of freedom's victory over causality. "With the recent development (1927) and general acceptance of the principle of uncertainty, no physicist could now subscribe to La Place's thesis," Compton announced at Yale; "Natural phenomena do not obey exact laws." And that meant, Compton declared, that "it is no longer justifiable to use physical law as evidence against human freedom":

> The main arguments for the view that our actions are mechanistically determined are (1) the assumption of a determined physical world, and (2) the predictability of a person's actions. We now know that events in the physical world are not definitely determined by past history, and we have seen that uncertainties of the Heisenberg type may very probably be of significance in the actions of organisms with nervous systems. . . . I may confess, however, that even if logic appeared to favor determinism, as it has at many stages of our scientific knowledge, I should be unable to avoid a strong scepticism of a conclusion so contrary to the dictates of common sense.[23]

The pragmatic climate dissolved whatever objections might have arisen from harder-edged forms of logic or harder-edged forms of physics. "Whether or not indeterminateness, uncertainty, actually exists in the world is a difficult question," mused John Dewey, but "fortunately for us we do not have to settle the question." That is settled for us by the fact that the "world . . . is at points indeterminate enough to call out deliberation and to give play to choice to shape its future." By contrast, "only deductive reasoning from certain fixed premises" — which was exactly the sort of certainty Dewey in particular and pragmatism as a whole identified with absolutism and au-

22. George Herbert Palmer, *The Problem of Freedom* (Boston: Houghton Mifflin, 1911), pp. 46-47.

23. Arthur Compton, *The Freedom of Man* (New Haven: Yale University Press, 1935), pp. 6-7, 29, 56-57, 59.

thoritarianism — "creates a bias in favor of complete determination and finality."[24]

But liberty, as we have discovered in the post-World War II years, was a more ambivalent concept than the pragmatists had thought. Quantum mechanics turned out to be neither so indeterminate or uncertain as its popularizers (like Compton) unwarily advertised, and advances in neurobiology reawakened the unquiet potential of the man-machine model. Above all, the incapacity of pragmatism, merely by invoking intelligence and benevolent intentions, to impose order on the unruliness of American public life has stealthily returned many of the problems Edwards dealt with in *Freedom of the Will* back to the center of the stage, and perhaps not incidentally, in precisely the terms in which Edwards originally addressed the free will problem in 1754.

2

The return of the will in the last two decades in American thought has come along four basic paths — the theological or metaphysical, the experiential, the analytic, and the mental (by which I mean, through the current conflict over the nature of consciousness) — two of which Edwards embraced and two of which he rejected, and for what he thought good reason. Of them all, the theological path to the will would seem, at first, to be the one in least need of a "return," since worries about determinism never seemed to have entirely left American theology. But that is only superficially true, and it invites an imprudent slide past one of the major premises in Edwards's theological thinking. For Edwards, the ontology of an eternal God who holds an infallible foreknowledge of all events *ipso facto* eliminated any notion of human self-determination, and he was confident enough that this ontology was shared by his Arminian opposition that it never seems to have occurred to him that they would do anything but retreat as soon as he beat his drum. Curiously, it could be said that the modern theological discussion of freedom of the will began in 1965, when Nelson

24. John Dewey, *Human Nature and Conduct: An Introduction to Social Psychology* (New York: Henry Holt, 1922), pp. 309-10; see also Sidney Hook, *The Metaphysics of Pragmatism* (Chicago: The Open Court Publishing Company, 1927), pp. 136, 144.

Pike made precisely the same claim about divine eternality and free will as Edwards on the pages of *The Philosophical Review*. "If God exists at a given time and holds infallible beliefs concerning what human agents will do in the future relative to that time, then the actions of those agents are not free."[25] Pike, in fact, had set the case even more starkly than Edwards, since his dictum was unqualified by Edwards's claim that a proper definition of necessity and liberty would still permit a reasonable definition of *free* to exist alongside divine eternality.

What was different was the opposition's response, which was, this time, to insist that, if push came to shove, God should not be regarded as eternal or infallible. This was not the voice of some *quondam* Arminianism, but rather of "process theology," which has owed more to Jamesian pragmatism than most interpreters have been wont to concede.[26] And what was especially curious in this response to Pike was that the most forceful criticisms of divine eternality came from individuals like Alvin Plantinga, William Hasker, and Nicholas Wolterstorff, whose roots lie in traditionalist forms of Protestant orthodoxy removed theologically only by time from the categories of Jonathan Edwards. As Wolterstorff, with a provocatively dramatic flair, wrote in 1975, "God the Redeemer cannot be a God eternal. This is so because God the Redeemer is a God who *changes*."[27] The influence of process thinking on these responses has varied a good deal (Plantinga invokes, for instance, not the ghost of Whitehead, but of William of Ockham), and some of them would probably manifest some testiness at the association; but I think the overall congruities are reasonably plain. "I find within myself a deep love and admiration for the Augustinian theology," acknowledged Hasker in 1989, but "I do not find permanence to be inherently preferable to change; a workable universe, it seems to me, needs both in full measure" — whatever else Hasker might have intended, that certainly locates him far closer to Whitehead and

25. Nelson Pike, "Divine Omniscience and Voluntary Action," *The Philosophical Review* 74 (1965), pp. 27-46, and "Divine Foreknowledge, Human Freedom and Possible Worlds," *The Philosophical Review* 86 (1977), pp. 209-16.

26. Bruce Kuklick, *The Rise of American Philosophy: Cambridge, Massachusetts, 1860-1930* (New Haven: Yale University Press, 1977), 530-32.

27. Alvin Plantinga, *God, Freedom and Evil* (New York: Harper Torchbook, 1974), and "On Ockham's Way Out," *Faith and Philosophy* 3 (1986), p. 240; and Nicholas Wolterstorff, "God Everlasting," in *God and the Good*, ed. C. J. Orlebeke and L. B. Smedes (Grand Rapids: Eerdmans, 1975), p. 64.

Hartshorne than Jonathan Edwards.[28] This "evangelicalizing" of process pragmatism has most recently taken the form of what Hasker, David Basinger, and Clark Pinnock have called "the openness of God," and they have in large measure turned Edwards on his head by insisting that the only way to ensure a viable theism, as well as the devotional piety Edwards prized, is to abandon eternality and embrace a theology of "openness" in which "God invites us to participate with him to bring the future into being," and which incidentally "grants humans significant freedom to cooperate with or work against God's will for their lives."[29] This is because, as Basinger explained in 1995, God possesses only "Present Knowledge":

> According to this perspective, God's infallible knowledge extends over everything that is (or has been) actual and that which follows deterministically from it. . . . God understands exactly how the laws of nature that he has created function, he knows how any part of nature which is governed by deterministic laws will develop and unfold. But God does not possess infallible knowledge of any future state of affairs that includes free human decision-making as a causal component.[30]

"Openness" theologians would thus be considered, at best, to be compatibilists, but a compatibilism only between God's present-moment omniscience and possible future events, and a compatibilism altered decisively away from the divine initiative. On the other hand, as in the case of Hasker, openness also allows for a repudiation of compatibilism in favor of outright contingency in the universe. "Incompatibility is real and must be accepted," Hasker insisted, "The *best* Christian theodicy will . . . affirm forcefully that *God the Creator and Redeemer is a risk taker.*"[31]

Edwards would, I suspect, have found this simply incoherent. In the most basic sense, Edwards believed that "all material existence is

---

28. William Hasker, *God, Time and Knowledge* (Ithaca: Cornell University Press, 1989), pp. 183-84.

29. Clark Pinnock et al., *The Openness of God: A Biblical Challenge to the Traditional Understanding of God* (Downers Grove: InterVarsity Press, 1994), p. 7.

30. David Basinger, "Can an Evangelical Christian Justifiably Deny God's Exhaustive Knowledge of the Future?" *Christian Scholars Review* 25 (December 1995), pp. 134-35.

31. Hasker, *God, Time and Knowledge*, pp. 186, 205.

only idea," and therefore the existence of anything "is in God's supposing of them" and then "rendering complete the series of things — to speak more strictly, the series of ideas — according to his own settled order."[32] To surrender infallible knowledge of any aspect of creation is inconceivable in a creation which is, after all, an idea; it would be to alienate God's creation from himself, and worse, to ensure that this alienated creation would, with Peircean inevitability, swallow up God himself. This did not mean that Edwards thought of the world as an immaterialist illusion: ideas, remember, are real entities for Edwards in much the same way they were for bishop Berkeley, and so both time and creation possess real existence. Nevertheless God's communication with the world is in the nature of a one-way diffusion of his own being rather than a location within time or an adjustment to elements of human struggle. "Though these communications of God, these exercises, operations, effects and expressions of his glorious perfections, which God rejoices in are in time," Edwards wrote in the posthumously published *Two Dissertations*, "yet his joy in them is without beginning or change . . . is eternally, absolutely perfect, unchangeable and independent. It can't be added to or diminished by the power of will of any creature; nor is in the least dependent on anything mutable or contingent."[33]

This may, of course, mean only that Edwards is a particularly grievous example of what Hasker, Wolterstorff, Basinger, and Pinnock believe has been the problem all along: a "Neoplatonic-Augustinian metaphysic" that hijacked Christian theology into an ontology of eternality.[34] But Edwards was quite conscious of what the alternatives to an ontology of eternality were — in *Freedom of the Will* he as much as accused Samuel Clarke and Isaac Watts of promoting the same "openness" touted by Hasker and Pinnock — and he believed that "openness" (a) posed serious problems in Christology, (b) tended to indulge itself in

32. Edwards, "The Mind," no. 40, *The Works of Jonathan Edwards*, 6, *Scientific and Philosophical Writings*, ed. Wallace E. Anderson (New Haven: Yale University Press, 1980), pp. 357-58.

33. Edwards, "Concerning the End for Which God Created the World," *Works*, 8, *Ethical Writings*, ed. Paul Ramsey (New Haven: Yale University Press, 1989), pp. 432, 448.

34. Hasker, *God, Time and Knowledge*, p. 182; Wolterstorff, "Suffering Love," in *Philosophy and Christian Faith*, ed. T. V. Morris (Notre Dame: University of Notre Dame Press, 1988), pp. 196-237.

"declaiming, rather than arguing; and an application to men's imaginations and prejudices, rather than to mere reason," and (c) dodged what seemed to Edwards the perfectly commonsensical proposition that, all things in the universe considered, it was "better, that the good and evil which happens in God's world, should be ordered, regulated, bounded and determined by the good pleasure of an infinitely wise Being . . . than to leave these things to fall out by chance, and to be determined by those causes which have no understanding or aim."[35]

Still, whatever his disagreements with "openness," this kind of theological argument was, at least, something which Edwards would have been prepared to recognize as the kind of thing liable to raise its head in any discussion of free will that went on long enough. Edwards would probably have less patience with the injection of an argument from experience into the construction of free will; he would, in other words, have shook his head in disbelief at Robert Nozick's proposition that the most significant factor in any consideration of free will is whether it grants to us a sense of worth or value. Nozick writes, "Our concern is to formulate a view of how we (sometimes) act so that if we act that way our value is not threatened, our stature is not diminished." Nozick has no absolute case to make for or against free will, but this is because he is less interested in making airtight logical cases than in establishing experientially that a person is "a being with originative value" which "can make a difference." He is driven, in other words, not so much by logic as by anxiety about the felt integrity of the person making choices. "Originatory value . . . is crucial to the problem of free will" because "what we would most want are decisions of originatory value that track bestness."[36] Peter Van Inwagen, similarly, argues that the only argument worth considering in connection with free will is an argument based on our sense of moral responsibility. "The only relevant argument would seem to be this: if we do not have free will, then there is no such thing as moral responsibility; therefore, since there is such a thing as moral responsibility, there is such a thing as free will." And as such, Van Inwagen freely confesses himself an incompatibilist: "since free will is incompatible with determinism, determinism is false."[37]

35. Edwards, *Works*, 1, pp. 375, 405.

36. Nozick, *Philosophical Explanations*, pp. 312, 314, 315, 396-97.

37. Peter Van Inwagen, *An Essay on Free Will* (Oxford: Clarendon Press, 1983), pp. 21-22.

Sometimes, as in the case of W. S. Anglin, the experiential argument against determinism is predicated on more explicitly theological considerations than Van Inwagen's "moral responsibility" or Nozick's "originatory value." The "effect" of determinism, argues Anglin, "would be a feeling of impotence and despair" and a rather crabbed notion of God, and on those grounds free willers should shed their inhibitions and "chide our opponents for their melancholy, repugnant, and unthinkable picture of the world."[38] But just as often, the experiential argument can turn into a simple reassertion of pragmatism. Morton White, for instance, has given the experiential argument an enterprisingly Jamesian twist by suggesting that what the free will problem requires is a "holistic" theory "which implies neither the truth or the falsity of determinism" but instead a "relativism or pluralism" which can shift between free will and determinism as any given moral situation dictates.

> I reject the view that we *must* accept anti-determinism as a consequence of the correct analysis of the statement that the agent can make these choices. I also deny that a correct analysis of it requires us to accept determinism. In the language of William James, I hope to show that neither the truth of determinism nor the truth of anti-determinism can be logically forced down our throats when we say that we have free will.[39]

One might be tempted to say that this is precisely the kind of surrender to contingency which Edwards predicted would wreck all notions of the moral entirely. But Edwards's most energetic criticism of Van Inwagen, Anglin, and White would have been for putting the cart before the horse. For Edwards, if experience entered into the free will debate at any point, it was as a response subsequent to the sovereignty of God: what confirmed the virtue of Calvinism was how it led towards the purest form of experience (in terms of worship, life, and adoration), not how the purest experience could suggest an idea of God.

---

38. W. S. Anglin, *Free Will and Christian Faith* (Oxford: Clarendon Press, 1990), pp. 3-4, 17.

39. Morton White, *The Question of Free Will: A Holistic View* (Princeton: Princeton University Press, 1993), pp. 30, 46; see also Steven Cahn's project for "pragmatizing" ontology so as to make it yield indeterminism, in *Fate, Logic and Time* (New Haven: Yale University Press, 1967), pp. 129, 136-37.

"The notion of liberty, consisting in a *contingent self-determination of the will*," Edwards wrote to John Erskine in 1757, "is almost inconceivably pernicious . . . and wholly inconsistent with, and subversive of, the main things belonging to the gospel scheme." Give Arminian free will free rein, and the experiential result was "vice, profaneness, luxury and wickedness of all sorts, and contempt of all religion, and of every kind of seriousness and strictness of conversation," and all because "their doctrine excuses all evil inclinations . . . because in such inclinations, they are not self-determined."[40] Consult the nature of God first, then see what experience ensues.

But Edwards would probably not take any more comfort from the more rarefied constructs of analytic philosophers who have come at the problem of free will from roughly the same methodological perspective as he did — namely, the analysis of the terms involved — and that is because modern analytic philosophy has sung an almost exclusively incompatibilist song of hard determinism. This is a curious turn, since the long history of American analytic philosophy, up until the last two decades, had been generally friendly to various forms of compatibilism. But now Richard Double dismisses "Free will and moral responsibility" as "merely honorific and subjective" terms which "are not to be counted as candidates among the class of real entities."[41] This, ironically, is exactly the sort of argument which filled Edwards with embarrassment and his critics with joy, since hostile commentary on Edwards from James Dana onwards has accused Edwards's compatibilism of being built out of the same "honorific and subjective" terminology, and therefore merely a smoke-screen for hard, incompatibilist determinism. Edwards himself was unpleasantly surprised in 1757 to discover that *Freedom of the Will* was being passed around in Scotland as a friend to Lord Kames's *Essays*, which treated free will as a delightful illusion which was nevertheless necessary to slide us through life. Edwards put into John Erskine's hands a short pamphlet which made it very clear that the terms by which he had constructed a Calvinistic compatibilism were not illusions; if anyone, it was the incompatibilists who were under

40. Edwards, *Works*, 1, pp. 421, 422.
41. Richard Double, *The Non-Reality of Free Will* (New York: Oxford University Press, 1991), p. 9; see also Ted Honderich, *How Free Are You? The Determinism Problem* (New York: Oxford University Press, 1993), p. 59.

the spell of "artfully contriving to put them on care and industry for their own good. . . ."[42]

What Edwards did not have to deal with in 1757, and which certainly accounts for Double's decision to dismiss compatibilist language as meaningless, is the impact of neurobiology and "cognitive studies." In some ways, neurobiology is the lineal descendant of nineteenth-century mechanism, mediated through turn-of-the-century American psychology's drift toward behaviorism and psychoanalysis (both of which operated with deterministic premises in hand). Here, the spectre of the "man-machine" which in Edwards's day had too little empirical force to command much of an audience has now matured into the single most forceful argument for incompatibilist hard determinism. The great enemy of neuroscience, one might say, is René Descartes and Cartesian dualist distinctions between the brain (as a physical organ) and the mind (as an immaterial spiritual substance); neuroscience dismisses all such distinctions. Understood rightly and empirically, all minds are brains and all human consciousness is the function of brains. What this means for free will is that, in the sense of freedom being the possession of reflective, self-conscious, moral beings, there simply isn't any. Francis Crick, for instance, reduces free will to a location "in or near the anterior cingulate sulcus" in the brain and retails stories of patients who had lost all ability to act spontaneously when damage was done to that area. Crick did not deny that the function of the brain in this context was "free," but he also understood the brain to be functioning in this way as a "machine" which "will appear to itself to have Free Will, provided it can personify its behavior. . . ." There was, in other words, free will, but its reduction to a physical location created some difficulty for understanding whether the entity which had such a freedom was still a personality.[43]

This was very close to suggesting that mental states did not exist at all, a conclusion which some cognitive philosophers like John Searle have treated with horror. Searle has vigorously attacked any suggestion that the mind resembles in structure or in function a Turing machine, arguing instead that consciousness is simply as much a biologi-

42. Edwards, *Works*, 1, p. 461.
43. Francis Crick, *The Astonishing Hypothesis: The Scientific Search for the Soul* (New York: Scribners, 1994), pp. 265-68.

cal attribute of the brain as digestion is of the stomach.[44] But this still gave Searle no very good ground for resisting a mechanistic view of willing, and it gave the more radical "computational" cognitive philosophers an easy opening for asserting a full-blown theory of mechanistic determinism. Daniel Dennett, for instance, does not balk at describing human minds as Turing machines and human subjects as "zombies" — he argues that "consciousness" as we experience the phenomenon is really only a higher-order form of complexity than the "artificial intelligence" which can now be built into robots — and as such, the only free will we should concern ourselves with is whatever "free will" notion helps us in good pragmatic fashion to come to terms, individually and socially, with our environment. "Whatever responsibility is, considered as a metaphysical state, unless we can tie it to some recognizable social desideratum, it will have no rational claim on our esteem," Dennett argued in 1984, which became an interesting way of insisting that there were recognizable social desideratums, even for zombies. Steven Pinker, similarly, remarks simply that "Free will is an idealization of human beings that makes the ethics game playable." When we want real explanations of human behavior, we adopt "the mechanistic stance," but "when those discussions wind down for the day, we go back to talking about each other as free and dignified human beings."[45] The point was that Dennett's unspecified desideratums or Pinker's intellectual happy hour just might be well served by some notion of "free will" as a way of satisfying our desires, but whether this free will existed as an ontological or psychological reality, apart from our desires, was as unlikely for Dennett as for Pinker.

> What we want when we want free will is the power to decide our courses of action, and to decide them wisely, in the light of our expectations and desires. We want to be in control of ourselves, and not under the control of others. We want to be agents, capable of initiating, and taking responsibility for, projects and deeds. All this is ours, I have tried to show, as a natural product of our biological endowment, extended and enhanced by our initiation into society.[46]

44. John Searle, *The Rediscovery of the Mind* (Cambridge: M.I.T. Press, 1992), pp. 208-12.

45. Pinker, *How the Mind Works*, p. 56.

46. Daniel Dennett, *Consciousness Explained* (Boston: Little, Brown, 1991), p. 406; and *Elbow Room: The Varieties of Free Will Worth Wanting* (Cambridge: M.I.T.

Dennett has not wanted to be found guilty of denying intentionality, or suggesting that "any mechanistic (or causal) explanation of human motivations takes priority over, indeed renders false, any explanation in terms of desires, beliefs, intentions." What undermines the success of that protest is his admission that intentionality can be "settled pragmatically, without reference to whether the object *really* has beliefs, intentions, and so forth."[47] Free will is thus a socially useful component of an intentionality which in fact turns out not to be necessarily distinguishable from computational mechanism.

Oddly, mechanism of this all-embracing sort was what Edwards *expected* to be charged with as a way of rendering him ridiculous; and if there is anything in modern constructions of the free will problem which might genuinely leave him speechless it is the confident acceptance of a form of mechanism, not as a bludgeon to beat others, but as a platform on which to stand. But as Paul Boller has warned, we could not make a greater mistake than to suppose that the cognitive philosophers have invented a wholly new form of discourse about free will: "Modern scientific determinism had its roots in theological predestination and originated as a metaphysical affirmation rather than as a hypothetical presupposition to guide empirical or experimental research."[48] From Edwards to Dennett, we have been locked in a wordy embrace with the same gargoyle. That prospect leads us, then, to a highly troubling question in the development of the free will problem; for if the questions we have asked of free will over the last 250 years have tracked Edwards's questions to a remarkable degree, what accounts for the startling reversal of the answers? Of evangelical theologians who depreciate the eternality of God, of philosophers who freeze terminology meant for compatibilism into hard determinism, or scientists who regard zombie-ism as a worthwhile description of human consciousness?

Part of the answer may lie half-imbedded in *Freedom of the Will* it-

---

Press, 1984), pp. 163, 169. Dennett includes a footnote to his assertion that "We're all zombies," in *Consciousness Explained*, insisting that "It would be an act of desperate intellectual dishonesty to quote this assertion out of context!" (p. 406), but this leaves us wondering why the statement was then made in the first place.

47. Dennett, "Mechanism and Responsibility," *Brainstorms: Philosophical Essays on Mind and Psychology* (Cambridge: M.I.T. Press, 1978), pp. 234, 238.

48. Paul F. Boller, *Freedom and Fate in American Thought* (Dallas: Southern Methodist University Press, 1978), p. 20.

self, because even as he wrote *Freedom of the Will,* it is evident that Edwards was climbing a darkening hill. He knew all too well in the final pages that "a great alteration . . . has been made in the state of things in our nation . . . by the exploding of so generally Calvinistic doctrines," and he meant that in more than doctrinal terms. Arminianism meant not just free will-ism, but "vice, profaneness, luxury and wickedness of all sorts"; and *luxury* was too loaded a term in the eighteenth century for it to have had no connection with the spirit of "luxury" which revolutionary republicans decried in the next generation. *Arminianism* itself was hardly less loaded, since for Edwards's New Englanders it was virtually synonymous with English culture and especially the Church of England. Taken together, *luxury* and *Arminianism* were Edwards's first inkling that it was the entire British imperial context, and especially the commercial revolution which supplied those luxuries, which would be the most seductive argument against the necessitarian limits of Calvinism.[49] Thomas Haskell has suggested, in a provocative exchange with David Brion Davis and John Ashworth, that the peculiar association of capitalism and moral reform (such as anti-slavery) in the north Atlantic world after 1760 is explainable in terms of the long-distance outlook which capitalism trained people to, a habit of thinking which convinced those same people that they could take far greater responsibility for their lives, their societies, and the ills of those societies, than they had previously thought. Haskell did not intend to talk about Calvinism, and admittedly the Haskell thesis has some serious flaws in it; but to the extent that the market revolution — the commercial invasion of *luxuries* — of the late eighteenth and early nineteenth century gave people that power of foresight, it also depreciated their need for divine foreknowledge.

This was, at the end of the day, no more than an inkling on Edwards's part; he never intimated more than a predictable Puritan dislike for the excesses of freedom and power, and in fact his own failed career in Northampton and Stockbridge stands as a mark of how little he understood the dynamics of power and disorder. His New Divinity disciples conned the threat of luxury no more skillfully than Edwards himself, since they alternately condemned and condoned the new transatlantic market in "luxuries." But the inkling was there all the same, and time would soon enough tell the tale of an economic uni-

49. Edwards, *Works,* 1, pp. 422, 438.

verse in which Arminianism — in the form of more power, more indulgence, more affluence — would end up in zombiedoms of more regimentation, more boredom, and more hopelessness.

The great allure of "luxury" in the eighteenth century, and the characteristic which linked it in Edwards's mind with Arminianism, was the excess of freedom and power which it promised to its manipulators, both in technological and commercial terms. What we have discovered since Edwards's day is that the more "luxury" we have achieved in controlling environments, economies, and even our own self-identities (the ultimate Arminianism, so to speak), the more thinned-out and vapid the modern self has become. The postmodern industrial state (not to mention the practice of postmodern theory) grants us the unheard-of power to make ourselves over into our desire; but at the same moment, it also demands levels of planning and personal regulation at every stage beyond anything even the maddest Calvinist could have dreamt of. By the same token, the luxury of power has rendered us incapable, to a point no eighteenth-century Arminian could have anticipated, of either setting or recognizing limits on our demands for an endless vista of economic and technological progress. In that way, both the dark turn to determinism *and* the flight from eternality are testimonies that the scientific and commercial "luxuries" which promised to carry us beyond the trammels of inability to ultimate freedom and self-definition have led us instead to a sense of the self so insubstantial that personal agency is inconceivable.

The harmony of necessity and free will which Edwards sought to retrieve in 1754 was a workable dream only within a hierarchical, premodern agricultural society; even he must have sensed that time and the market were on the side of Arminianism. I suspect that what has brought us back to "Edwards on the will" was his sense of asking the right questions about human ability at the dawn of the liberal era; the problem he poses for us is whether we are still humane enough to believe his answers.

PART III

PREACHING AND REVIVAL

The Pastor as Revivalist

WALTER V. L. EVERSLEY

Jonathan Edwards, the eighteenth-century preacher, has become widely known as a practitioner of revivalism, a proponent of conversion. It would seem anomalous then for him to lose his pulpit, after more than twenty years, in defense of his views about communion, as if he were a sacramentalist. But that is what happened.

Using Edwards's experience, I wish to explore the differences between conversionism and sacramentalism as two approaches to ministry which, when simultaneously implemented, engender tension because of their contrasting theological presuppositions. Edwards understood this potential for tension. As an evangelist he advocated conversion. As a pastor he needed to support communion. He really wanted to be a genuine revivalist and a pastor simultaneously, so he integrated his beliefs concerning conversion and communion within the conspectus of his overarching theology of the glory of God.

With accommodating intent, Edwards redefined the conditions of participation in communion according to convictions which he held for a long time but did not implement for nearly twenty years. Neither his motivation nor his patience sufficed to make this change successful. His convictions differed too radically from the understandings which had obtained previously in his congregation where his grandfather, Solomon Stoddard, had worked out a tenable position.

In this examination of Edwards's ecclesiology, I will suggest that his theological integrity actually undermined his pastoral role. It prompted a disastrous political miscalculation in his particular ecclesial context. This aspect of Edwards's experience in ministry can be instructive for the contemporary pastor who aspires to lead a congregation by supporting both conversion and communion. It provides the occasion for us to evaluate the compatibility of the two emphases, and, hence, their place in ministry today. I shall explore the issues by examining, first, the pastor's role, and then considering in turn both revivalism and sacramentalism. I will then look at the nature of the church Edwards knew, and conclude by drawing out implications for ministry today.

Edwards the Pastor

In the minds of many, Jonathan Edwards personifies the pastor as revivalist. A pastor all his life, an indefatigable writer and scholar, he was also an occasional evangelist throughout New England. The merger of these two vocations is rare. In the long tradition of American evangelism, few revivalists have held a pastoral charge. Revivalists, moreover, have a tendency to be anti-intellectual. By contrast, Edwards, the intellectual, makes conversionism an appealing proposition for the academically inclined. He thought matters through. The ontology and typology which informed his erudite preaching, biblical by any definition of the term, rescued him from descending to the fundamentalism to which revivalism often degenerates.

Richard Stoll Armstrong tries to make a case for the pastor as evangelist today,[1] but the responsibilities of a pastor and a revivalist differ sufficiently in content and character to make of a pastor-evangelist an ecclesiastical hybrid. The pastor has civic duties. The pastor has to visit the sick and counsel the troubled. The pastor presides at the administration of communion. While the pastor might repeat some of his sermons, as did Edwards, his ministry depends on regular study and fresh insights; evangelists, on the other hand, tend to repeat the same sermons in many different places. Edwards the pastor preached and taught about the Christian life — charity and its fruits, sanctification, and obedience — as did the average pastor. Some of Edwards's particular pastoral concerns are evident in the se-

---

1. Richard Stoll Armstrong, *The Pastor as Evangelist* (Philadelphia: The Westminster Press, 1984).

lection by Kenneth P. Minkema of a significant sample of the civic and sacramental sermons which engaged his attention during his early ministry.[2]

Edwards the pastor had an obligation to act soberly in supervising the flock of God. Excesses of emotionalism would not do. Indeed, concern about this particular aspect of revivalism shaped Edwards's greater emphasis on maintaining steadiness and stability in his cure of souls. The highly emotionally charged language of revivalist preaching frequently provoked excesses of emotional response.

Early in his ministry, in a 1741 Yale Commencement Address which later became *The Distinguishing Marks of a Work of the Spirit of God*, Edwards referred with sympathy to the "tears, trembling, groans, loud outcries, agonies of body, or the failing of bodily strength," which accompany revival. He argued that although Scripture did not specifically mention them all, God could not be confined to using for his glory only those signs which Scripture mentioned.[3] Five years after the Yale address, however, Edwards's change of opinion on this subject is evident in his *A Treatise Concerning Religious Affections*, a work of noteworthy sobriety regarding the emotionalism associated with the revivals.[4] Rather than merely regarding emotional responses per se as neither proving nor disproving the presence of the Spirit, *Religious Affections* excoriates dependence on the unsanctified imagination which leads to emotional excesses.[5]

Edwards amplifies the meaning of "affections" to include a compendium of Christian spiritual gifts, graces, and works. He modifies his original near-neutrality about emotionalism to reject manifestations of emotion as proper marks of the conversion experience. He considers such manifestations to be untrustworthy guides to a per-

---

2. Jonathan Edwards, *The Works of Jonathan Edwards*, 14, *Sermons and Discourses 1723-1729*, ed. Kenneth P. Minkema (New Haven: Yale University Press, 1996).

3. *The Works of Jonathan Edwards*, 4, *The Great Awakening*, ed. C. C. Goen (New Haven: Yale University Press, 1972), pp. 230-35.

4. *The Works of Jonathan Edwards*, 2, *Religious Affections*, ed. John Smith (New Haven: Yale University Press, 1959).

5. Frequently, Edwards disparaged the imagination. For helpful discussions of his attitude see Conrad Cherry, *Nature and Religious Imagination* (Philadelphia: Fortress, 1980), pp. 26-35, 56-57; Wilson Kimnach, "Jonathan Edwards' Pursuit of Reality," in *Jonathan Edwards and the American Experience*, ed. Nathan O. Hatch and Harry S. Stout (New York: Oxford University Press, 1988), pp. 102-17.

son's spiritual standing before God and other people. But the most remarkable shift in his thinking appears in his emphasis on a change of nature as the seventh gracious sign or affection[6] which must have its "exercise and fruit in Christian practice," the twelfth and last sign.[7]

By proposing right conduct as the critical criterion of Christian commitment, Edwards chooses an indicator of the evidence of the Spirit which any pastor or layperson could see. This is primarily a pastor's identification of that which surpasses all the intellectual options by which one might define the affections. But this Calvinist pastor is not crudely advocating "works righteousness." He sees conduct as the outgrowth of inner transformation. As a pastor, resident in a particular geographical location and attached to a particular congregation, Edwards here exhibits distinctly pastoral preferences. He is not a roving revivalist. He can verify whether church members have implemented the message in their conduct on the basis of their own testimony and reports by their neighbors.

Pastors have time for the cure of souls and for reflection on their development. Revivalists might interest souls and encourage them to make a decision for Christ but pastors must have an abiding concern for the continuity of the life of the community over which they have oversight. Unlike the typical revivalist, they interact directly with individuals. They not only exhort parishioners to avail themselves of all the means of grace but have a duty to place them at the disposal of believers for their spiritual growth.

All these factors create the significant divide between pastors and revivalists, and underscore Edwards's new emphasis on conduct and his demand for a profession of faith before communion. Inevitably, the means of grace include the sacrament of communion and its administration. Communion is integral to the practice of pastoral ministry. It aids stability and conduces to Christian maturity. Evangelists may choose not to think through the theology of communion and who should or should not attend. Jonathan Edwards the pastor did not have that luxury. The very success of revivalism which added active members to the congregation prodded him to examine the importance of communion in his ministry and in the life of his parishioners. Who

6. *Works*, 2, p. 340.
7. Ibid., p. 383.

should participate? Is communion a saving ordinance? How should the pastor proceed?

Edwards's newly articulated emphasis on conduct seemed inconsistent with revivalism. For revivalists, conversion was not a protracted event; hence, all who claimed conversion would be immediately eligible to attend communion. But it was not consistent with sacramentalism either, since sacramentalists presumed that all baptized persons were eligible to attend communion. The latter fact, as much as the first, presented political complications for Edwards. Politically, he had to live with the larger community of clergy and with a congregation whose members were also leading citizens of Northampton. Edwards was to prove more a theologian of integrity than an adept politician on this issue.

In writing *Religious Affections,* Edwards demonstrates more than a mere awareness of ecclesiastical politics. Revivalist and anti-revivalist clergy far and near became embroiled in acrimonious debates about the course of revivalism, its theology, and its effects. Clergy, then and now, often fight for influence in theological terms about issues of power. They choose sides. In this instance, the Old Lights, defenders of tradition, battled the New Lights, Edwards and his compatriots who advocated revivalism and defended it. A few laypersons became involved in these "testings of the spirit," as the debates were called, but revivals continued because of indispensable lay involvement, not clergy leadership.[8] Revivals were about the conversion of laypeople.

Edwards, long in the theological fray, produces in *Religious Affections* a political manifesto. It attempts the balancing act of siding with the defenders of revivalism while trying to placate its detractors. It is a rigorous scholarly work for pastors, not for theological novices. It demands close reading. It still stands on its own for its nuanced analysis of religious experience. As Wayne Proudfoot argues, it speaks in theological terms about psychological states, as distinct from speaking in psychological terms about religious states, as William James did much later in *Varieties of Religious Experience.*[9]

8. C. C. Goen provides a useful account of the struggle in his "Editor's Introduction" to *Works,* 4, pp. 46-85.

9. Wayne Proudfoot rightly considers it inadequate to think of Edwards as a psychologist but discovers in this treatise enough psychological acuity to broaden our sense of the psychological valence of human experience of the divine. *Harvard Theological Review* 82/2 (1989), pp. 149-68.

But within the contemporary context, *Affections* expresses the interplay between Edwards's conversion theology and his right-conduct requirement for attendance at communion. His insistence on a godly profession as prerequisite to church membership (and, hence, attendance at communion) amounts to an application of his rigorous demand for right conduct as visible evidence of conversion. Conversion, even mental assent, ought to occur before participation in communion, the community's response to the glory of God. Edwards sees conversion and participation in communion as complementary, not contradictory. For Edwards, God's divine glory, which is manifested in human redemption, is also experienced in communion.

Although the glory of God may connect them intellectually, the issue of reconciling Edwards's new conduct/profession requirement with the former practice, which assumed participation by anyone who wished to do so, had political ramifications which needed attention. Theology dominated Edwards's ecclesiology but he lived in a context which demanded sensitivity to the public impact of his actions. He had some awareness of this for years before he anticipated that his requirement would generate "public noise and excitement."[10] Edwards fought for evidence of conversion on the battleground of communion and assumed he was defending the glory of God on both counts.

Although requirements for attending communion and conduct which defines visible Christians were separate issues, people perceived a connection and saw them as parts of a new and unacceptable obligation. Edwards himself drew a connection between conduct and a public profession of faith for admission to communion. In his "Narrative of Communion Controversy," he states: "I also designedly gave some intimations of my notions of visible Christians in my work on *Religious Affections*."[11] However, in order to specify how Edwards tried to balance communion and conversion in parish life, synopses of his views of both conversion and communion are necessary.

10. *The Works of Jonathan Edwards*, 12, *Ecclesiastical Writings*, ed. David D. Hall (New Haven: Yale University Press, 1994), p. 507.
11. Ibid., p. 29.

Edwards and Conversion

In his helpful essay introducing *The Great Awakening,* C. C. Goen speaks of "revivalism as a technique of mass evangelism."[12] Revivalists may have an arsenal of techniques which include the ability to frame their message in readily accessible phrases, to add graphic and arresting illustrations of the terrors of hell and the joys of heaven, to manage the ebb and flow of their sermons with emotional appeals at the right psychological moment, and they may be endowed with exceptionally stentorian voices with which to express the robustness of the message, but the ultimate purpose of the entire undertaking, as Goen sees it, is conversion.

Revivalists were the catalysts of the so-called Great Awakening — actually a series of "awakenings" — of the eighteenth century. Jonathan Edwards himself presided over two significant awakenings, 1734-1735, and 1740-1743, in the congregation he served from 1727 to 1750. But revivalism was not a novelty to his flock, nor was he striking out in a new direction. His revivals came within a local tradition of revivalism. The parish had in fact experienced five awakenings (in 1679, 1683, 1696, 1712, and 1718) during the sixty-year tenure of Solomon Stoddard, Edwards's grandfather, whom he succeeded.[13] So when Edwards spoke of the 1734-35 revivals during his own pastorate as a "surprising work of God,"[14] we may, perhaps, in charity, assign this designation to a lapse of memory.

By the time Edwards became pastor at Northampton, however, the general ecclesiological climate had undergone a sea change. Itinerant evangelists ignored pulpits to preach in the open air, with unwonted enthusiasm. Conversion theology dominated their sermons. Multitudes went to hear them because of their style, their readily understood theology, and "the show." All this made established clergy in their pulpits jealous. Controversy, long a staple among New England religionists, flared.

Jonathan Edwards remained in his pulpit but became the champion of revivalists. Harry Stout says of him: "Evangelicalism's popular

---

12. "Editor's Introduction," *Works,* 4, pp. 2-4.
13. Ibid., p. 5.
14. "A Faithful Narrative of the Surprising Work of God in the Conversion of Many Hundred Souls in Northampton," *Works,* 4, pp. 130-211.

orientation and theological rigor fused in one towering intellectual figure, Jonathan Edwards."[15] He encouraged revivalists through his writings. He began a ten-year period of publication on the nature and effects of revivalism.

The first sally came in "A Faithful Narrative of the Surprising Work of God in the Conversion of Many Hundred Souls in Northampton,"[16] where he recounts the state of local degeneracy, the breakdown of family life, and social contentiousness. He provides detailed accounts of the religious experiences of a few notable converts such as Abigail Hutchinson.[17] Elsewhere he tells us about the religious experiences of his disciple, David Brainerd, his wife, and other persons with whom he was intimately acquainted both before and after their conversions.

Edwards understood conversion as the personal experience of strong feelings of guilt before God, godly sorrow for sin in abject repentance, release from the bondage of sin, followed by a testimony to the fact of the new experience, often with ecstatic signs.[18] Conversion had inscrutable dimensions but also many visible ones. It brought about changes in the dispositions and aspirations of the converted. They exuded a sweetness of spirit, became involved in the enlivened praises of God, and often had a salutary effect on others. Conversions had a major impact on the life of the church as a whole. They caused an increase in church attendance and greater participation in the activities of the church.

Edwards noted also a change in the whole social climate of Northampton, particularly among the young adults of the town.

> Although people did not ordinarily neglect their worldly business; yet there then was the reverse of what commonly is: religion was with all sorts the great concern, and the world was a thing only by the bye. The only thing in their view was to get the kingdom of heaven and everyone appeared pressing into it.[19]

---

15. Harry S. Stout, *The New England Soul: Preaching and Religious Culture in Colonial New England* (New York: Oxford University Press, 1986).

16. *Works*, 4.

17. Ibid., pp. 191ff.

18. See sermons "True Repentance Required" and "The Value of Salvation," *The Works of Jonathan Edwards*, 10, *Sermons and Discourses, 1720-1723*, ed. Wilson H. Kimnach (New Haven: Yale University Press, 1992), pp. 506 and 308, respectively.

19. *Works*, 4, p. 150.

In his local community, Edwards used all the considerable means at his disposal — his office as a leader of Northampton society, and his suasion as pastor — to sustain converts and reinforce revivalism. He showed remarkable social awareness in his exhortations that the rich should be pursued and encouraged to support the cause financially: "If some of our rich men would give one quarter of their estates to promote this work, they would act a little as if they were designed for the kingdom of heaven."[20] He also encouraged converts to participate in communion.

When similar spiritual awakenings occurred in other churches (which were coterminous with the towns in which they were located), Edwards recommended a plan of action to promote their further success. He proposed reconciliation among persons involved as a means of removing stumbling blocks to revival[21] and promoted the reaffirmation of orthodoxy.[22] He also used his fame as a renowned speaker to further the cause. He saw the doctrine of justification by faith alone as the theological foundation of the movement; indeed, he believed that his sermon on that subject had actually sparked the revival.[23]

When invited to preach ordination and installation sermons, Edwards expounded on the responsibility of the pastor to propagate revivalism by bringing people to a saving knowledge of Jesus. These ordinations were of more momentous importance in the eighteenth century than are those of today, occurring less frequently because incumbents typically remained in parishes for a considerable number of years. (Stoddard's ministry of sixty years may have been a bit longer than most but it was not unexceptional. Nowadays, by comparison, we consider a pastorate of ten years a long one.)

These ordination and installation sermons extended Edwards's influence. His voice resounded from shore to shore and his writings spread from the New World to the Old. Without the public occasions attended by many far and near, Edwards might have been less influential during his lifetime since he was among the younger members of a considerable, wealthy family of important clergy. He served a parish made prestigious more by its pastor, Solomon Stoddard, "the pope of

20. Ibid., p. 515.
21. Ibid., p. 98.
22. Ibid., p. 502.
23. C. C. Goen, "Editor's Introduction," *Works*, 4, p. 19.

New England," than by its social and economic character. It consisted of 200 families and lay geographically many miles away from the significant centers of learning and commerce in Cambridge, Boston, New Haven, and New York.

Edwards preached relentlessly about conversion, even in his ordination sermons. In "Christ the Example of Ministers," preached at the ordination of the Rev. Mr. Job Strong, Edwards labored to show that "spiritual washing and cleansing of believers was the end for which Christ so abased himself for them." Pastors should help their hearers honor Christ by accepting that washing and cleansing.[24]

In Robert Abercrombie's ordination sermon, "The True Excellency of a Gospel Minister," Edwards invited the ordinand to imitate the excellencies Jesus admired in John the Baptist, "a burning and a shining light," full of the power of the Holy Spirit. Ministers had the responsibility "to discover, to refresh, and to direct [the church], to be the means of bringing men out of darkness into God's marvelous light, and of bringing them to the infinite fountain of light, that in his light they may see light." Edwards considered ministers ineffectual if they manifested light without heat, for light alone "will not be very likely to reach people's hearts, or to save their souls."[25]

He used the imagery of light and fire in this instance with a certain restraint appropriate to the occasion. However, he was unafraid, on other occasions, to graphically paint a picture of the fires of hell from which God in his mercy redeems. Edwards's famous hellfire and brimstone sermon, preached in the heat of summer at Enfield, has been regarded, much to the dislike of ardent philosophical Edwardseans, as prototypical of his preaching. However extreme they may seem, the convictions expressed in the Enfield sermon were by no means atypical of Edwards and its sentiments are vintage revivalism.

Edwards and Communion

Edwards's communion sermons show a development of a theology of the sacraments based on the glory of God. In one early sermon Edwards says, "The saints have communion with Christ in glory now

24. John 13:15, 16 (June 28, 1749).
25. John 5:35 (August 30, 1744).

and shall partake of the same glory in heaven." Here on earth, Christ invites us in the sacrament of communion to be "his friend, his near and familiar and intimate friend, to accept of the communication of his spirit, of his divine knowledge, of his peace, and his joy, and his glory."[26] Kindred sentiments appear in a later communion sermon where he says that in communion there are "represented those things that are the chief manifestations of the glory of God and his glorious perfection."[27] Although he is much more this-world oriented than his peers, there are many eschatological allusions in other sermons as well, where Edwards sees communion as a "representation of the blessed society above feasting."[28]

Communion is characterized in a variety of other ways as well. It provides for union with Christ — "legal union," "vital union." It is a seal of the covenant like the marriage bond, the bond of fellowship.[29] It also has aesthetic perfections: "If any event was more worthy to be commemorated, it is the death and last passion of Christ. The greatest that ever most wonderful and marvelously dispels the divine perfections considered with the design and events of it."[30] Communion is the essence of worship, the greatest Christian ordinance except for baptism.

Edwards rejects the doctrine of transubstantiation as horrid and monstrous. Nevertheless, he believes that the prayer of blessing transforms the elements of communion so that "our souls are united to the person of Jesus in beholding his excellencies and glory," and that the

26. Sermon on I Cor. 1:9, pre-1733. Edwards probably preached this sermon for the first time as early as 1729 but undoubtedly before 1733, when he began to date his sermons. He holds these ideas quite firmly. He preached a sermon on I Cor. 10:16 which contained similar ideas in August 1745 and twice in 1756. The sermons confirm Edwards's claim that he had formed his views long before the *Humble Inquiry*. (I am indebted to William Danaher, doctoral student in ethics at Yale, for pointing me to these unpublished manuscript sermons in the Yale Library.)

27. Unpublished sermon on I Cor. 10:16(b), preached before 1733.

28. Unpublished sermon on I Cor. 10:16(b), preached before 1745.

29. Sermon on I Cor. 10:16(b). Edwards preached other communion sermons on I Cor. 1:9, before 1733, and two sermons on I Cor. 10:17 between 1749 and 1751. Wilson Kimnach discovers more sacrament sermons than sermons on any other subject in Edwards's sermon notebook 45, the largest of the notebooks. There are 30 fast sermons, the next highest category, and then 22 ordination sermons. Wilson H. Kimnach, "Editor's Introduction," *Works*, 10, p. 137.

30. Sermon on I Cor. 10:16(b), preached before 1733.

communion elements become the body and blood of Christ within us. Christians partake of "the excellencies of the Person of Christ and his love [which] are their food." These elements "procure happiness for us" here on earth.[31]

While Edwards does not speak of the Lord's Supper as a mystery he comes very close to doing so. A Roman Catholic could scarcely place greater emphasis on the mystical nature of the Lord's Supper, in which the elements of communion undergo inner transformation within us. These elements are more than symbols, since they do not remain the same after the words of institution. They become a special infusion of grace, "metaphor," "sensible signs represented," to effect mystical and intimate union with Christ.[32]

Edwards's nuanced usage of "in him," "with him," "of him," and "to him" explicates a theosis, a high view of the eucharist by which Anglicans today would characterize the Real Presence of Christ.

The benefits and intrinsic sacredness of the eucharist should prompt every believer to attend. We honor God by our presence and dishonor God by our absence in a manner more grave than if we were to refuse the invitation to a banquet given by a great person, for at communion God condescends to commune with us.

> If the nature of this holy ordinance be thoughtfully considered, it will appear to be every way wisely ordered as an excellent means to promote strictness and holiness of life, and would undoubtedly prove so if it was attended seriously and carefully and with proper consideration of the nature and design of it.[33]

On reviewing the outstanding features of Edwards's communion theology, we notice the importance of covenant, mystery, the temporal and eschatological communion with all who sit at the Lord's Table here and hereafter in the Church Triumphant, mystery and grace. This breadth of understanding explains why Edwards raises communion to the highest liturgical level possible, to make it the absolute test of com-

31. Sermon on I Cor. 10:16(b).

32. Sang Lee, *The Philosophical Theology of Jonathan Edwards* (Princeton: Princeton University Press, 1988), pp. 143-44, elaborates on infusion in the theology of Jonathan Edwards. See Anri Morimoto, *Jonathan Edwards and the Catholic Vision of Salvation* (University Park: Penn State Press, 1995), pp. 13-36; 105ff.

33. Sermon on I Cor. 10:16.

mitment to Christ: "that which is equivalent to the most solemn oath imaginable."[34]

Evidently, Edwards makes communion and conversion equal in importance. Although intrinsically valuable in and of themselves, they acquire greater value because they conduce to the divine glory. This is their foundation. Edwards thereby makes a viable connection between the two. By doing so, he sets an intellectual example to pastors today, for all clergy can find useful a general theological construct upon which they may build and against which they may test their ideas in ministry.

But a major construct becomes almost irrelevant to the contemporary pastor who faces the problem of winning converts, unless one can build a church and sustain a ministry thereby. And the question remains whether one can do so on the basis of the choices Edwards made. An emphasis on conversion or, conversely, on communion represents two fundamentally different approaches to salvation and ecclesiology. The pastor needs to decide how far these approaches are reconcilable or whether in fact they are essentially different.

Building a congregation on the basis of conversionism entails requiring every member to make a decision for Christ, or to make a public confession of faith, as Edwards ultimately required. "I came to this determination, that if any person should offer to come into the church without a profession of godliness, I must decline being active in his admission."[35] In the conversion pattern, members date their Christian life from the time of their conversion. This becomes the basis of their participation in the Lord's Supper.

Those who rely on communion proceed in a different way. As Professor Goen has explained, "sacramentalism regards the Christian life as beginning with the bestowal of grace at baptism."[36] Sacramentalism considers all baptized persons Christians, so a personal conversion experience and profession of faith seldom become necessary. Indeed, people in the communion tradition may speak of multiple "conversions," a variety of religious experiences. But the basis for their partaking of the Holy Communion is their membership in the baptized community.

34. Sermon on I Cor. 10:16, preached before 1733 and repeated in August and October 1745, and October 1756. Evidently Edwards held this view very strongly.
35. *Works*, 12, p. 507.
36. "Editor's Introduction," *Works*, 4, p. 2.

Communion and conversion can thus be seen as two different doors into the church. Both offer options for increasing the membership of a given congregation but the one more frequently relied upon depends upon the history and identity of the particular parish and the particular pastor. This introduces a variety of permutations for resolution. Edwards usually saw such complexities clearly. However, his vision proved unreliable on these issues in Northampton.

Church, State and Communion

In 1743, three years prior to the appearance of *Religious Affections*, the spectacular religious awakenings at Northampton ended. Revivals depend on the Holy Spirit; revivals also depend on emotional contagion. The Northampton revivals came to an end when two suicides changed the psychological climate of Northampton.[37] Edwards hoped the awakenings would return for he considered them essential to the salvation of people. He could not predict their return but wanted to keep the core of his congregation, the gathered church, attuned to revival and keenly aware of the importance of professing a Christian faith. Attendance at communion became the issue which precipitated the crisis in the Northampton congregation.

Revivals did not impinge on the rights of those citizens who declined to participate. Communion was a different matter. All persons had a right to attend by virtue of their baptism, of their citizenship in the town; the Half-way Covenant, by which those devoid of evident personal faith were still deemed bound to God through their baptism, guaranteed this. Church and state intertwined in Northampton, a not unusual arrangement in New England at the time.[38] The pastor received his stipend from the public coffers; all citizens held membership in the local parish. Attendance at communion was thus a civic issue in spite of the status of communion as a religious ordinance.

When Edwards reached the psychological milestone which made him unwilling to admit to communion those persons who declined to

37. See Ola Winslow, *Jonathan Edwards, 1703-1758* (New York: Collier Books, 1961), p. 46; also Goen, "Editor's Introduction," *Works*, 4, p. 46.

38. Stout, *The New England Soul*, pp. 13-31, discusses the institutional setting of the sermon and also speaks about the social and political equities.

join the church by signing a statement of faith, he commenced his last battle over the theology of revivalism. Ostensibly, he was combating sacramentalism. In fact, he was defending his own brand of sacramentalism: a high church view of the sacraments with a very low church view of participation. Citizens of the town wanted to keep their garden-variety sacramentalism.

Throughout his ministry Edwards held essentially the same views about who could come to communion, views which differed radically from those of his grandfather. He gave political reasons for declining to make those views known until 1748, nineteen years after he succeeded Stoddard: "I am sensible, [it] would occasion much uneasiness and public noise and excitement."[39] Edwards may have guessed that at the time he lacked the political power to disagree publicly with Stoddard — at least while the old preacher was still alive. We would be hasty to equate the burgeoning integrity of the twenty-five-year-old assistant with the famous and mature pastor two decades later. Had Edwards made known his exclusionary intentions it is anyone's guess whether he would in fact have succeeded to the Northampton pulpit.

But Stoddard, long after his earthly demise, remained very much alive in his writings, in the pastoral practices he established, and in the hearts of many people. When Stoddard promulgated the Half-way Covenant in 1707, he was acknowledging both declining interest in the life of the church and the fact that participation in the activities of a parish inevitably sprang from mixed motives, including social obligations:

> In effect, the character of the church was changed. The old Congregational idea had been that the church was the fellowship of believers, and that only they had a right to its privileges, including the baptism of their children.[40]

Without surrendering a commitment to conversions and awakenings, Stoddard acted like any ordinary sacramentalist by baptizing the children of baptized persons and admitting to the Lord's Supper any baptized person, whereby he maintained his religious and political influence in the town and farther afield.

39. "Narrative of Communion Controversy," *Works*, 12, p. 507.
40. Frank Hugh Foster, *A Genetic History of the New England Theology* (New York: Russel & Russel Inc., 1963), p. 31.

Jonathan Edwards underestimated both the Christian generosity and political astuteness of his grandfather's Half-way Covenant. Having inherited, with Stoddard's mantle, many expectations, Edwards was to write, preach, and pontificate upon the religious issues of the day, and become involved in church politics. He fulfilled these expectations.[41] He quickly gained status, found a ready audience, and had wide support for his ministry. But he may have failed to see that that special commodity of political influence had value, too, when issues needed resolution. Votes counted.

He might have kept his views about attendance at communion to himself, or even continued to preach them, provided he avoided putting them into strict practice. But his unflagging confidence in the rightness of his convictions, his sense of leadership, and his integrity as a representative of God on earth caused him to make an issue of them. Finally, his interlocutors refused to let him preach about the issues anymore. They insisted that he write them out for a tribunal. Thus we have *A Humble Inquiry*. The communion controversy was an albatross of Edwards's own creating.

In *A Humble Inquiry*, Edwards attacked Stoddard. He forgot the advice he gave in an ordination sermon, "Another thing requisite in order to a minister's being a shining light, is that he be discreet in all his administrations."[42] Stoddard saw communion as a saving ordinance. Edwards disagreed vehemently. He also underestimated the power of his grandfather's Half-way Covenant, symbol of his legendary survival skills, testimony of his ability to be a pastor for all people.

Edwards's parishioners saw through the encomiums he heaped on his grandfather and recognized the attack on their revered patriarch. They saw in the attack a rejection of themselves. Edwards had committed a fatal political mistake. When the votes were counted the people rejected Edwards — in spite of the glory of God.

41. For example, Edwards became involved in such matters as the settling of clergy in their benefices. See "A Letter to the Author of the Pamphlet called an answer to the Hampshire Narrative," in *Works*, 12, pp. 91-163.

42. Ordination sermon on John 5:35 (August 1744).

Choices for Today

Communion and conversion offer distinct options for increasing the membership of established congregations — both in the traditional mainline denominations such as the United Church of Christ (successor to Edwards's Congregational Church), Episcopalian, and Presbyterian Churches and in some Baptist, Pentecostal, and Bible Churches of long standing. The first group of churches would be generally resistant to revivalism, the second to sacramentalism. But what makes the contemporary ecclesial scene more complicated than in Edwards's day is the side-by-side coexistence of revivalistic and sacramental congregations in the same denominations.

A pastor's choice to depend more heavily on the warmth and individualism of evangelicalism or the coolness and community of sacramentalism determines the direction of the ministry in a particular place. The erosion of membership in many churches sometimes tempts pastors to entertain thoughts about the joint role communion and conversion may have in their ministries. As a consequence, churches in both groups have added practices traditionally found only in the other, for, irrespective of the type of church, all churches gain new members by conversion or communion.

A pastor in the eighteenth century did not have as many options; he could not be a thoroughgoing adherent of both conversion and communion. The isolation which Edwards seemed to fear and which kept him quiet for a number of years did come to pass. He had to leave Northampton for the wilderness. We may, then, learn the revivalist lesson from Edwards but the pastor's lesson from his grandfather Stoddard. He knew that established churches could no longer restrict communion to visible saints or to those who signed sincerely a profession of faith.

On the other hand, pastors today have problems Edwards did not envisage: winning people to the parish and keeping them. He sought to convert members of his parish, his own town, ready-made candidates for induction into the gathered church. For good or ill, churches now compete for members from a broad general public. They do so both for institutional survival and in obedience to the Great Commission. Should a pastor become an ideologue bent on promulgating the pastor's personal convictions as Edwards did?

It seems to me that the nature of the established congregation, the ecclesial context, more than a theological doctrine ought to determine the appropriateness of the means pastors use for evangelism. Edwards failed to appreciate this adequately in the controversy which arose over communion. But though he lost his pulpit, revivalism won America — and Edwards deserves some credit for this. American evangelicalism can scarcely be understood without him, nor can he be understood without it.

H. R. Niebuhr thought that the role of conversionists and revivalists created a tradition indispensable to an adequate understanding of the national psyche.[43] Niebuhr knew Edwards, but Niebuhr's liberal brand of conversionism can scarcely be called revivalist. The revivalistic variety, even in the twentieth century, demands the straightforward Damascus Road experience which Edwards and his cohorts advocated. We hear it echoed in the preaching of that most renowned practitioner of revivalism, Billy Graham, who calls on his hearers to make a "decision for Christ."

Graham also follows the tradition of itinerancy which Americans identify with evangelicalism. Although Edwards was a resident pastor of a congregation, he helped to endow itinerancy with acceptability, if not respectability. Itinerants, unlike Edwards, were not amenable to direction from a whole town or even a denominational judicatory. They pursued their own theological bent without restraint. Because Edwards remained a pastor he remained accountable to others and vulnerable to their votes.

Pastors today who think of evangelicalism as a route to congregation-building ought to remember the occasional nature of revivals. Edwards could not institutionalize revivalism and make it a constant feature of his ministry. In addition, domesticating revivalism constitutes a departure from the itinerancy which contributes to its vibrancy. If Edwards could not do it we should question whether anyone could today.

Pastors of established congregations who wish to draw crowds to their churches often devise programmatic strategies to attract and maintain public attention. They may even invite itinerant evangelists to preach occasionally, without risking their pulpits. We can learn from Edwards that neither crowds nor the techniques of persuading people to come to church Sunday after Sunday make an evangelical. It needs a certain conviction to bring about conversion. Edwards had it but then he could not continue as a pastor.

43. *The Kingdom of God in America* (New York: Harper Torchbooks, 1937 [1959]).

Divinity's Design: Edwards and the History of the Work of Revival

HELEN P. WESTRA

Late-twentieth-century phenomena such as the "Concerts of Prayer" movement,[1] sports stadiums filled with Christian men pledging to be Promise Keepers, and the surges of spiritual renewal lately reported among groups of evangelical students on American campuses[2] are signal reminders that spiritual awakenings, revivals, and reformations continue to be a vital part of America's religious landscape. These contemporary events, bolstered by media attention, modern transportation and technology, promoters and publishers, denominational and interdenominational networking, and no shortage of money certainly differ in form from the religious awakenings in the colonial eighteenth century. Yet many of these recent manifestations of revivalist activity bear strong marks of kinship to the evangelistic impulses that flourished during the time of Jonathan Edwards. Today's "Concerts of Prayer" organization, fast becoming a world-wide movement, explicitly links itself to the ideas and writ-

---

1. Edward C. Lyrene, Jr., "Prayer and Evangelism," in *Evangelism in the Twenty-first Century*, ed. Thom S. Rainer (Wheaton: Harold Shaw, 1989), 90-102.

2. *Accounts of a Campus Revival: Wheaton College 1995*, ed. Timothy K. Beougher and Lyle W. Dorsett (Wheaton: Harold Shaw, 1995), focuses primarily on Wheaton College during the spring of 1995 and includes a chapter called "The Spreading Blaze," pp. 139-69, by Mike Yarrington, which reports in detail on revivals in dozens of other campuses around the country in 1995.

ings of Edwards.[3] Likewise, the author of *New Hope for the Nineties: The Coming Great Awakening*, published by InterVarsity Press, in calling for campus revivals, asserts that "the history of America can be written through the turning points of spiritual awakenings," and looks fundamentally to Edwards as a key eighteenth-century "model of empowered preaching" and a "prophetic voice" for spiritual renewal and a global view of the kingdom of God.[4]

The great colonial theologian, whose *Faithful Narrative of Surprising Conversions* became the prototype of American revival narratives,[5] was surely one of the earliest and most articulate religious leaders to press America's soul toward the notion of revivals as mass movements. Edwards's "original contribution to evangelical historiography" was, as Joseph Conforti's recent study has noted, to "place revivals at the center of the providential plan for human redemption."[6] Thus, to read Edwards's sermons spanning the three and a half decades of his preaching career is also to experience the range of pastoral approaches and strategies he used to stimulate renewal in his congregation. And to study Jonathan Edwards's full sermon corpus is to grasp how central the emphasis on revival was for him, not only during the mid-1730s and again for a time in the early 1740s but throughout his entire career. In his pulpit efforts to make God's redemptive design manifest and to serve as a means of grace that would open his parishioners' eyes and ears and move them individually and collectively, Edwards was by turns brusque, benevolent, belittling, bold, and beseeching toward his listeners as he variously delivered exhortations, jeremiads, and hell-fire sermons. Shaping his messages to call God's voice forth from contemporary events, he played upon the pride and reputation of his auditors (even as he disparaged them as hell-deserving), rhapsodized upon the ineffable and eternal benefits to be gained by conversion, and struggled ceaselessly to maintain his position and authority as revivalist and ecclesiastical leader.

3. David Bryant, *With Concerts of Prayer: Christians Join for Spiritual Awakening and World Evangelization* (Ventura: Regal Books, 1984), pp. 17, 57, 78, 155-56, 199.

4. David McKenna, *New Hope for the Nineties: The Coming Great Awakening* (Downers Grove: InterVarsity Press, 1990), pp. 39, 30, 32, 47.

5. Michael Crawford, *Seasons of Grace: Colonial New England's Revival Tradition in Its British Context* (New York: Oxford University Press, 1991), p. 189.

6. Joseph A. Conforti, *Jonathan Edwards, Religious Tradition, and American Culture* (Chapel Hill: University of North Carolina Press, 1995), pp. 47-48.

In a very early sermon fragment Jonathan Edwards posed a deceptively brief question: "How, where, and by what means may God be found?"[7] Each additional volume in the Yale edition of the *Works* makes increasingly apparent that Edwards's life was fully absorbed in pondering the enormous pastoral, theological, epistemological, metaphysical, and psychological complexities lodged in that youthful inquiry. His now famous letter penned near the end of his life to the trustees of the College of New Jersey remains a poignant reminder of his unfulfilled plan to provide answers within a systematic and comprehensive "body of divinity" that would demonstrate the harmony and beauty of "the grand design of God [in redemption] . . . as it has been brought forth to view, in the course of divine dispensations, . . . [and] successive acts and events."[8] Although death prevented Edwards from completing this proposed work, his collected sermons of almost thirty-five years — certainly his most extensive, systematic, continuous public attempt to illuminate what he believed was God's mind, will, and ultimate redemptive design — may be viewed and valued together as a body of divinity.

Among Edwards's early writings is a sermon on Psalm 95:7-8 expounding on God's "fourfold voice," that is, "his creating, his providential, his verbal, and spiritual voice."[9] Like Edwards's previous question on how and where to find God, this message adumbrates much of what Edwards would persistently enlarge upon during his career as preacher and student of divinity. For Edwards, God's will and mind is "brought forth to view" in *all* of creation. Likewise, God's voice calls out in *all* of history. At the threshold of his ministerial career, Edwards declared in his exegesis of Psalm 95:7-8 that God communicates not only "by his voice to us in the Scriptures" and "his voice by his ministers and ambassadors"; the voice of God is also audible in creation and in events because "the whole creation of God preaches"[10] and the whole of the "providence of God preaches aloud." Indeed, the sermon insists, it is divinity's design that the Holy Spirit's gracious "internal" voice or "call" comes to hearts softened and readied by

7. *The Works of Jonathan Edwards*, 10, *Sermons and Discourses, 1720-1723*, ed. Wilson Kimnach (New Haven: Yale University Press, 1992), p. 380.

8. *The Works of Jonathan Edwards*, 9, *A History of the Work of Redemption*, ed. John F. Wilson (New Haven: Yale University Press, 1989), pp. 55-56.

9. *Works*, 10, p. 443.

10. Ibid., p. 440.

means of the "external call" in the "preaching" of God's creating, verbal, and providential voice.

Ever attentive to preaching as a means of redemption and as his professional imperative, Edwards underscored the importance of his pulpit efforts by noting that "the word commonly used in the New Testament that we translate 'preach,' properly signifies to proclaim aloud like a crier."[11] Future sermon volumes and transcriptions of the sermon corpus to be made available on CD ROM will allow manuscript sermons unheard and unseen for centuries again to "proclaim." These will no doubt strengthen previous assertions that Edwards's sermons, of all his works, best chronicle both his professional and artistic efforts because they are "most revealing of his innermost thought" and are "the pre-eminent genre and the primary vehicle for the articulation of his thought."[12]

Dating from 1720 to 1758, the sermons offer themselves to various textual, topical, and chronological divisions as well as groupings by occasion and function — fast sermons, covenant sermons, sacrament sermons, ecclesiastical sermons, military sermons, funeral sermons, thanksgiving sermons, sermons for children, for parents, for various private meetings, for deacons, for Stockbridge Indians, etc.[13] These discourses provide almost limitless opportunities to chart the intricate relationship between the eighteenth-century colonial minister and his parish through the contexts of numerous circumstances and passing years.[14] Given Edwards's pastoral and theological interest in events as

11. *Some Thoughts Concerning the Revival,* in *The Works of Jonathan Edwards,* 4, *The Great Awakening,* ed. C. C. Goen (New Haven: Yale University Press, 1972), p. 389.

12. *Edwards and the American Experience,* ed. Nathan Hatch and Harry Stout (New York: Oxford University Press, 1988), p. 9. Wilson Kimnach, "The Literary Techniques of Jonathan Edwards" (dissertation, University of Pennsylvania, 1971), p. 1.

13. While Harry Stout for his purposes in *The New England Soul* (New York: Oxford University Press, 1986), pp. 27-31, carefully defines the Puritan "occasional" or "week-day" sermon to distinguish it from the Sunday sermon in terms of the relative emphasis on corporate or personal covenants, I use the term "occasional" sermon here in a less restricted sense to refer to any of Edwards's sermons, week-day or Sabbath, in which the message gains much of its force and significance from its treatment of a contemporary circumstance, occasion, or providence as event-text.

14. Patricia Tracy's *Jonathan Edwards, Pastor: Religion and Society in Eighteenth-Century Northampton* (New York: Hill and Wang, 1979) is an example of a work

providence, many of his Northampton sermons are particularized redactions of local episodes and incidents in which, according to Edwards, "the providence of God preaches." In these sermons the minister speaking for God stands before his congregation renarrating local situations and explaining current affairs as divine design to be clearly heard as God's "providential voice" calling for revival or awakening in the hearts of the hearers. While a number of these sermons contain interesting self-referential remarks and comments, their most distinguishing features are their authoritative tenor and their impressive "exegetical" use of contemporary events-become-texts as exhortations, warnings, entreaties, and means of grace, all presented "as God's voice by his messenger" specifically to the people gathered in Northampton.

In the "Editor's Introduction" to *Apocalyptic Writings*, volume 5 in *The Works of Jonathan Edwards*, Stephen Stein describes Edwards's extensive investigations of historic events, and he claims that Edwards's "pastoral obligations did not dull his fascination with the more speculative apocalyptic issues" related to these events.[15] Edwards's notebooks indeed reveal his millennialist fondness for speculative readings and extensive listings of such event-texts as contemporary political upheavals, naval battles, military encounters, and ecclesiastical struggles around the world. In these he searched for evidence and patterns as to how such far-flung dispensations or providential occurrences might be affecting Christ's church and work of redemption; in this his habit was generally to exercise "speculation in private but discretion in public."[16] By contrast, his pulpit expositions of *local* circumstances and events in Northampton (death, illness, politics, dissension, economic developments, drought, floods, earthquake, fire, accidents) are seldom speculative but rather convey unblinking pronouncements of what God is saying and doing in the event.[17] These sermonic utter-

---

which uses many of Edwards's unpublished sermons as sources of local, psychological, political, and ecclesiastical history. Another such example is Ola Winslow's *Jonathan Edwards, 1703-1758: A Biography* (New York: Macmillan, 1940).

15. *The Works of Jonathan Edwards, 5, Apocalyptic Writings*, ed. Stephen J. Stein (New Haven: Yale University Press, 1977), p. 17.

16. Ibid., p. 19.

17. Much work has been done on Edwards's use of typology and images of divine things. See Perry Miller's introduction to *Images and Shadows of Divine Things* (New Haven: Yale University Press, 1948) and Mason Lowance, Jr., *The Language of Canaan: Metaphor and Symbol in New England from the Puritans to the Transcendental-*

ances offer complex expressions of Edwards's vision of the role of gospel ministry in action, practical applications of his doctrine of revival, his interpretations of God's providential voice, and the ways in which these shaped his pulpit messages and rhetoric.

Edwards's Concept of Ministry and Revival

Much of Jonathan Edwards's confidence in his homiletic interpretations of local events sprang from his concept of gospel ministry; following in the New Testament tradition of the apostle Paul, Edwards believed that the faithful minister is God's holy, ordained agent, divinely delegated and bound in covenant with Christ as a co-laborer in the work of redemption. His words to the Northampton congregation in his famous "Farewell Sermon" summarize the view he held throughout his career: "Ministers are [God's] messengers, sent forth by him; and, in their office and administrations among their people, represent his person, stand in his stead, as those that are sent to declare his mind, to do his works, and to speak and act in his name."[18] As God's voice and proxy to parishioners, the gospel minister "above all others"[19] must faithfully attend both to the care of souls and to the study of divinity, "those truths and rules which concern the great business of religion."[20] In exercising pastoral duties, gospel ministers must be gentle "like lambs to men's persons" but fearlessly roaring "like lions to guilty consciences"[21] because God's greatest work, the work of

---

ists (Cambridge: Harvard University Press, 1980). As John Wilson has indicated, there were times when Edwards "moved decisively beyond a conservative typological hermeneutic," particularly when he "detached the typological framework from its exclusive linkage to scriptural sources," and "explicitly located in the events of history (not only in canonical scriptural accounts) patterns constraining both the redeemed and the rejected of God." In so doing, Edwards's "typology broadened to the point that paradigmatic events outside Scripture had a figural relationship to the rest of history." "Editor's Introduction," *Works,* 9, p. 49.

18. "Farewell Sermon," in *The Works of Jonathan Edwards, A.M.,* ed. Edward Hickman, 2 vols. (London: William Tegg & Co., 1879), I:ccxlv.

19. *Works,* 4, p. 374.

20. "The Importance and Advantage of a Thorough Knowledge of Divine Truth," in *The Works of President Edwards,* ed. S. Austin, Worcester Edition, 1808, 8 vols. Reprinted in 4 vols. (New York, 1843), 4:1-3.

21. *Works,* 4, p. 423.

redemption in the lives of individuals and in the church of Christ, shall be brought to pass "principally by the labors of his ministers."[22]

From his probing studies of Scripture and divinity and his scrutiny of history within and outside the canonical accounts came Jonathan Edwards's ideas on revival as he beheld what he considered essential patterns in God's redemptive plan. His most elaborate exposition of these patterns appears in the series of thirty sermons he delivered in 1739 on Isaiah 51:8 — published posthumously as *The History of the Work of Redemption* — in which he traces the "many successive works and dispensations of God" through the ages to reveal what he believed was an utterly compelling, conspicuous, and overarching truth. Multitudes of events and details in history that "might appear like confusion" can, if viewed rightly, be seen as parts of God's one "grand design" of redemption,[23] that is, a succession of spiritual revivals and gradual increases of divine light until the ultimate defeat of all God's enemies and the full revival and eternal restoration of Christ's kingdom. An additionally important insight for Edwards was that "the increase of gospel light and the carrying on the Work of Redemption as it respects the elect church . . . is very much after the same manner as the carrying on of the same work and the same light in a particular soul. . . . The work in a particular soul has its ups and downs. Sometimes the light shines brighter: at other times it seems to languish for great while . . . and then grace revives again."[24] Accordingly, of deepest personal and professional concern to Edwards was the gospel minister's collaborative role in this pattern of revival within the design of God's grand redemptive plan.

The work of revival and redemption, as understood by Edwards, is no human work but a divine and mysterious plan administered in God's own time through human instrumentality — i.e., through weak and flawed earthen vessels — the more fully to reveal God's sovereignty and glory. In the progress of Christ's church and the "increase of light," the recurring patterns of spiritual declension and revival, of backsliding and reformation, are particularly intriguing to Edwards: he sees declensions as times of unhappiness, selfishness, disinterest in spiritual things, and a turning away from God, eventually followed by

22. Ibid., p. 374.
23. *Works,* 9, p. 121.
24. Ibid., p. 144.

revivals as seasons of spiritual vitality, gracious love toward God, great joy, and a flourishing of Christ's kingdom. Accepting this revival-declension-revival pattern as integral to divinity's design for redemption and the gradual increase of light thus offered Edwards a unitive framework for hearing the many expressions of "God's providential voice" and for communicating them in his role as God's messenger. God's providential utterances over time, although they might seem to have a kind of periodicity or disconnectedness, are for Edwards surely linked and connected in their design, for as he wrote in a 1750 notebook, "the ages are all continuing [and] the last half of our age is the first half of another, and so all are interlaced."[25]

Because Edwards saw the revival-declension-revival pattern as uncertain in its timing and intervals yet utterly reliable in its sequence, his yearnings to assist as a godly means in the positive movements pressed him to formulate revivalist principles to bring his own ministerial design into conformity with his view of the divine design. A fundamental principle which moved Edwards as a preacher to bear down on his people with seeming relentlessness was his abiding conviction that no gathered and visible people could stand in an equivocal relationship to God: a person's or a group's lack of response to God's Spirit (and voice and providence) indicates a disposition against God. There is no neutral ground. Another motivating principle held by Edwards was that God's work of redemption is particularly glorious and effective when numbers of people are converted, because "the amia-

---

25. From Edwards's notebook on "Subjects of Enquiry" (Yale collection). Cited in Wilson Kimnach's "Preface" to *Works*, 10, p. 257. In *A History of the Work of Redemption, Works*, 9, in efforts to establish the patterns of revival and declension, Edwards traces the extraordinary outpourings of the Spirit, beginning with the first "large effusion" of the Holy Spirit "bringing in an harvest of souls to Christ," which occurred in the days of Enoch (143). Edwards then identifies numerous successive spiritual declensions, each followed by and overcome by increase of light through outpourings of the Holy Spirit, each "outpouring" or revival signaling an "awakening" among God's people and a time of prosperity for the church. Edwards studies these "awakenings" as they occur among the children of Israel under Moses and Joshua (190-92); in the "blessed revivals . . . in Hezekiah's and Josiah's time" (192, 233); the awakenings under Ezra's ministry (265); the great outpourings following Christ's ascension and Pentecost (375-81); the gospel success under Constantine (422); the glorious work of the Spirit in the first Reformation, and the flourishing of the gospel "in one country and another," including New England and America "which is now full of Bibles" (434).

bleness of true religion" is more evident collectively in "their walk and conversation" and thus will have a larger "effect in others' minds to stir them to seek after a like blessing."[26] The conversion of numbers can be a greater means to awaken greater numbers of souls to enlarge Christ's church as a greater and finally irresistible force in the world.

Because Edwards held that there is no work, no business, no knowledge so absolutely necessary as "divinity," his spoken messages as Christ's ambassador and proxy attempt to make the abstract ideas in divinity's design manifest and palpable by capitalizing on the "impression" his "words made on the heart" of the hearers "in the time of it." His revivalist strategies thus tend to rhetorical intensification, extremity, and reiteration to fix these impressions "deeper and deeper in the mind,"[27] and his sermonic discourse often deliberately follows "the method God takes with the world — to first reveal his dreadful justice and then reveal his grace,"[28] "first by that which [is] terrible, then by that which [is] comfortable."[29] Edwards takes this to be a gracious means (a providence) to ready and awaken people for the gift of the Holy Spirit; "from the fall of man to this day wherein we live," writes Edwards in *A History of the Work of Redemption*, "the Work of Redemption in its effect has mainly been carried on by remarkable pourings out of the Spirit of God . . . at special seasons of mercy."[30] Thus, as Michael Crawford has indicated, Edwards "made the phenomenon of the revival the key element in the drama of redemption," and his preaching consistently reinforced his conception "of revivals as the engine that drives redemption history."[31] Serving as part of that engine, Edwards's sermons regularly attempt to clarify "God's meaning in his external providence towards a people" to show how these events are related to a people's spiritual flourishing or declension and to their being "rewarded or punished according to their deeds in this

---

26. From a yet-to-be published manuscript sermon on Matt. 5:14, delivered in 1736. All sermons quoted here are housed in Beinecke Rare Books and Manuscript Library, where they are available for reading. I am grateful to Ken Minkema for sharing a transcription of this sermon and several others with me.

27. *Works*, 4, p. 397.

28. *The Works of Jonathan Edwards*, 13, *The "Miscellanies," a-500*, ed. Thomas A. Schafer (New Haven: Yale University Press, 1994), pp. 412-13.

29. Ibid., p. 459.

30. *Works*, 9, p. 143.

31. Crawford, *Seasons of Grace*, p. 132.

world."[32] That is, God so "orders all his dispensations towards us . . . that his voice may be heard in them"[33] as blessings, warnings, or curses; preaching from a local event-text accordingly becomes a vital element in Edwards's revivalist efforts.

Sermons on Event-Texts

Like his well-known June 22, 1750, "Farewell Sermon," many of Edwards's sermons derive their power from their striking — both in the sense of remarkable and hard-hitting — use of superlatives and from their theological applications to hometown happenings cast within the declension-revival pattern of God's design for redemption. To illustrate these traits so abundant in Edwards's many occasional sermons, one could choose examples from almost anywhere along the continuum of his ministerial career. The examples included here come from the beginning, the middle, and the end of Edwards's Northampton pastorate; they are messages related to the death of Stoddard, to the awakenings in the mid-30s, and to the now famous communion controversy between Edwards and his congregation in the 1740s. Each of these selected "occasional" sermons was delivered during a time of perceived declension in Northampton. Each gains its potency from the pastor's intimate knowledge of his auditory. By elevating the providential happening as text, each attempts to shame and startle the unawakened or backslidden listener — and to place the burden of revival and reformation squarely upon the Northampton parishioners. In these sermons, the voice of providence is represented, one might say restated or renarrated, so pointedly through the mouth of the minister-messenger that contemporary drama and details often nearly overshadow the biblical passage upon which the sermon is based.

Jeremiah 6:29-30 (1729)

Vivid use of a contemporary event-text occurs in *Living Unconverted Under an Eminent Means of Grace,* a sermon on Jeremiah 6:29-30 delivered in 1729 to the Northampton congregation shortly after the death

---

32. Sermon on Ezek. 20:21, March 1737.
33. *Works,* 10, p. 440.

of its pastor, Edwards's elderly grandfather, Solomon Stoddard. Having newly taken over the pulpit, the youthful pastor presents a sermon that views this time in the parish's history as one of "extraordinary dullness in religion." He adroitly manipulates the event-text of Stoddard's death to move the listeners to an awareness of their danger in living in such a state of declension. Bruce Kuklick, in discussing *Some Thoughts on the Revival* and *Life of Brainerd,* indicates that Edwards was not above creating literary texts that "distorted" events "for maximum effect."[34] In Edwards's view, of course, careful shaping of providential particulars was not distortion but worthy "use" of material at hand for the readers' or hearers' spiritual "improvement." Having served for several years as his grandfather's apprentice in Northampton, Edwards's familiarity with the church's history under six decades of Stoddard's leadership provided him with insider information to construct the sermon on Jeremiah 6:29-30 for "use of awakening to the unconverted of this town." The message is unsparing and accusatory, intending to sting. It castigates those in the audience whose hearts he believes have hardened by having long resisted the privilege of Stoddard's eminently "powerful preaching." Says Edwards in the emphatic rhetoric typical of this sermon: "Wicked professors of Christianity" who have lived under great gospel light and "eminent means of grace" are the greatest of sinners because they sin "with more presumption, with more obstinacy and more ingratitude" than even the "most wicked" heathen who have not heard the gospel.

Edwards frames the sermon's doctrine ominously: "It argues great danger of being finally left of God when sinners have lived long unconverted under eminent means of conversion." Positioning the recently deceased and silenced Stoddard at the sermon's emotional center, the young preacher aims his verbal arsenal at those who have grown "sermon proof" and charges them with culpability in the death of Stoddard. He alleges that the unconverted members of the parish spiritually abused and trampled on their pastor by rejecting his eminent pastoral care until he could no longer preach. Using Jeremiah's

34. "The Two Cultures in Eighteenth-Century America," in *Benjamin Franklin, Jonathan Edwards, and the Representation of American Culture,* ed. Barbara Olberg and Harry Stout (New York: Oxford University Press, 1993), p. 104. Patricia Tracy in *Jonathan Edwards, Pastor* also demonstrates that Edwards used "artistic liberty (117) in placing the conversions of Abigail Hutchinson and Phebe Bartlett before the Hawley suicide rather than after, when they actually occurred.

bellows-fire-foundry metaphor, through repetition and variation Edwards drives home multivalent phrases such as "base metal," "hypocrite silver," "refuse metal." And he presents vivid images of Stoddard the preacher serving as God's bellows until "worn out by trying." Edwards then warns his listeners that God himself after "a long time trying" is weary, and in removing Stoddard's means, may also be finished "trying." The sermon offers no consolation to a people mourning the death of a beloved pastor and "eminent means" of grace, for Edwards's strategy is to reiterate the phrase "eminent means" so often that it becomes a battering ram on the ears of listeners.

Though the sermon doctrine has a polemical edge ("it argues great danger . . ."), its message does not attempt to convince the "sermon proof" by close reasoning or logic. Instead, Edwards first suggests they are in eternal danger because they are refuse, base, reprobate, dross, and waste. Then with heavy irony, he taunts them for their strength of ego in withstanding roaring cannons (Stoddard's messages) and overcoming a holy champion (Stoddard himself). However, in God's view, the "sermon proof" now appear as utterly "stupid" eternal losers. For those who have turned a deaf ear on eminent preaching, Edwards's message is "Woe to them that go to hell out of Northampton and have lived under Mr. Stoddard's sermons!"

The sermon ends bluntly on the theme that God "takes away his spirit from a people when he takes away eminent means of grace." Although Stoddard's death was that of a very old man, Edwards's interpretation indicates it may well be a divine warning that the listeners' "days of grace are past." In Edwards's sermon the event becomes a threat that God has tried Northampton "till he [is] weary," and the day of grace "is at an end." The sermon's cutting words are those of a diligent gardener intent on pruning a tree for its own future benefit, for the message follows the design Edwards records in his notebook on "Images of Divine Things," where he states, "God is wont to wound his saints . . . before he revives them, after . . . long seasons of deadness, and to purge them and prepare his church."[35] Therefore, the sub-text of this harsh sermon is hope and longing for the spiritual revival that follows declension in the pattern of redemption history. But the sermon is also a clear example of how Edwards's revivalist principles —

35. *The Works of Jonathan Edwards*, 11, *Typological Writings*, ed. Wallace E. Anderson and Mason I. Lowance (New Haven: Yale University Press, 1993), p. 116.

on the one hand pressing down relentlessly to threaten parishioners and on the other holding up a vision of eminent life and faith to arouse parishioners — jostle painfully against each other and create tensions to be relieved only by the converting and purging of a heart.

Matthew 5:14 (July 1736)

Five years after Stoddard's death, Northampton indeed evidenced the softening of hearts Edwards had prayed for. In his abrasive 1729 sermon Edwards had wielded the word "eminent" to describe Stoddard's faithful preaching to hardened listeners. By 1734-35, under the heat of Edwards's proclamations, hearts previously frozen or "sermon proof" had seemed to melt, and the parish became renowned for the revival its pastor carefully described and celebrated in a letter to Benjamin Colman (written in May and June, 1735).[36] For a time Northampton demonstrated great spiritual vitality and gracious behavior, yet by mid-1736, in the eyes of Edwards the parish again seemed to be in declension. In July 1736 the revivalist mounted his pulpit to address the Northampton parishioners in a dramatic sermon on Matt. 5:14 in which he plays upon the congregation's eminence. As "eminent professors" of religion, they have themselves, he reminds them, become "eminent means" of grace in America and abroad. If they fail in the continuing spiritual responsibilities accompanying their fame and visibility as "a city set on an hill," the consequences will be extraordinarily dire. With extensive references to details, names, and places, Edwards uses recent providential happenings related to the Northampton community to insist that the listeners are not ordinary but have become extraordinarily distinguished for their "great and remarkable influence on others. . . to awaken them and reform 'em and to cause religion to flourish among 'em." Because of God's reviving work in Northampton, "the whole country has been filled from one end of it to the other with the fame of what has been here done and what is here professed." And, says Edwards, stressing both temporal eminence and its eternal import, "there probably never was any town in this land under so great obligations . . . to honor their profession by their practice as this town."

36. In *Works*, 4, pp. 99-110. Later Edwards would agree to expand his letter for publication as *A Faithful Narrative of Surprising Conversions* (London, 1737).

While Edwards's doctrine states, "When any professing society is as a city set on an hill, 'tis a very great obligation upon them to honor religion in their practice," his exposition is shaped by deep fears that an embarrassing, dishonoring religious declension has already begun in Northampton following its much publicized revival. Coming shortly after the suicide of Joseph Hawley, a man whom Edwards believed the devil had driven "into despairing thoughts,"[37] the sermon warns of declension: "If we in this town, whom God has of late remarkably set up as a city on an hill, should carry ourselves so as remarkably to dishonor that profession, there seems to be no people that will be more exposed to temporal chastisement."

Repeated references to Hawley's death treat the event as Satan's violently jealous efforts to obstruct revival in Northampton and "bring a blot upon the work of God amongst us." Attempting to resuscitate and uplift the corporate body, Edwards extols the "eminence" which the town's revival had attained in capturing the admiration of many he had conversed with in his 1735 journey through "the Jerseys," Long Island, and the "Highlands on Hudson's River," and in attracting the keen interest of prominent divines in England now wishing to publish Edwards's account of the revival for all the world to read. Clearly, in this sermon, Edwards as God's agent who had promoted and recorded the Spirit's wonderful works in Northampton can now be seen struggling to sustain this revival which has acquired such interest in the colonies and abroad.

Through the rhetoric of intensification and superlatives Edwards's sermon turns the logic of consequence relentlessly upon his listeners. Eminence can be a people's greatest blessing or, when followed by failure, its greatest curse. Edwards tells his listeners that because of the visibility of their "profession and shows of religion" before the world and their "great and remarkable influence" beyond Northampton, they are the more required "by their walk and conversation" to ensure "that Christianity appears in them untainted." Through the extraordinary outpourings of the Spirit, the people of Northampton have become, says Edwards, in comparison to other people, more distinguished, more blessed, more influential, more renowned, more honored, more eminent in their profession of religion; however, if they fail, they will, compared to other people, be more guilty of hypocrisy, dishonor, scandal, spiritual harm to others, and

37. Ibid., p. 109.

the "great wounding of the credit of the glorious work of God." And because of their "great and remarkable profession," Satan is now more active in their midst. Thus, if the people of Northampton "do not honor religion, they will above all people appear inconsistent with themselves." If they decline in obedience and gratitude to God, they will be more degenerate, more conspicuously judged and disgraced, more worthy of being despised and discredited, "more extensively dishonored," more deserving of eternal punishment, and more of an abomination to God than other people are. The entreaties marking the sermon's end touch on the problems again troubling the community — quarrels over money spent "for the honor of God's public worship," enticements offered by the world, and the growing popularity of Arminianism. In Edwards's view, all these temptations are not surprising because "Satan's spirit has been chiefly against Northampton, . . . the original and principal seat of this work of God." Now, to prove to the world that their revival is genuine and is being sustained by God's Spirit, the people of Northampton must work more zealously to resist the devil and to live up to their glorious reputation as people exceptionally enlightened and blessed by God.

Less than a year after the Matt. 5:14 "city on a hill" sermon in mid-1736, Edwards delivered a number of messages that clearly reveal his deep concerns over events that to him signify the spiritual declension he had hoped to prevent in a town he now saw terribly tainted by backsliding, division, and wrangling. God's providence, it seemed to him, was loudly warning of the grave danger faced by those in the parish who had again become "lifeless" and "shiftless," "lazy in religion and service to God." For Edwards the meeting house itself where he perceived "a drowsy sleepy spirit" must have seemed to whisper that things were not as they had been previously when "persons were eager to attend" public worship, when "if a sermon [was] preached, how [they] crowded in" and availed themselves of "all opportunities, as if they could not have enough of them."[38]

Ezekiel 20:21 (March 1737)

By the spring of 1737, Edwards's sermons are increasingly marked by urgent efforts to rekindle the spiritual vitality the town had previously manifested. Not surprisingly, in some sermons Edwards turns almost

38. Sermon on Ezekiel 20:21, March 1737.

as frequently to providential happenings as to biblical texts and theological insights, asserting that God does "designedly" and vividly "contrive his works and . . . dispose things in the common affairs of the world in such a manner as [to] represent divine things and signify his mind as truly as his Word."[39] The central message of the sermon on Ezekiel 20:21 (March 1737) is extracted from the astonishing collapse of Northampton's meeting house gallery in which many were shocked and terrified but no one was fatally injured. The message stands as a monumental example of Edwards's deftness in interpreting the mind of God in events. Fundamentally, the sermon reconstructs not only the gallery accident but also incorporates the physical details of a number of other contemporary local event-texts that to Edwards spoke God's providential warnings which, if heard with the heart, might be followed "by remarkable pouring out of the Spirit of God . . . [in a] special season of mercy."[40]

The Ezekiel 21:20 sermon doctrine contains manifold implications: "When God's professing people behave themselves unanswerably to great things that God has done for 'em, God sometimes appears ready in an awful manner to destroy them, and yet in undeserved and wonderful mercy withdraws his hand and spares them." Upon first reminding listeners of the richness of God's blessings to them in the late wonderful outpouring of the Spirit in Northampton, Edwards highlights physical details to demonstrate the spiritual importance of local circumstances. Movingly, he stresses God's "marvelous and distinguishing temporal mercies" in sparing Northampton during the "sore and sweeping sickness" that had hit New England the previous year and devastated many other communities.[41] To underscore God's mercy to the "particular town" of Northampton, Edwards paints heart-rending pictures of surrounding towns and "parents [who] have had all their dear children snatched away from them, . . . had several

39. "Miscellanies," no. 201, *Works*, 13, p. 125.

40. *Works*, 9, p. 144.

41. See "Cornerstones, Cannons, and Covenants: The Puritan Clergy as Cultural Guardians," in *Pro Rege* 19 (1990): 24-31, for my discussion of a number of other unpublished Edwards sermons relating to the deaths of children from epidemics and illnesses. See also John Duffy's *Epidemics in Colonial America* (Baton Rouge: Louisiana State University Press, 1953), pp. 113, 116-19, a study of the virulent outbreaks of diphtheria in 1735-36 which proved fatal to large numbers in New England.

laid out dead in their houses at the same [time], and others sick and drawing near to death." He reminds Northampton of its "great measure of health," while other communities "that used to be filled with children" playing in the streets are now "in a great measure emptied of their young." Thus, he says to his congregation, "We have rejoiced while others have mourned. We have had our children about us in health" and by God's grace "no such bitterness mingled with our meat and drink." Offering such providence as evidence of God's generosity to Northampton, Edwards then moves abruptly to the recent accident in the meeting house, highlighting God's patience with a backsliding and undeserving people: "God has besides mercies bestowed [on us], appeared in many awful rebukes. And now in the late surprising providence has in an awful manner appeared just ready to destroy a multitude of us but in a most wonderful manner has spared."

Above all, this sermon insists, to disregard God's voice in the gallery's collapse is to disdain all the momentous meanings "in this providence [in which] we were immediately threatened with the most awful blow that perhaps ever happened in the town." When the balcony "began to sink," says Edwards, "those that were on it and under" were being told that they "were in God's hand" and likely to be "sent into eternity in a moment." As the sermon was brought to a halt by hideous "shrieking and crying in all parts of the meeting house," God made the listeners' own terrified voices to be a providential means of warning them to prepare for eternity. The calamity occuring on the Sabbath and in God's house was divinity's design to send "us out of his presence with an awful rebuke" as people unworthy to "set our feet within the doors." God's "manifestation of displeasure" was justly directed toward his people, says Edwards; but in preventing fatalities, God's tender hand was "turning aside his wrath" just at the moment a punishing dart was "within a few inches" of the people's hearts. Of great import was God's providential plan to keep the worshippers "insensible of the state that the meeting house was in" so those present in it could not "take any care for [their] own preservation" but would come to know fully that it was divine mercy alone that turned aside divine wrath, and "so wonderfully [took] care of every individual person that was exposed [so] that not one life [was] hitherto lost, either of young or old, and not a bone broken."

Edwards's sermon application specifically names the reasons the "remarkable frowns of divine providence" have come to Northampton: in behavior indicative of spiritual declension, people have not kept the Sabbath suitably, have not attended public worship amiably, and have slept during sermons. God has therefore "shown you how he can speak so as to wake you effectually" and has "shown you how he can cause that you shall never wake more in this world." And there has also "been too much of a backward spirit," he scolds, and dissension over land and "expense of building an house for the worship."[42] Indeed, contends Edwards as he offers a catalogue of local sins, it is the evils of complaining, stinginess, worldliness, ingratitude, seeking after gain, and the lack of a becoming cheerfulness in matters related to religion that have brought God's threatening providence upon the town. The community's fretfulness and disagreements about the costs of a new meeting house have obviously demonstrated a lack of faith in God's provisions for them and a failure to believe that God's people never lose by "laying out [their] estates for religious uses" and honoring their Creator with their substance. Furthermore, says Edwards, their ungrateful attitudes have become habitual: "Remember what was told you from the pulpit last year, viz., that such complaining of the heaviness of the burden was the way to make it much heavier." And also remember how God clearly manifested his "frowning on us in outward concerns" last year — "by the flood in bridges and mills and damage to the seed in the ground," by "the exceeding backwardness of the spring and afterward by drought," and by a diminished harvest and then sickness among the cattle and sheep. To Edwards's ears, the divine message in all of these events calls for revival as surely as night calls for day, for "God will take away our substance still by one judgment or other if we behave no more answerably to God's expectations than we have."

Ultimately, not to hearken to God's mind and voice in his providence is in Edwards's view equivalent to turning a deaf ear to God's Word and his appointed servants in the work of redemption: "As I am the messenger of the Lord of Hosts to you, God calls me to reprove and warn you at such a time of rebuke . . . and he requires you to accept the reproof as his reproof." A faithful minister must expose the underlying truths in specific events that reveal God's relationship to a people. A

42. Referring to his own previous sermons on this subject, he asks, "When such a backwardness was gently reproved from the pulpit, was it not taken ill by some persons? Did not they show that they did not like it?"

faithful minister must communicate God's justice, warnings, and anger as well as his mercy, love, and compassion as it is spoken and revealed. Thus Edwards unhesitatingly presents his sermonic renarrations of local events so that his interpretations, like the events themselves, can serve as means of grace and a call to repentance and awakening. Though his own voice colors the message defensively at times, his sermon's rhetorical power comes from its skillful layering of a multiplicity of texts — historical, biblical, local, spiritual, providential — which Edwards insists are all speaking the same message from God, the same warning, the same plea for revival.

II Samuel 20:19 (May 1737)

In May 1737, within a few weeks of the gallery sermon, Edwards preached another message of warning to Northampton, this one revealing his mounting distress over what in his view is the contentious, grudging, quarrelsome, back-biting "spirit of strife" and "public division" prevailing among the townspeople — conditions profoundly troubling to the leader of a church that had lately become an eminent example of religion to the world. On the one hand, this sermon on II Samuel 20:19[43] boldly rebukes all self-righteous, hypocritical, "little-souled men" whose sin is to "oppose contention in a contentious manner" and in so doing dishonor God and the Spirit of God that had been "of late . . . so remarkable." On the other hand, the sermon praises those in the parish who have demonstrated that "a peaceable spirit is a divine spirit" and who have been a "peaceable and faithful," "calm and sedate" example in the church and community.

Although the first lines of the sermon application contain Edwards's claim "I would only apply my self to one sort of persons, viz. those that have [been] peaceable and faithful amongst us in the time of the late strifes and divisions and parties," this extremely tough, castigating sermon uses its most impressive rhetoric and illustrations to bear down on the Northamptonites who have been disgracing the community's eminent reputation by behavior that is "nauseous," "a stink in the nostrils." His heavy censure of those who call themselves Christians but engage in "a great deal of secret contriving and cabal-

---

43. This manuscript sermon at Beinecke has recently been transcribed but is not yet published.

ling" becomes both a plea for listeners to be truly reformed and a warning that only God can purge the seeds of evil that lie deep in their hearts and in the town's history. Edwards emphasizes the depth of the problem:

'Tis most notorious that there has been much of a spirit of strife seen in this town of late. Contention and a party spirit is the old iniquity of this town. It has been remarkably a contentious town. I suppose for this thirty years people have not known how to manage scarce any public business without siding and dividing themselves into parties. Though it be a great disgrace to a town to have any such [contention] true of them, yet 'tis too notorious to be denied of this town. When the Spirit of God of late was so remarkably [poured out], this spirit [of contention] seemed to cease, but . . . this hateful serpent has again put forth his head and of late time after time that old party spirit has appeared again and particularly this spring.

There is great irony here in the fact that Edwards is speaking to the very people whose eminent manifestations of grace in 1734-35 had stirred him to pen a narrative of which Rev. Isaac Watts and John Guyse in Britain would say glowingly, "Never did we hear or read, since the first ages of Christianity, any event of this kind so surprising as the present narrative before us."[44] Northampton, the "place of wonders" where the Spirit of God had moved extraordinarily and where people had been divinely "preserved" when their church balcony collapsed, had now fallen into bickering and divisions about the location, the cost, and the politics of a new house of worship. The degree to which Edwards is vexed by this declension of good will and piety noticeably shapes his message and its inability to remain focused — according to his stated intent — on the blessedness of persons who have shown exemplary "faithfulness and peaceableness" in the community. Instead, he repeatedly fixes on the "fomenters" of contention who "have given great wounds to the honor of the town . . . and grand wounds to the honor of religion" and immense wounds "to their own souls." And he is also defensive, justifying his sermon against those who "say that I make too much of things . . . not worth the while to . . .

44. "Preface to the First Edition" of *A Faithful Narrative, Works,* 4, p. 130. Goen details the very interesting publishing history of this text in his "Editor's Introduction," pp. 32-46.

preach about." In answer to critics, he calculates (hyperbolically, it would seem) Northampton's current contentions as "ten times" more lamentable and bringing "ten times the guilt upon the town" than "any contention that has been in the town [since] it was a town." In conclusion, his sermon strategy is to shame the proud, the self-righteous, and quarrelsome by beseeching the pious and faithful to pray for a change of heart in the contentious. This is utterly necessary for the community's revival and reform, for "God don't love to hear the prayers of contentious persons." In describing temporal and verbal divisions in Northampton, Edwards ultimately identifies what he sees as a far deeper and more destructive division, the spiritual and eternal one as viewed from God's eye and divine design.

John 14:2 (December 25, 1737)

Later that year, on December 25, 1737, in a sermon on John 14:2 Edwards tries another approach to the community's jealousies over status and position which had by then become reified in the seating plans for the new church. The sermon's theme — "heaven is God's house" — pushes beyond the debate over temporal placements in a church's pews to the "infinite and everlasting concern" of having "a seat in God's house above." Place and status in a meeting house seating chart will mean nothing if one does not prepare for a place in heaven. In fact, to quarrel over one's seating in church will likely jeopardize one's seating in heaven, says Edwards. Using the recent deaths of a local father and son as "warnings of providence" about the shortness of life and the importance of a comfortable seat in eternity, Edwards reminds his listeners of the dangers of rancor and declension, for after death, "there is no middle place"; one either dwells with God or with the devils in hell. And "if you die unconverted, you will have the worst place in hell for having had a seat or place in God's house in this world."

After some years of inability to sustain the effects of the glorious outpourings in 1734-35, the Northampton parish in 1740-42 experienced another spiritual renewal, nourished in part by the visit of English revivalist George Whitefield to Northampton in October 1740 and also stimulated by revival activities in many neighboring communities. This "awakening" wave throughout New England was highly complicated by lay preachers, critics of the learned clergy, and by over-zealous, even bizarre, behavior on the part of some converts. These extraordinary manifestations of piety and religious affection became the flashpoint of contention between Old Light and New Light camps, with Edwards, a moderate New Light, writing and publishing at least three documents[45] that addressed distinctions between true and false piety and upholding the traditional role of the ministry over against the laity in rightly defining these.

But no amount of writing or reasoning could push the new wine of emotional excess, individual expression, and spiritual egalitarianism back into old bottles. The Great Awakening of 1740-42 and its concomitant effects in Northampton severely threatened Edwards's identity and status as a pastor, ministerial authority, and church leader.[46] From his elevated ministerial position, Edwards had for many years assumed that, "It is enough for you to whom I have spoke . . . that I have demonstrated that what I have delivered is the mind of God" (Malachi 3:10, July 1743). As a gospel minister and leader in the community, he had applied persistent pressure upon the parish and its individuals to live a life of revival. Likewise in his regular readings of the divine design in local events, he had unceasingly warned of causes for guilt and alarm and repentance. But as increasing numbers in his parish would no longer defer to their pastor or tolerate the threats that were an inextricable element in his revivalist strategies but would instead construct their own interpretations of the mind of God in providence, the party spirit among the town's citizens began severely to test their pastor's authority and credibility.

Isaiah 30:20-21 (February 1749)

In 1749, in a context of highly charged theological and ecclesiastical controversies between Edwards and his parishioners on church membership, profession of faith, and the role of communion,[47] Edwards

45. *The Distinguishing Marks of a Work of the Spirit of God . . .* (1741), *Some Thoughts Concerning the Present Revival of Religion in New England* (1742), and *Treatise Concerning Religious Affections* (1746). The first two are available in *Works*, 4. The third constitutes *Works*, 2.

46. *The Works of Jonathan Edwards*, 12, *Ecclesiastical Writings*, ed. David Hall (New Haven: Yale University Press, 1994), offers both an excellent "Editor's Introduction" and Edwards's own works documenting this very difficult time in his ministerial life. See also Tracy, *Jonathan Edwards, Pastor*, pp. 147ff.

47. Edwards's position on communion is clearly stated in an Ezek. 44:9 sermon doctrine: "'Tis the mind and will of God that none should be admitted to full com-

continued his practice of using the pulpit to press for spiritual reformation and renewal as the only way in which there could be an increase of light in the church, souls could be saved from declension,
and Northampton could again shine as an eminent example of faith
and piety.

Edwards's sermon delivered in March 1749 is particularly noteworthy because it is his public answer to his congregation's denial in
February 1749 of his request to present from the pulpit his views on
church membership and the errors of open communion. The sermon
draws its doctrine from Isaiah 30:20-21: "One great end and design of
God in appointing the gospel ministry is to shew his people which is
the way of duty when they [ministers] see they [people] mistake their
way and to be a means of an increase of light in the church." For a
group militating against its pastor's elevated sense of authority and
doctrinal correctness, this must have been an extremely trying sermon
and doctrine to hear, yet arguably it is one of Edwards's most complex
and conflicted revival sermons because in it he reworks the meanings
of declension, division, revival, and righteousness as he purposefully
presents his and Northampton's position in divinity's design for the
church of Christ.

In explaining God's plan for the "increase of light in the church,"
Edwards offers a carefully developed view of providence that does not
speak directly of religious affections, piety, awakening, or renewal, but
rather suggests that a people's respectful relationship with their pastor, their teachableness, their submission to his correction, their will-
ingness to "hear" him as the messenger of God and to see him as a
"light" to lead them out of darkness has historically been a vital indicator of their righteousness and relationship to God himself. In "the
way of truth," the sacred duty of a gospel minister is to "hold forth the
light" and to deliver his people from errors in matters of religion. On
their part, the people must see their pastor as their "special benefit"
from God and must not place him "into a corner," "persecute" him, or
"deny" him "opportunity to speak publicly." They owe the minister

---

munion in the church of Christ but such as in profession and in the eye of a reasonable judgment are truly saints or godly persons." His position is also presented at
length in *An Humble Inquiry Into the Rules of the Word of God, Concerning the Qualifications Requisite to a Complete Standing and Full Communion in the Visible Christian
Church*, written in March and April of 1749 and published in the fall. *An Humble Inquiry* is included in *Works*, 12.

"free liberty to speak" and hold forth light so the people can "receive instruction" from it. Edwards, with this Isaiah 30:20-21 sermon, sees before him souls he believes are proceeding in a declining, "dangerous way" of self-righteous stubbornness. His call for revival is his plea to them to repent their willful pride and arrogance: "Take heed that . . . you don't refuse [the light] under a notion that you have sufficient light already and no remaining darkness to be removed," for a people who act as if they love "darkness rather than light" will find that "God departs from 'em and give 'em his blessing no more."

Throughout this sermon, Edwards's elevated view of ministerial authority never wavers. The message is an ardent attempt to convince his listeners that, faithfully administered, his pastoral work of admonition and correction in matters of religion is part of his covenant with Christ and is integral to divinity's design for church revival and "the gradual increase of light." This design has been often repeated, Edwards reminds his listeners, in the Old Testament and the New, the post-apostolic church, the Reformation, and in recent events in the colonies. Whenever God through his messengers introduces "an increase of light to correct mistakes," the awakening that follows is like a dawning "when the light of the day comes . . . and gives opportunity to see things in their true shapes and colors so as they were not seen before." And woe to those who try to stand in the way: they interfere with their minister's obligation to Christ and "do therefore hurt Christ and expose themselves to calamity."

In February 1749, as in the 1720s and 1730s, Edwards was still zealously probing divisions and contentions among his people, earnestly hoping that he might overcome them and be a means to revival and increase of light. However, by 1749 the divisions were primarily between increasingly self-assured and secularized parishioners and a pastor intent on saving them from themselves and their doctrinal errors. Highlighting his detractors' feeble reasoning, Edwards's sermon on Isaiah 30:20-21 ridicules those who would argue that because pastoral correction "tends to make division," he as pastor should desist from showing people their mistakes. If this fallacious principle were universally applied in the church of Christ, says Edwards, it would terribly interfere with God's design for revival and redemption, for "this reasoning would effectively establish all factions all over the world in their errors . . . to the end of the world without any ordinances to propagate truth and answer errors for fear it will make divisions." As often before, here, near the conclusion of his pastorate in Northampton, we find Edwards "in the way of truth and duty" still presenting local event-texts as divine messages pointing to the dangers of apathy, hypocrisy, and declension. Inevitably in Edwards's sermons the voice of God in his providence is understood as a warning against spiritual lethargy and a call for a revived sense of God's glorious sovereignty, justice, and mercy.

Conclusion

In Edwards's 1749 sermon on Isaiah 30:20-21, as in so many of his other sermons, we hear him addressing events and cultural circumstances at hand and we find strong elements of what has become the classic profile of American revivalists to this day — enormous zeal for saving souls, certainty that revival is central to the work of redemption, confidence in one's role as God's delegated messenger, emphasis on God's Word and providential voice, boldness in presenting God's dreadful justice *and* saving grace, stress on concerted prayer and repentance as means of spiritual renewal, and the belief that great awakenings transform individual believers and the world. Edwards's views of divinity's design and his example of fearless preaching have nourished many revivalists who have claimed that "the great business of our calling is to advance the divine life in the world; to make religion sway and prevail; and . . . to waken men out of their deadly sleep. We are the instruments of God for effecting these great designs."[48]

What Edwards did so forcefully in the 1700s, argues William G. McLoughlin, that is, warning those he viewed as guilty sinners but also telling them as "distressed individuals in a time of cultural distortion that God still loves them and is ready to help them out of their confusion"[49] by offering them his divine word and light for their lives, American evangelists and revivalists still do today — but with new technologies, reaching far larger and wider audiences, and speaking to a dramatically more fragmented, secularized society. Edwards contin-

48. *The Importance and Difficulty of the Ministerial Function* (New York, 1846), pp. 206-7.

49. *Revivals, Awakenings, and Reform: An Essay on Religion and Social Change in America, 1607-1977* (Chicago: University of Chicago Press, 1978), p. 46.

ues even now to influence the work of revival, as for instance in the recent and wide-reaching "Concerts of Prayer" movement. David Bryant's book, *Concerts of Prayer: Christians Join for Spiritual Awakening and World Evangelization,*[50] draws much of its inspiration directly from Edwards's *Humble Attempt.* Also, in books such as *Accounts of a Campus Revival: Wheaton College 1995,* one hears strong echoes of *A Faithful Narrative,* Edwards's eighteenth-century publication which, among evangelical Christians, became "canonized as the prototype of . . . the revival narrative."[51] Likewise, when David McKenna's book *New Hope for the Nineties: The Coming Great Awakening* looks to eighteenth-century American religious history for inspiration and examples, it vigorously embraces Edwards's vision of church renewal and revival as central to God's design for expanding Christ's kingdom and redeeming the world. Recent theological discussions continue to elevate Edwards as a key figure in American philosophy of religion and in the development of modern faith.[52] And in pointedly bringing Edwards's revivalist writings to bear on contemporary religious thought, Nancey Murphy speaks for many who assert the continuing value "of Edwards's claim that Christians are able to have a set of criteria to an assortment of religious phenomena in order to recognize those that are caused by the activity of the Holy Spirit."[53]

In short, it is not difficult, even in these post-modern times, to find in the spirit and motivation of late-twentieth-century movements among evangelical Christians in America much that continues ideas and beliefs articulated by Edwards some two-and-a-half centuries ago. And though it might seem whimsical, it is not altogether unreasonable to imagine that Edwards — the man who envisioned a time when peoples from "distant extremes of the world shall shake hands together

50. Bryant's book makes many references to Edwards's *Humble Attempt* as an exemplary document. The movement Bryant represents has a worldwide network and has developed seminars, videos, handbooks, discussion guides, training manuals to support the emphasis on concerted prayer as a tool in spiritual revival. See also Lyrene, Jr., "Prayer and Evangelism."

51. Conforti, *Jonathan Edwards, Religious Tradition, and American Culture,* p. 44.

52. *Reason and the Christian Religion: Essays in Honour of Richard Swinburne,* ed. Alan G. Padgett (Oxford: Oxford University Press, 1994), pp. 96-117, and *Modern Christian Revivals,* ed. Edith L. Blumhofer and Randall Balmer (Chicago: Chicago University Press, 1993).

53. *Theology in the Age of Scientific Reasoning* (Ithaca: Cornell University Press, 1990), pp. 130-73.

and all nations shall be acquainted, and they shall all join the forces of their minds in exploring the glories of the Creator, their hearts in loving and adoring him, their hands in serving him"[54] — could indeed find much for which to be gratified in today's expanding arena of global missions, world evangelism, and international revival movements.

54. *Works*, 13, p. 213.

PART IV

ESCHATOLOGY

The End Is Music

ROBERT W. JENSON

I

From time to time, the public prints report the death of a theological *locus*, often as murder at the hands of modernity. These reports are usually exaggerated. But in the case of the traditional doctrine of "last things," at least coma is undeniable. Faced with the simplest question from a child, e.g., "What did Jesus mean, 'the Kingdom of Heaven'?" what would *you* do?

Blanche Jenson and I are happy with our current preacher. He is an intelligent and serious priest, not much addicted to denominational ideologies, who actually seems to believe the gospel. It is all the more instructive to observe his homiletical elisions when faced with an explicitly eschatological passage.

All essayists in this volume are assigned to consider how Jonathan Edwards speaks in some way to our present situation. I am a systematic theologian, and will therefore start with the present debility of the church's eschatology and ask how Edwards might ameliorate it.

I should say immediately what I understand under the rubric "eschatology." It is surely an ecumenical characterization of the church's message, the gospel of Jesus' resurrection, that it is a "promise." Eschatology is the effort to say *what* the gospel promises, insofar as this is something specific to the gospel, i.e., not enabled except as Christ lives with death behind him, and so not enabled by or within the otherwise obtaining continuities of history.

The Scriptures are forthcoming with descriptions, and traditional church doctrine has been in large part simply an attempt to organize them. Let me put my own such attempt up front: the gospel promises the advent of a human community gathered as what the Fathers called the *totus Christus*, the one person of the Son-with-his-church, "deified" by this inclusion in the triune life.

II

It may be useful to look at a few actual instances of eschatology's suppression in the theology of modernity. I shall caricature — for that is what must happen in the compass I can allow myself — first, Friedrich Schleiermacher; second, the properly so called "liberal theology"; and Rudolf Bultmann. It may be seen that the instances were not picked at random.

Schleiermacher follows his rather unwilling expositions of church teaching about the "return of Christ," the "resurrection of the flesh," the "last judgment," and "eternal blessedness," with a *"Zusatz."* Discourse about such things, he there says, inevitably becomes "mythical, i.e., the historical depiction of something beyond history" or "visionary, i.e., the earthly depiction of something not of this earth." And he concludes: myth and vision "have always been the linguistic modes of 'prophecy,' which in its higher intention makes no claim to yield knowledge. . . ."[1]

There is no mystery about why Schleiermacher cannot grant prophecy informative power. Doing so would involve supposing that the world, as something distinct from the church, could change its spots. Salvation for Schleiermacher is a transformation of human life historically carried on in and by the church. The church's "prophetic teachings" promise a conclusion of this transformation. But it can in fact never be concluded, because "the church continues . . . to take the world into itself, therefore always remains . . . conflicted, and therefore is never perfected."[2]

1. *Der Christliche Glaube*, II: §163.
2. Ibid., §157.

The liberal theology, properly so called, went behind Schleier-macher to Kant himself for its starting analyses.[3] There were several reasons for this, but one was perhaps most important. In the later nineteenth century, idealism's hope dimmed of overcoming the determinism seemingly dictated by science, and theologians decided they had after all to reckon with an inexorable world-system. Kant's God is legislator both of the world-system's laws and of the moral demand for free action. Just so, the liberals said, he is the condition of moral action within the determined world, and faith in him the subjective possibility of such action.

Such freedom is possible within the world-system precisely because it does not challenge its regularities. The liberals were great biblical exegetes, and read that the destiny of human freedom is "the Kingdom of God." They reconciled their principles with their biblical faith by construing the Kingdom as a realm resident within the world-system yet innocuous to its determinisms: the realm of moral endeavor. Notoriously, the shock from which liberal theology never recovered — besides liberal Europe's suicidal war and the ever more manifest flaws of liberal theology's sibling social theories — was the discovery by her own exegetes that Jesus probably meant all that apocalyptic stuff.

Liberalism was overthrown, as a serious option, by the "dialectical theology." Of those briefly gathered under that label, one remained forever faithful to its key positions. Rudolf Bultmann is particularly appropriate to our purpose because he upheld Karl Barth's maxim that Christianity must be "altogether eschatology." The question is: What then did he — along with many other twentieth-century theologians — mean by "eschatology"?

The eschaton, Bultmann read in Scripture, is a halt of history in face of God. Scripture tells of this halt narratively. But any *narrative* of action between God and what is not God is exactly the "myth" which, according to Bultmann, moderns cannot entertain in good faith. The eschaton must therefore be so construed as to be historically real while occupying no temporal space — just like the liberal "Kingdom of God."

It is, thinks Bultmann, the dimensionless moment of personal de-

---

3. For a longer version of the following, see Carl E. Braaten and Robert W. Jenson, *A Map of Twentieth-Century Theology* (Minneapolis: Fortress, 1995), pp. 1-18.

cision that satisfies these requirements. By any genuine decision, I surrender security in what already is and risk myself to the contingent future: thus history breaks, though the event occupies no time and so is not perceptible to historical observation. There will not exactly be an eschaton, but there can at any moment be "eschatological existence": repeated punctual openness to openness, hope to be able to hope.

III

By my diagnosis, three chief problems have afflicted eschatology through the modern period, in Sunday school and elite theology alike. I had omitted one, but since John Smith has developed it, above, I can simply and very briefly reinsert it. Each is demonstrated by our sample caricatures.

It is no great divinatory feat to discern at least the first: normal modernity was founded by the Enlightenment's awe before science's seventeenth-century achievements, and has thought that reality other than God is a closed determined system. Newtonian physics itself does not entail this view, but the metaphors do by which the culture interpreted Newton to itself. The world, modernity has thought with greater or lesser naiveté, is a cosmos-machine: a system that indeed encloses great energies and movements but constrains them within an encompassing diachronic immobility.

Clearly, if the world of which we are part is so describable, then the gospel's eschatological expectations, as displayed throughout Scripture, must be reductively explained, and that pretty severely. For the appearance of a perfectly loving human community with a heaven and earth ordered to accommodate it, would be the very paradigm of the sort of radical novelty, of temporal fracture, from which the cosmos-machine is supposed to protect us. Denial of "miracle" was a defining achievement of modernity; the coming to pass of any significant part of what Christians once awaited at the end would be a miracle of miracles, would be the ultimate monkey-wrench in the world-works.

It is important in this connection — as in others — to remember that the wider conceptual and ideological impact of science is not made by the body of scientific discourse itself in its mathematical purity, but by a para-scientific discourse that accompanies it. And this is true not only for non-scientists, but for the practitioners themselves.

Moreover, what we may call everyday metaphysics generally outlives its occasion. Every medium of what in the modern world goes without saying continues to implant it at the back of our minds that according to "science" all events could in principle be predicted using "the laws of nature," despite the quite well-known fact that the current state of science offers little occasion for this belief. We do not expect a biblically dramatic eschaton because without thinking we think we know such a thing cannot happen.

But now — what if mechanism were an error? And what if that could be seen not by the lights of mere traditionalism but by modernity's own best lights? What if Schleiermacher and the liberals and Bultmann and most of us have been all those years accommodating a phantasm? It is this ironic and hopeful possibility that Jonathan Edwards revealed, almost in advance of its occasion.

I need not rehearse here Edwards's dismantling of mechanism, physical and psychological. It is the position he thereby achieved that I want to praise. Edwards rewon the freedom to tell a *story* of the world, and to tell it together with the triune story of God as a single dramatically coherent narrative. And he did this not by looking for "gaps" or limits of science but by taking the Newtonian vision more severely and with greater ontological seriousness than others did.

Edwards's interpretation of the newly burgeoning scientific knowledge was austerely phenomenalist and operationalist. He saw no need to posit entities that "possess" the qualities which appear in physical or phenomenological propositions. He saw no need to attribute observed regularities to occult "causes." He regarded the mechanist world view as an obscurantist anachronism, produced by a hangover of antique notions. But unlike many others who have held such positions, he had an answer to the question, Is there then nothing *to* the play of phenomena? There is, he said, and it is "God himself, or the immediate exercise of his power. . . ."[4]

God has neither constructed a machine nor instituted a game of craps. The play of phenomena is the play of God's imagination, their law-like coherence the coherence thereof.[5] God thinks movements and

4. *The Works of Jonathan Edwards*, 6, *Scientific and Philosophical Writings*, ed. Wallace E. Anderson (New Haven: Yale University Press, 1980), p. 214.

5. Robert W. Jenson, *America's Theologian: A Recommendation of Jonathan Edwards* (New York: Oxford University Press, 1988), pp. 27-34.

resistances in universally mutual harmony, and *that* is what underlies the appearances.[6] Therefore the world delineated by Newton's physics can be experienced as a finite harmony perfectly flexible to the infinite triune harmony that is God himself.

This will only do, of course, with so drastically biblical and therefore triune a God as Edwards knew. Indeed, that God himself was creation's immediate support and coherence would only imprison us in *pantheos*, were God a monadic divinity. As God is, he is the "supreme harmony"[7] of Father, Son, and Spirit. And since this triune harmony is a *social* harmony, it can open to embrace others within itself without abolishing them, so that the triune harmony and the harmony of created persons can intersect, just *thereby* enabling the meta-harmony of the infinite and the finite harmonies.[8] According to a favorite passage of mine: "There was, [as] it were, an eternal society or family in the Godhead, in the Trinity of persons. It seems to be God's design to admit the church into the divine family as his son's wife."[9]

God "infinitely loves himself," just so to *be* infinite and so to be God.[10] And this love of God for himself is not simply reflexive consciousness; it is rather that he "*exerts* himself toward himself . . . in the mutual love of the Father and the Son."[11] Moreover, and decisively for our present point, the exertion going on in God is contingently identical with the reality in God of the events narrated by the gospel;[12] the loving that happens in the triune life is a love *story*, the one Exodus, Isaiah, and the Gospels tell. Edwards had not been reading current trinitarian theorists, but nevertheless obeys the Rahnerian maxim in not separating the "immanent" and "economic" trinities: the immanent relation "among the persons of the Trinity" is precisely "with respect to their operations and actions *ad extra*." For Edwards, as for the

6. Ibid., pp. 20-21, 28-34.

7. "Miscellanies," no. 182, *The Works of Jonathan Edwards,* 13, *The "Miscellanies," a-500,* ed. Thomas A. Schafer (New Haven: Yale University Press, 1994), pp. 328-29.

8. Perhaps for the evidence and argument here I may be permitted to refer to the book on account of which I am writing this paper, *America's Theologian,* pp. 92-98.

9. "Miscellanies," no. 741, Yale MSS, Beinecke Rare Book and Manuscript Library, Yale University.

10. *Works,* 6, p. 381.

11. Ibid., p. 364. Emphasis added.

12. E.g., "Memoirs of President Edwards," *The Works of President Edwards in Four Volumes* (New York: Leavitt and Allen, 1852), 1:16. Emphasis added.

Greeks but not usually for the Latins, the indivisibility of the triune persons' works *ad extra* is not that they are interchangeable among the persons, but that "all the persons of the Trinity do *concur*" in them.[13] All action of God beyond himself is a dramatically *mutual* work of Father, Son, and Spirit.

Having won the conceptual right to do so, Edwards loved to trace the plot of the divine-human history. The particulars of his plotting have been much and fruitfully studied, but for our purpose we may elide them; the great "design" can suffice us. The presence of the Son-and-his-spouse in the triune life is the *telos* of all things: "Heaven and earth were created that the Son of God might be complete in a spouse."[14] Edwards's deconstruction of mechanism and his radically trinitarian interpretation of God allow him to understand all reality as one history, coherent by the intention with which God imagines it.

Thus Edwards can conceive the connectedness of events very differently than did his usual contemporaries. All events are "done immediately by God, only in harmony and proportion," the harmony given by their envelopment in God's own harmonious life. The ordering of *all* events is their coherence by appropriateness within God's imagining them; events lying outside the usually expected order of things differ from others only as they are "done in the most general proportion, not tied to any particular proportion, to this or that created being, but the proportion is with the whole series of [God's] acts and designs from eternity to eternity."[15]

It is the final truth here proposed by Edwards — and it *is* the truth if the gospel is to be true: the stories told by cosmological physics or evolutionary narrative, or by such a proposition as "Water always runs downhill," or by a history of England or a religious history of humankind, are not the fixed presupposition of the "history of salvation," of our history with God, but are each merely one or another abstracted part or aspect of it. If miracles are regarded as events that violate some regularity, this is only by reference to such a *partial* ordering of events.

Thomas Aquinas said, "If we speak with reference to God and his power, there are no miracles."[16] Edwards displays "God and his

13. "Miscellanies," no. 958, Yale MSS.

14. "Miscellanies," no. 103, *Works*, 13, p. 271.

15. "Miscellanies," no. 64, *Works*, 13, p. 235.

16. *Summa Theologiae*, i.105.8: *Nihil potest dici miraculum ex comparatione potentiae divinae.*

power" in a more radically trinitarian way than did Thomas, and so rescues us from a conceptual and spiritual imprisonment darker than any Thomas had to reckon with.

There is no reason why a real, dramatic, biblical-style eschaton cannot happen. Anything *can* happen that within God's harmony is dramatically appropriate to what has gone before and to the final intent of God's imagining. Aristotle said a good story is one where each new event occurs unpredictably, but so that after the fact one can see it was just what had to happen.[17] The totality of being is that good story, and God the imaginer thereof.

IV

The next point I can now quickly recruit from John Smith. Modernity's "nominalism," as Smith labels it, prevents dramatic narration from having metaphysical status, since the subject of a dramatic narrative must be a community. But for there to be what the church has meant by eschatology, precisely *humanity* must be a narrative subject.

I will add just one point. Smith uses the term "realism" for Edwards's anti-nominalism. But a realism of *kinds* also prevents apprehension of a universal narrative. Such realism had to be overcome, if only that resulting nominalism be in turn overthrown by what one may perhaps call "narrative realism."

V

The third problem is perhaps somewhat less obvious, but it can, I think, be discerned as a suppressing factor in all three sketched instances of debilitated eschatology. I have elsewhere called it "the antinomy of hope."

It would seem that if what one hopes for comes, the hope itself must cease. What then of an object of final hope? Must not its advent be the end of all hope, *that is,* be more or less equivalent to death? One can perhaps hope to stop hoping, but this is the defining hope of nihilism, the attempted anticipation of damnation. Bultmann and his

---

17. Aristotle, *Peri Poietikes*, 1452a, 3.

school tried to solve the antinomy by emptying eschatological hope of specific content; the future to which we are to be "open" is each time whatever future is at hand. But this is simply the same emptiness historicized. I recall as a small child sitting in a pew and trying to comprehend the pastor's talk of eternity; I decided that it would make little difference whether one were in heaven or hell, since a truly endless on and on and on. . . would merely in itself be intolerable.

Some years ago Wolfhart Pannenberg and I — and, for all I know, others — independently proposed that *love* resolves the antinomy. Love is a specifiable object of hope: if my hope for love is disappointed, I will recognize its absence. Yet when love comes, neither does life become static nor do we need to move to something else to move on with life. The advent of love can occur and be followed by no other advent, without the lovers having to cling to something finished and merely persistent. For love is in itself perfect openness to possibility. Perhaps we may say that love is the one thing that is both subject and object of hope.

So far, I allow myself to think, so good. Yet I have to say that this analysis still feels to me somehow too, as the Germans say, *massif.* The stricture is perhaps only a matter of post-modernity's particular conceptual taste, but we cannot bypass our own palates. It may even be that the stricture displays a moment of truth in the errors we have just renounced.

Surely, many levels of language will be distinguishable in right bespeaking of the eschaton. If my instinct is right, systematic theology would be fully satisfied only by language that peeled away all *Massifität,* that is, in the present case, perfectly united description of the eschaton as a specifiable event with respect for the undescribable break between the eschaton and all that goes before it. This apex is perhaps unreachable and merely geometrical. But can we find language a little closer to it? Is there anything desirable simply and solely for its own sake, so that if it is granted no empty infinity opens? God is, according to St. Augustine, but why? Can we ask *what* is so wonderful about love? Indeed, about living in and with God?

Jonathan Edwards identifies the heart of mutual love as music. You know the passages, but I cannot refrain from them. What we must not do is take them as similes; "metaphorical" they may be, if by that overworked label we intend no contrast with "conceptual." "The best . . . way that we have of expressing a sweet concord of mind to each other, is music. When I would form an idea of a society in the highest degree happy, I think of them . . . sweetly singing to each other."[18] "Singing is amiable, because of the proportion that is perceived in it . . .";[19] and we must remember that "amiable proportion" would be as close to a *definition* of deity as Edwards would care to come.

Explicitly eschatological application of this principle is infrequent in Edwards but decisive. The Kingdom will be constituted by the perfecting of harmony "between all . . . minds and Christ Jesus and the supreme Mind."[20] And the "exquisite spiritual proportion" of this perfected harmony will be that of a "very complex tune, where respect is to be had to the proportion of a great many notes together." Thus there must be "in the future world . . . that which will be a far more lively expression of this harmony [of singing], and shall itself be vastly more harmonious . . . than our air or ear . . . is capable of."[21]

Eschatology is about God before it is about us, for if there is to be an eschaton it is because he is the Eschatos. The deity of Edwards's God is his beauty,[22] and this is the archetype and possibility of the eschatological "exquisite proportion."[23] God, moreover, is according to Edwards beautiful only because he is triune.[24] What would be a triune beauty? If not a beauty constituted in the *"perichoresis"* of identities who are one with each other precisely by what distinguishes them? Edwards did not say it, but I will, not knowing whether he would go so far: the final specification of God's being is that he is the infinite *fugue.* And the harmony of our love, finally perfectly harmonized with the supreme harmony, can only be the inclusion in the divine fugue of as many voices as there are blessed creatures.

If we are, with another essayist, to say that God is a semiotic field,[25] whether to interpret Edwards or on our own behalf, we should, I think, consider that this phrase is itself impressively polyvalent.

---

18. "Miscellanies," no. 188, *Works,* 13, p. 331.

19. "Miscellanies," no. 153 (143), *Works,* 13, p. 303.

20. "Miscellanies," no. 42, *Works,* 13, p. 224.

21. "Miscellanies," no. 153 (143), *Works,* 13, p. 303.

22. *The Works of Jonathan Edwards,* 2, *Religious Affections,* ed. John E. Smith (New Haven: Yale University Press, 1959), p. 298.

23. "Miscellanies," no. 182, *Works,* 13, pp. 328-29.

24. "Miscellanies," no. 117, *Works,* 13, pp. 283-84.

25. See Stephen H. Daniel, "Postmodern Concepts of God and Edwards's Trinitarian Ontology," pp. 45-64 above.

Construal of the "semiotic field" as signifier, signified, and significa-tion is after all historically contingent, created — at least for the West — by Augustine. We might remember that Augustine feared the arts. Overcoming that fear, and deconstructionism's unconscious tradition-alism, we should be thinking instead of counterpoint.

We would speak strictly systematically about the eschaton, I said, if we could evoke a perfection in which the difference between what can be described and what cannot was transcended. Perhaps we can now do that. We speak of "absolute music," meaning music without text and without program. But surely the truly absolute music would be music in which text and setting were so perfectly at one that there was no more reality to the distinction, and in which again narrative plot was so formally perfect that it simply was the musical structure. We will call beatitude "absolute music" in this sense.

And would not singing and being sung in such music indeed be the heart of love? The one thing desirable for itself? The one thing that can be hoped for without hoping to stop hoping? I think I have Ed-wards on my side in saying at least "Maybe."

A Possibility of Reconciliation: Jonathan Edwards and the Salvation of Non-Christians

GERALD R. McDERMOTT

Most students of early New England remember the Robert Breck affair as a bizarre episode in which western Massachusetts ministers in 1735 arranged to have a young preacher from Harvard arrested and carried off to jail on charges of heresy. Students of Edwards also know that the Northampton theologian publicly defended the ministers' actions, agreeing that Breck was preaching dangerous heresy. What most historians have overlooked, however, is that one of the three Breck doctrines deemed to be heretical concerned the eschatological destiny of the "heathen," and that it was this doctrine that seemed to bother Edwards the most.[1]

According to his accusers, Robert Breck (1713-1784) had told his Windham County (CT) auditors that some portions of the Scriptures were not inspired, that predestination gave "no Encouragement to Duty," and that "the heathen[2] doing what they could would entitle 'em

---

1. For the most recent overview of the affair and relevant bibliography, see *Works of Jonathan Edwards*, 12, *Ecclesiastical Writings*, ed. David D. Hall (New Haven: Yale University Press, 1994), pp. 4-17.

2. By "heathen" Breck, Edwards, and nearly everyone else in this period meant religionists who were outside the pale of Jewish, Christian, and Muslim communities. Most frequently they meant classical Greeks and Romans, less frequently Buddhists, Hindus, the Chinese, and assorted animists.

to salvation." It was this last accusation to which Edwards devoted the majority of his attention in his published account of the heresies.[3]

1. Deism and the Scandal of Particularity

Edwards was probably not surprised to learn that Breck was a disciple of Thomas Chubb,[4] the most accessible guide to deism[5] in the 1730s. For it was the deists who most prominently raised the issue of the heathen's eschatological destiny. In the seventeenth century the Cambridge Platonists[6] also challenged the view, usually attributed to Calvinism, that those who never heard the gospel were doomed to eternal damnation. But the deists were bolder, seemed more relevant, and were far more popular than the Cambridge Platonists. Beginning with Lord Herbert of Cherbury, they suggested that the Calvinist God who sent people to hell because they didn't believe in one of whom they had never heard, and who created human beings with the knowledge that they would burn in hell forever, was a monster.[7]

3. *A Letter to the Author of the Pamphlet Called An Answer to the Hampshire Narrative* (orig. 1737), in *Works*, 12, pp. 91-163. Edwards discusses Breck's objectionable teachings at pp. 155-61.

4. *A Narrative of the Proceedings of those Ministers of the County of Hampshire, etc. That have disapproved of the late Measures taken in order to the Settlement of Mr. Robert Breck, in the Pastoral Office of the first Church in Springfield, with a Defence of their Conduct in that Affair. Written by Themselves* (Boston, 1736), p. 5; *Works*, 12, pp. 6, 159.

5. Although I reify "deism" in this paper, the term is of more heuristic than historic value. There was little that united the writers often called "deists" beyond the determination to accept from the Christian tradition only what seemed commonsensical. Yet the eighteenth-century Reformed writers, including Edwards, commonly referred to the "deists" as a coherent group. For the purposes of this study, I have stipulated that the term refers to Lord Herbert of Cherbury, Charles Blount, John Toland, Anthony Collins, Matthew Tindal, Thomas Gordon, John Trenchard, and Thomas Chubb. I will discuss the historiographical problems with the term in chapter one of *Jonathan Edwards Confronts the Gods: Christian Theology, Enlightenment Religion, and Non-Christian Faiths* (forthcoming).

6. For secondary treatments, see Gerald R. Cragg, ed., *The Cambridge Platonists* (New York: Oxford University Press, 1968); C. A. Patrides, ed., *The Cambridge Platonists* (London: Edward Arnold, 1969).

7. For secondary treatments of deism, see Gerald R. Cragg, *Reason and Authority in the Eighteenth Century* (Cambridge: Cambridge University Press, 1964); Peter Byrne, *Natural Religion and the Nature of Religion: The Legacy of Deism* (London:

For many deists, this "scandal of particularity" was the greatest theoretical[8] problem of Christian orthodoxy. That the Jewish and Christian God revealed himself to only one-sixth of the world[9] seemed manifestly unjust, particularly if eternal happiness depended on knowledge of that revelation. For example, Lord Herbert, typically regarded as the father of the movement, developed his five "common notions," supposedly common to all religions, because he was scandalized by the suggestion of many church fathers that most human beings were doomed because they lived outside the light of Christian revelation. No revelation, he concluded, could be normative unless it is known and promulgated to the whole world. "Otherwise the Gentiles must be supposed to be universally lost and damned, which it were cruel and injurious to God to imagine."[10]

Routledge, 1989); Peter Harrison, *'Religion' and the Religions in the English Enlightenment* (Cambridge: Cambridge University Press, 1990); J. A. I. Champion, *The Pillars of Priestcraft Shaken: The Church of England and Its Enemies 1660-1730* (Cambridge: Cambridge University Press, 1992); Ernest Campbell Mossner, *Bishop Butler and the Age of Reason* (New York: Macmillan, 1936); Stephen H. Daniel, *John Toland: His Method, Manners and Mind* (Kingston and Montreal: McGill-Queen's University Press, 1984); John Redwood, *Reason, Ridicule and Religion: The Age of Enlightenment in England, 1660-1750* (Cambridge, MA: Harvard University Press, 1976); Alfred Owen Aldridge, "Deism," in Gordon Stein, ed., *The Encyclopedia of Unbelief* (Buffalo, NY: Prometheus Books, 1985); Leslie Stephen, *History of English Thought in the Eighteenth Century,* 3rd ed., 2 vols. (New York: Peter Smith, 1949); Frank E. Manuel, *The Changing of the Gods* (Hanover, NH: University Press of New England, 1983), esp. pp. 5-129. The best contemporary account is John Leland, *A View of the Principal Deistical Writers,* orig. ed. 1755-1757 (New York and London: Garland, 1978).

8. There were also practical problems — the avarice and self-indulgence of the clergy, and persecution by the state of all who did not toe the line. See Champion, *Pillars of Priestcraft Shaken.*

9. This was a figure used in the late seventeenth and first half of the eighteenth centuries by many of those who reflected on the religious state of the heathen. See, for example, William Turner's *History of All Religions* (London, 1695), p. 606; and Thomas Broughton's *Bibliotheca Historico-Sacra: or, an Historical Library of the Principal Matters Relating to Religion Antient and Modern; Pagan, Jewish, Christian and Mohammedan* (1737), p. 116. It seems to have come from a mid-seventeenth-century geographer.

10. Quote cited by Leland in *A View,* p. 17. For Lord Herbert's distaste for Calvinism's treatment of the heathen, see Edward Lord Herbert of Cherbury, *On Truth in Distinction from Revelation, Probability, Possibility, and Error,* 3rd ed. (London, 1645 [1st ed. 1624]), p. 77; Lord Herbert, *The Antient Religion of the Gentiles* (London, 1705 [1st ed. 1663]), pp. 2-3, 29, 119.

Charles Blount, John Toland, and Anthony Collins agreed with Lord Herbert that God must have no favorite nations or parts of the world, and hence a religion must be generally known if it is to expect all human beings to subscribe to it. The plight of those who have not heard runs throughout the argument of Matthew Tindal's *Christianity as Old as Creation* (1730), sometimes called "the Deists' Bible." Tindal argued that if God is good, then all would know his revelation; but if he reveals himself to only a part of the world, God is "cruel and unmerciful." This proves that God, whom Tindal knew to be good, reveals himself by the light of nature to all, and has done so since the creation.[11] Thomas Chubb, Thomas Gordon, and John Trenchard, with all of whom Jonathan Edwards was familiar,[12] were similarly disturbed by the implications of Calvinist soteriology for those who had not received Christian revelation.

2. Heterodox Soteriologies

Jonathan Edwards seems to have been as fascinated as the deists by the flood of travelogues and other reports of heathen religions coming to England in the seventeenth and early eighteenth centuries.[13] His

11. Matthew Tindal, *Christianity as Old as the Creation* (London, 1730), p. 401; see also pp. 5, 11, 48, 64, 242, 256, 391-93.

12. Edwards quoted Chubb at length on the atonement in "Miscellanies," no. 1213, and paraphrased Leland's treatment of him in "Miscellanies," no. 1297. In *Freedom of the Will* Chubb was one of Edwards's principal antagonists; *Works of Jonathan Edwards*, 1, *Freedom of the Will*, ed. Paul Ramsey (New Haven: Yale University Press, 1957), pp. 132, 232-33, 226-38, 343-48, 418. Trenchard and Gordon's *Independent Whig*, a newspaper with strong deist views, is no. 210 in Edwards's "Catalogue" of reading. Chubb's complaints about Calvinism's unfairness to the heathen are in *A Discourse Concerning Reason* (London, 1733), pp. 1-6, 12, 22, 71, 209. Similar sentiments can be found in Trenchard and Gordon's *The Independent Whig* (1720-21), 1:333-34; 2:13.

Edwards in fact was nearly obsessed with deism and its challenges to Reformed orthodoxy. More than 357 (25%) of the 1412 entries in the Miscellanies are directed to issues which deists raised. It cannot be determined whether Edwards's ruminations on the destiny of the heathen were provoked by deist speculation on the same or simply by his own confrontation with what seemed to be remarkable convergences between Christianity and heathen religions. But it is clear that he used these ruminations to support his attacks on deism.

13. For a review of this literature, see Donald F. Lach, *Asia in the Making of Europe* (Chicago: University of Chicago Press, 1965), 3:549-97.

very first Miscellanies entry, written in 1722 or 1723 when he was about twenty years old, makes mention of the "heathen" ("Miscellanies," no. a). In 1743 or 1744 he began writing detailed descriptions of non-Christian religious beliefs and practices ("Miscellanies," no. 953). Most of these entries were extracts which he copied from seventeenth- and eighteenth-century Christian writers such as Theophilus Gale (1628-78), Hugo Grotius (1583-1645), Isaac Barrow (1630-77), Humphrey Prideaux (1648-1724), Samuel Clarke (1675-1729), Samuel Shuckford (ca. 1694-1754), Isaac Watts (1674-1748), Philip Skelton (1707-87), Chevalier Ramsay (1686-1743), and Johann Friedrich Stapfer (1708-1775).

Edwards seems to have become more interested in other religions the older he became; most of the sixty entries devoted to the religions were penned during his years at Stockbridge, in the last decade of his life. The majority of these entries purport to show that non-Christian thinkers and religions actually contain Reformed Christian doctrines. For example, "Miscellanies," no. 1181, is an extract from Chevalier Ramsay's *Principles of Natural and Revealed Religion* (Glasgow, 1749). It claims to find the Trinity in the Tao Te Ching, expectations of a suffering Messiah in one of the Confucian classics, and a supposed statement by Confucius that a saint will come from the west to banish sin and suffering.

Edwards appears to have read voraciously about the religions; he knew of, tried to get, and perhaps read many of the travelogues, dictionaries and encyclopedias of religion available in his time. The books cited in his "Catalogue" include George Sale's translation of the Qur'an, reports of the Jesuits in China, an analysis of the Qabbalah, comparative mythology, and a wide range of dictionaries and encyclopedias of religion — from skeptic Peter Bayle's *Historical and Critical Dictionary* to Daniel Defoe's *Dictionary of All Religions Antient and Modern*.[14]

Edwards was therefore exposed to many heterodox soteriologies. Many of these authors speculated explicitly or implied discreetly that

14. He also read or tried to get William Turner's *History of All Religions* (1695), Isaac Watts's *Harmony of All Religions* (1742), Samuel Shuckford's *Sacred and Profane History* (1727), Ephraim Chambers's *Philosophical Dictionary* (1728), Broughton's *Historical Library of Religion Antient and Modern* (1737), and Thomas Dyche's *A New General English Dictionary* (1725) — all of which featured articles on non-Christian religions. "Jonathan Edwards' Reading 'Catalogue' With Notes and Index," prepared by L. Brian Sullivan, Works of Jonathan Edwards office.

the heathen could be saved, and often chose to hypothesize how they could find salvation. Two of Edwards's favorite[15] writers on the heathen believed that God would use transmigration of the soul to help the heathen find heaven. Philip Skelton (1707-87), a Church of Ireland divine whose anti-deist volumes *Deism Revealed* (London, 1751) were used extensively by Edwards, suggested that the merits of Christ's death may be extended to those heathen who use reason rightly and live moral lives by the transmigration of their souls into the bodies of those born under the light of the gospel.[16] Edwards also quoted copiously from Chevalier (Andrew Michael) Ramsay (1686-1743), a Scotsman who lived with both Fenelon and Madame Guyon, converted to Roman Catholicism, and later wrote a tract defending Freemasonry. Influenced by Origen, Ramsay held that all humans sinned in a preexistent state, are reborn into earthly bodies, and eventually receive universal pardon. He believed that pagans can live in the bosom of paganism without partaking spiritually of the idolatry and superstition that surrounds them.[17] Other writers on the religions whom Edwards read praised certain heathen for their worship of the true God[18] and often constructed an inclusivist ladder to heaven for them.[19] That is, they believed it was possible to go to heaven without having confessed Christ on earth.

3. The *Prisca Theologia*

Many of the writers whom Edwards read, particularly Skelton and Ramsay, understood the religions in terms defined by what was called the *prisca theologia* (ancient theology). This was a tradition in apolo-

---

15. If we can judge "favorite" by the amount of space he devotes in his private notebooks to their writings.

16. Skelton, *Deism Revealed*, 1:171; 2:155.

17. Andrew Michael Ramsay, *Philosophical Principles of Natural and Revealed Religion* (Glasgow, 1748-49), 1:347, 410-11, 430; 2:457.

18. Turner, *History*, pp. 4, 15ff., 323; Defoe, *Dictionary*, pass.; Broughton, *Historical Library*, vi; Shuckford, *Sacred and Profane History*, p. 15; Sale, *The Koran*, pp. v, 97.

19. According to Isaac Watts, for example, experience tells those without written revelation that they are sinners. If they fear God and work righteousness, and hope in a merciful God, they shall be accepted through an unknown (to them) mediator. Watts, *Harmony*, pp. 92-94.

getic theology, resting on misdated texts (the Hermetica, Chaldean oracles, Orpheia, and Sybilline oracles), that attempted to prove that vestiges of true religion were taught by the Greeks and other non-Christian traditions. Typically it alleged that all human beings were originally given knowledge of true religion (monotheism, the Trinity, *creatio ex nihilo*) by Jews or by tradition going back to Noah's good sons (Shem and Japheth) or antediluvians such as Enoch or Adam. The *prisca theologia* was developed first by Clement of Alexandria, Origen, Lactantius, and Eusebius to show that the greatest philosophers had stolen from the Chosen People, and then in the Renaissance by Marsilio Ficino and Pico Della Mirandola to synthesize Neoplatonism and Christian dogma. In the seventeenth and eighteenth centuries it was revived by the "Jesuit Figurists," who tried to win acceptance of their mission in China by claiming that China worshipped the true God two thousand years before Christ, and a number of other, mostly Protestant, thinkers. Four of these were read carefully and taken seriously by Edwards. We have already seen Skelton and Ramsay, the latter of whom found trinitarian monotheism among the ancient Egyptians, Persians, and Greeks. Ramsay tried to prove that God gave complete revelation of the essential Christian doctrines to the earliest patriarchs, so that most pagan religions teach a trinity similar to the Neoplatonic triad.[20]

Theophilus Gale (1628-78) and Ralph Cudworth (1617-88) were

20. On the *prisca theologia,* see D. P. Walker, "Orpheus the Theologian and Renaissance Platonists," *Journal of the Wartburg and Courtauld Institutes* 16 (1953), pp. 100-120; idem, *The Ancient Theology: Studies in Christian Platonism from the Fifteenth to the Eighteenth Centuries* (London: Duckworth, 1972); idem, *The Decline of Hell: Seventeenth-Century Discussions of Eternal Torment* (London: Routledge, 1964); Frances A. Yates, *Giordano Bruno and the Hermetic Tradition* (Chicago: University of Chicago Press, 1964); Charles B. Schmitt, "Perennial Philosophy: From Agostino Steuco to Leibniz," *Journal of the History of Ideas* 27 (Oct.-Dec. 1966), pp. 505-32; Arthur J. Droze, *Homer or Moses? Early Christian Interpretations of the History of Culture* (Tubingen: J. C. B. Mohr, 1989); Jean Seznec, *The Survival of the Pagan Gods: The Mythological Tradition and Its Place in Renaissance Humanism and Art* (New York: Bollingen, 1953).

On China and this tradition, see Arnold H. Rowbotham, "The Jesuit Figurists and Eighteenth-Century Religious Thought," *Journal of the History of Ideas* 17 (1956), pp. 471-85; Rowbotham, *Missionary and Mandarin: The Jesuits at the Court of China* (Berkeley: University of California Press, 1942), esp. pp. 141, 144, 249-64; Walter W. Davis, "China, the Confucian Ideal, and the European Age of Enlightenment," *Journal of the History of Ideas* 44 (1983), pp. 523-48.

two earlier proponents of the *prisca theologia* who influenced Edwards. Gale's magnum opus, *The Court of the Gentiles* (1677), was a massive four-volume work dedicated to the proposition that all ancient languages and learning, particularly philosophical, were derived from the Jews. As Numenius of Apamea put it in a line noted by Edwards, "What is Plato but Moses speaking in the Attick language?" ("Miscellanies," no. 1355).[21] Cudworth, the great Cambridge Platonist, used much of his *True Intellectual System of the Universe* (1678) to show that the wiser pagans were trinitarian monotheists, not unacquainted with the true (Christian) God.

Edwards was clearly impressed by these proponents of the *prisca theologia*.[22] He copied enormous extracts from their works into his private notebooks, but not slavishly. As Diderot said, imitation is continual invention. From his marginal notes and recapitulation of the tradition in other private notebooks, it is clear that Edwards was selectively and creatively refashioning the tradition to serve his own polemical needs. His principal purpose was to show, against the deists, that nearly all humans have received revelation, and therefore all knowledge of true religion among the heathen is from revelation rather than the light of natural reason.

4. Trickle-Down Revelation and Religious Entropy

Edwards went to great lengths detailing in his notebooks the religious truths possessed by the heathen. From Grotius he learned that the Greeks said that the Spirit moved on the waters at the beginning, and that they knew that one can commit adultery in the heart and that one must forgive and love one's enemies ("Miscellanies," no. 1012; "Miscellanies," no. 1023). Vergil, Seneca, Juvenal, and Ovid, Edwards noted, confessed that our original nature was corrupt ("Miscellanies," no. 1073). Ramsay taught him that the Hindu *Vedas* and the Chinese *I Ching* contain stories about a hero who expiates crimes by his own sufferings,

21. Droze, *Homer or Moses?* p. 199; the quote is cited by Edwards in his extract from Ramsay's *Philosophical Principles* on p. 942 of the Miscellanies notebook.

22. Edwards may have been introduced to the *prisca theologia* by Samuel Johnson, his tutor at Yale; Norman Fiering, *Moral Philosophy at Seventeenth-Century Harvard* (Williamsburg and Chapel Hill: Institute of Early American History and Culture and University of North Carolina Press, 1981), p. 15.

and that many heathen from different traditions acknowledged a divine Incarnation and realized that virtue comes only by an infusion of grace ("Miscellanies," nos. 1351, 1355). Edwards noted in his Blank Bible[23] that heathen stories about gods and goddesses were actually distortions of Hebrew counterparts. Saturn, for example, is a transmutation of Adam, Noah, and Abraham; Hercules is a Greek rendition of Joshua, and Bacchus of Nimrod, Moses, and the Hebrew deity; Apis and Serapis are Egyptian retellings of the Joseph story (pp. 6, 11, 39).

In his own appropriation of the *prisca theologia,* Edwards said that the heathen learned these truths by what could be called a trickle-down process of revelation. In the "first ages" ("Miscellanies," nos. 953, 986, 984) of the world the fathers of the nations received revelation of the great religious truths, directly or indirectly, from God himself.[24] These truths were then passed down, by tradition, from one generation to the next. Unfortunately, there is also a religious law of entropy at work. Human finitude and corruption inevitably cause the revelation to be distorted, resulting in superstition and idolatry. So the original purity of divine truth is continually breaking down, corrupted by profane and demonic mixture ("Miscellanies," no. 986). God uses the Jews to retard the process of degeneration by periodically acting on their behalf with miracles, which remind the heathen of the traditions they once learned from their fathers but subsequently forgot ("Miscellanies," no. 350).

In his private commentary on selected biblical passages Edwards recapitulated this drama (Notes on the Scriptures, Acts 17:26-27, no. 387[25]). "The knowledge of true religion was for some time kept up in

---

23. A large Bible with wide margins in which he commented on the biblical text; Edwards Papers, Beinecke Rare Book and Manuscript Library, Yale University.

24. Usually Edwards is ambiguous about the location of the original deposit of revelation. Only occasionally does he pinpoint Adam; in "Miscellanies," no. 884, he says that Adam learned the moral law from God and taught it with great clarity to his descendants. In *Original Sin* he says that Adam "continued alive near two thirds of the time that passed before the flood," so that most people alive until the flood heard from Adam what "passed between him and his Creator in paradise" (*Works of Jonathan Edwards*, 3, *Original Sin,* ed. Clyde A. Holbrook [New Haven: Yale University Press, 1970], p. 170). Most often, however, he simply refers to the fathers of the nations as identical to or descended from Noah's sons. Presumably, Noah's knowledge was passed down by tradition from Adam and his descendants.

25. *The Works of Jonathan Edwards,* 15, *Notes on the Scriptures,* ed. Stephen J. Stein (New Haven: Yale University Press, 1998), pp. 369-72.

the world by tradition. And there were soon great corruptions and apostasies crept in, and much darkness overwhelmed great part of the world." By the time of Moses, most of the truth that had previously been taught by tradition was now lost. So "God took care that there might be something new, [which] should be very public, and of great fame, and much taken notice of abroad, in the world heard, that might be sufficient to lead sincere inquirers to the true God." Hence the heathen nations in the Ancient Near East heard about the exodus of the Jews from Egypt, the miracles God performed for them in the wilderness, Joshua's conquests of the Canaanites, and the sun standing still. The defeated Canaanites fled to Africa, Asia, Europe, and the isles of the sea "to carry the tidings of those things . . . so that, in a manner, the whole world heard of these great things."

After these wondrous acts of God, knowledge of true religion was maintained for several generations. But by the time of David, much had been forgotten and distorted. So God acted once more, this time for David and Solomon, "to make his people Israel, who had the true religion, [be] taken notice of among the heathens." The diaspora after the Babylonian captivity spread knowledge of the true God even further abroad, so that "the nations of the world, if their heart had been well disposed to seek after the truth, might have had some means to have led 'em in their sincere and diligent inquiries to the knowledge of the true God and his ways."

Edwards was always quick to note that heathen religion and philosophy contained "many absurdities" (e.g., "Miscellanies," no. 1350). But he learned from the *prisca theologia* that among the absurdities there were enough "scraps of truth" to show the way to salvation ("Miscellanies," no. 1297; Notes on the Scriptures, no. 387). Edwards found one way, then, to respond to the scandal of particularity which reports from the East had posed. He agreed with the deists that the problem could not be ignored, and disagreed with earlier Reformed scholastics who saw nothing beyond knowledge of God the Creator in non-Christian religions.[26] God's justice and goodness were not sufficiently protected by the received tradition, so Edwards appropriated

26. Following Calvin, they distinguished between knowledge of God the Creator which is given through nature and conscience but has been distorted by sin, and knowledge of God the Redeemer which is given through Scripture; Richard A. Muller, *Post-Reformation Reformed Dogmatics*, vol. 1, *Prolegomena to Theology* (Grand Rapids: Baker, 1987), p. 119.

an old tradition to make Reformed history anew. In Edwards's new history God was still good, in the context of the new knowledge of pluralism, because knowledge of God the Redeemer had been available from the beginning.

5. Dispositional Soteriology

Edwards filled hundreds of pages in his private notebooks with evidence that the pagans had received knowledge about God the Redeemer from the Jews and the *prisca theologia*. As far as he knew, the vast majority of the heathen failed to take advantage of this knowledge, which was used for their condemnation rather than salvation. But the question of God's fairness that deists had posed could now be answered with integrity. God had not limited his revelation to a minority of humankind, as Calvin and his successors had suggested, but had generously displayed throughout history his redemptive purposes for (most) all the world to see. If non-Christians had not received grace, blame could not be laid at God's feet. It was, as Edwards might have put it, in quite literal fashion, their own damned fault.

If Edwards differed from Calvin on the extent of revelation, he also viewed salvation differently — in a way that contains intriguing implications for the salvation of non-Christians. This new approach to soteriology emerged not from a history of religion but out of his philosophical reflection on being. To be more precise, Edwards used his own dispositional ontology[27] and applied it to soteriology. This move helped him determine what distinguishes saved heathen from unsaved heathen.

For Edwards, the essence of all being is disposition or habit. Drawing on a tradition that originated with Aristotle's *hexis* and developed through Thomas's *habitus* and Reformed scholastic permutations, Edwards held that "[a soul's] essence consists in powers and habits" ("Miscellanies," no. 241). By disposition (when discussing being in general he usually uses the term "habit," but in reference to salvation he prefers

27. For the importance of habit or disposition in Edwards's thought, see the seminal work by Sang Hyun Lee, *The Philosophical Theology of Jonathan Edwards* (Princeton: Princeton University Press, 1988).

"disposition"[28]) he meant an active and real tendency, not merely custom or regularity. This tendency has ontological reality even when it is not exercised; indeed, its exercise is necessary and inevitable when the opportunity for exercise presents itself. So when Edwards spoke of a "holy disposition," i.e., the disposition of the regenerate, he meant "an active and causal power" that, if it had opportunity to be exercised, would certainly produce holy effects. As Edwards put it, "All habits [are] a law that God has fixed, that such actions upon such occasions should be exerted" ("Miscellanies," no. 241).

What are these actions or effects? In other words, if a regenerate disposition is an active tendency that constitutes the essence of what-it-means-to-be-regenerate, what is it an active tendency towards? Very early in his career Edwards answered this question, and never diverged from its basic outline in the years following. In "Miscellanies," no. 39, he concluded that "conversion under the old testament was not only the same in general with what it is commonly under the new, but much more like it as to the particular way and manner, than I used to think." In what amounts to a phenomenology of true religious experience, Edwards declared what he thought to be common to Christians, Old Testament Jews, and all other true religionists "from the beginning of the world": "a sense of the dangerousness of sin, and of the dreadfulness of God's anger . . . [such a conviction of] their wickedness, that they trusted to nothing but the mere mercy of God, and then bitterly lamented and mourned for their sins."

Just a short time earlier Edwards had written that it is this inner religious consciousness (disposition) that is the only prerequisite to salvation. No particular act, even the act of receiving Christ, is necessary: "The disposition is all that can be said to be absolutely necessary. The act [of receiving Christ] cannot be proved to be absolutely necessary. . . . 'Tis the disposition or principle is the thing God looks at." For an illustration of this point Edwards used the Old Testament Jews. They did not receive Christ in any conscious or explicit man-

---

28. In other contexts he uses the following synonyms: "tendency," "propensity," "principle," "temper," and "frame of mind." See *Works of Jonathan Edwards, 2, Religious Affections,* ed. John E. Smith (New Haven: Yale University Press, 1959), pp. 206-7, 283-84; Lee, *Philosophical Theology of Jonathan Edwards,* pp. 15-46; *Works of Jonathan Edwards, 6, Scientific and Philosophical Writings,* ed. Wallace E. Anderson (New Haven: Yale University Press, 1980), pp. 124-29.

ner, but they had the proper disposition, which alone is necessary for salvation:

> It need not be doubted but that many of the ancient Jews before Christ were saved without the sensible exertions of those acts in that manner which is represented as necessary by some divines, because they had not those occasions nor were under circumstances that would draw them out; though without doubt *they had the disposition, which alone is absolutely necessary now, and at all times, and in all circumstances is equally necessary.* ("Miscellanies," no. 27b; emphasis added)

Now Edwards in this passage was not considering the heathen, and was not imagining salvation apart from belief in Christ. His point was that in conversion the most essential ingredient is a certain disposition, so that the manner of expressing that disposition by receiving Christ is secondary. Only the disposition is primary, and the Old Testament Jewish saints are a case in point. Edwards also used the illustration of a man who dies suddenly, "not in the actual exercise of faith." This man is still saved nevertheless, because "'tis his disposition that saves him." Yet this entry reveals an important structure in Edwards's thinking about salvation: faith is subsumed by the category of disposition. As becomes clear elsewhere in Edwards's writings, disposition functions as the ontological ground of forensic imputation.[29]

Seven years later Edwards made it clear that the disposition is more important than religious and moral behavior, for while the character of a saving disposition is constant, religious and moral expectations differ according to the degree of revelation available. The obedience required in the Old Testament era was "in considerable part different" from what was required during the New Testament. "And so there are duties that respect the Messias and his salvation and another world that are necessary now to salvation, that were not then, by reason of the different state of the church and of revelation. Though they could not be saved without the same principle and spirit of old, yet they might be saved without such explicit exercises and explicit acts thereof" ("Miscellanies," no. 439). The inner disposition, not any particular acts and exercises, is the only essential prerequisite to salvation. Therefore, Edwards added at the close of his Northampton so-

---

29. Anri Morimoto, *Jonathan Edwards and the Catholic Vision of Salvation* (University Park: Penn State Press, 1995), pp. 78-101.

journ, God "was pleased in a great measure to wink at and suffer (though he did not properly allow) . . . under that dark and imperfect, and comparatively carnal dispensation"[30] polygamy, divorce, blood revenge, and worship at the high places. God could overlook ungodly behavior in his saints because their disposition was pleasing.

God also overlooked faulty religious knowledge. Early in his pastorate at Northampton Edwards conceded privately that the Jewish saints of the Old Testament did not know about love for enemies, universal love for all humanity, monogamy, or loving one another as Christ has loved us ("Miscellanies," no. 343). Yet they were saved. In Edwards's last decade he became convinced that some heathen had more religious knowledge and knew more about virtue than many Old Testament saints. Greek and Roman moralists, for example, knew that we ought to love and forgive our enemies, return good for evil, and be monogamous ("Miscellanies," no. 1023). Other pagan philosophers knew about infused grace, the necessity of grace for virtue, the Trinity and Incarnation, and redemption by the suffering of a middle god ("Miscellanies," no. 1355). Even the (Muslim) Persians and Turks knew true humility and disinterested love for God ("Miscellanies," no. 1257). In the margins of an extract describing Plato's vision of God's beauty, Edwards scribbled, "Right notions of God and religion." At the end of an extract detailing many pagan ideas, he added, "All the chief philosophers have right views of virtue and religion."[31]

---

30. *An Humble Inquiry into the Rules of the Word of God, Concerning the Qualifications Requisite to a Complete Standing and Full Communion in the Visible Christian Church,* in *Works,* 12, p. 281.

31. This note is significant because it comes at the end of "Miscellanies," no. 1355, which immediately follows a long series of extracts from Philip Skelton ridiculing pagan notions of God ("Miscellanies," no. 1354). This is an illustration of how Edwards took some Reformed polemics against the heathen with a grain of salt. He believed that the heathen were generally lost in darkness but nevertheless was convinced that "the wiser heathen" possessed considerable religious and moral truth.

A similar pattern can be seen in the contrast between "Miscellanies," no. 965 (in which Gale scores the spiritual pride of heathen philosophers), and "Miscellanies," no. 1357 (an extract from John Brine that criticizes pagan philosophers for their lack of humility and failure to depend on God for virtue), on the one hand, and "Miscellanies," nos. 986 and 1028, on the other, where Edwards praises Socrates for showing humility by not trusting in himself, and Xenophon, Plato, and Seneca for knowing that virtue is impossible without divine grace.

These reflections on the religious knowledge and virtue of the heathen may have caused Edwards to rethink, or at least refine, his thinking on justification and regeneration. In a Miscellanies entry from the mid-1730s, he began to reflect on justification and regeneration as phased, and in one respect life-long, processes rather than instantaneous events. Jesus' disciples, he pondered, were "good men *before*" they met Christ, "already in a *disposition* to follow Christ" ("Miscellanies," no. 847; emphasis added). The same was true, Edwards thought, of Zacchaeus and the women of Canaan.[32]

If some are "good," because they have a regenerate disposition before they are outwardly converted to Christ, then perhaps conversion in those cases comes *after* they are already regenerate: "Conversion may still be necessary to salvation in some respect even after he is really a saint." In these cases justification is already a fact in one sense but in another sense depends on "these after works of the Spirit of God upon the soul" ("Miscellanies," no. 847). That is, the condition of justification still remains to be fulfilled after conversion. Hence saints are still in a state of probation until the end of their lives.[33]

If in a certain sense justification is in stages and finally complete only at death or the end of one's probation on earth, then regeneration can be viewed similarly: "The whole of the saving work of Gods [sic] Spirit on the soul in the beginning and progress of it from the very first dawnings of divine light and the first beginnings of divine life until death is in some respect to be looked upon as all one work of regeneration. . . . There is as it were an unregenerate part still in man after the first regeneration that still needs to be regenerated" ("Miscellanies," no. 847).

These views show startling similarity to the Roman Catholic view

---

32. This was simply an application of the principle he articulated in 1729 — that "a person according to the gospel may be in a state of salvation, before a distinct and express act of faith in the sufficiency and suitableness of Christ as a Savior" ("Miscellanies," no. 393).

33. Edwards also speaks of God justifying, "as it were," a person being received into the visible church on the "presumption" and "supposition" that the person is sincere, which is proved by later "faithfullness" ("Miscellanies," no. 689). This "visible covenant" is different from the "covenant of grace," but in each case there is a condition to be fulfilled. In the covenant of grace, however, God covenants "with those that before his allseeing eyes perform that condition of the covenant of grace" (ibid.).

that justification is a long and gradual process of transformation that includes sanctification. Several caveats are in order. First, Edwards qualifies his statements by inserting the pregnant phrases "in some respect" and "as it were," as a reminder that these remarks should not be taken in isolation from his other, extensive discussions of these topics. Second, Edwards's understandings of justification and regeneration are exceedingly complex. It is impossible to do justice to them here, and therefore place these remarks in their proper context; it is far better to refer the reader to several studies of these subjects.[34] But an observation relevant to our purposes can nonetheless be made: Edwards's soteriology seems in some respects to depart from Reformation distinctives. Martin Luther's salvation by faith *alone* becomes for Edwards salvation by faith *primarily*.[35] While Luther emphasized that in justification sinners are *counted* as righteous, Edwards stressed the fact that sinners are actually *made* holy in the act of regeneration.[36]

It should be said that Edwards did not follow the Protestant scholastic tendency to collapse all of soteriology into justification, and that he saw no contradiction or inconsistency between justification by Christ's righteousness and justification by good works.[37] In addition, Edwards followed the "Lombardian tradition" (of positing the radical contingency and dependence of the created virtues on God) far more consistently than most of his Reformed predecessors.[38] But his emphasis on disposition as primary and faith as secondary, and the dispositional structure of his soteriology, undermine the Reformation contention that salvation is the justification of the ungodly.[39] It is for

34. Conrad Cherry, *The Theology of Jonathan Edwards: A Reappraisal* (Indianapolis: Indiana University Press, 1990), pp. 90-106; Thomas A. Schafer, "Jonathan Edwards and Justification by Faith," *Church History* 20 (1951), pp. 55-67; Morimoto, *Jonathan Edwards and the Catholic Vision of Salvation,* pp. 71-130.

35. I am indebted to George Hunsinger for this characterization.

36. See Morimoto, *Jonathan Ewards and the Catholic Vision of Salvation,* pp. 82, 153.

37. "Miscellanies," nos. 793, 996; see also Morimoto, *Jonathan Edwards and the Catholic Vision of Salvation,* pp. 115, 113.

38. Morimoto, *Jonathan Ewards and the Catholic Vision of Salvation,* pp. 60-61.

39. In "Miscellanies," no. 218, faith is subsumed under the category of disposition; there is one disposition with many names: faith, hope, love, and obedience. In "Miscellanies," nos. 315 and 412, faith is subtly relativized by statements that both faith and works are conditions for salvation, though Edwards is quick to note that works are secondary and follow faith inevitably as fruit. In "Miscellanies," no. 712, Edwards says there is real goodness in the human subject prior to justification. On

this reason, in part, that Thomas A. Schafer concluded that Edwards "went beyond the doctrine of justification."[40]

It is also for this reason that Edwards's soteriology resembles Roman Catholic theology in ways that make it easier to consider the salvation of the heathen. If regeneration and justification can be considered, at least from one perspective, as processes that unfold in stages, and if one can therefore be a saint before conversion, then theological groundwork has been laid for the position that (some of) the heathen can be saints before they come to Christ if they have the proper dispositions. If their knowledge of Christ is incomplete, it may be because they are still in the initial stages of regeneration and justification, which may be completed in glory, just as it is for infants. Edwards never reached this explicit conclusion, at least in his published writings or private notebooks. But his own theology had laid the groundwork for such an interpretation.

Even more suggestively, Edwards described four types of persons without explicit knowledge of Christ who may nevertheless find salvation. For all four types disposition is the critical determinant of their eschatological destiny. Very early in his career Edwards wrote that infants can be regenerated at birth without knowledge of Christ ("Miscellanies," no. 78), and that salvation is based on disposition: "The Infant that has a Disposition in his Heart to believe in Christ if he had a capacity & opportunity is Looked upon and accepted as if he actually believed in Christ and so is entitled to Eternal Life through Christ" (Book of Controversies, p. 17, section 65).[41]

When Edwards asked himself how he was to understand the salvation of Old Testament saints "when yet they had no distinct respect to [Christ]," he reasoned that it was "the second Person in the Trinity" who appeared to them "as the author of temporal salvation and benefits," and whenever God is said to have manifested himself to Israel ("Miscellanies," no. 663). Hence they already believed in Christ in some sense ("Miscellanies," no. 840), and were saved by faith in Christ

---

this last point, see Morimoto, *Jonathan Edwards and the Catholic Vision of Salvation*, p. 93.

40. Schafer, "Jonathan Edwards and Justification by Faith," p. 64.

41. "Miscellanies," no. 492, suggests that Edwards considered the state of infants as analogous to that of the heathen, since both have less than full knowledge of revelation. In this entry he speculates that without revelation we would not know "who are liable to punishment, whether children, whether heathen."

("Miscellanies," nos. 884, 1283). In an early comment that is fascinatingly relevant to our interests, Edward wrote that conversions from wickedness to righteousness in the Old Testament era were just as "frequent" as in the New Testament era ("Miscellanies," no. 39).

New Testament saints followed a similar pattern. "Cornelius did already in some respect believe in X [Christ] even in the manner that the Old Testament saints were wont to do" ("Miscellanies," no. 840). Before he met Peter, that is, Cornelius in some sense believed in a Christ of whom he had not yet heard. Edwards said the same about the apostles. Cornelius, Nathaniel, "probably" John's two disciples, and several others were *"good men* before [they met Christ], for they seemed to be found already in a *disposition* to follow [Christ] when [Christ] first appeared to them in his human nature and this seems to have been the case with Zacchaeus and with the women of Canaan." Edwards infers from this that "conversion may still be by divine constitution necessary to salvation in some respect even after [a person] is really a saint" ("Miscellanies," no. 847; emphasis added). Once again we see that Edwards is suggesting instances where a person can be regenerate before conversion to an explicit knowledge of Christ. At this point, probably mid- to late-1730s, Edwards is returning to an inference he had reached very early in his career (1723), that "a man may have the disposition in himself for some time before he can sensibly feel them [the exercises of that disposition], for want of occasion or other reason" ("Miscellanies," no. 27b).

This notion of regeneration before conversion, and our observation of similarities with Roman Catholic soteriology, invite comparison to Karl Rahner's conception of "anonymous Christians." Like Edwards and unlike Luther, Rahner looks more to the human subject and its condition (rather than to God's free decision or Christ's person and work) when explaining the justification of those who never hear the gospel. Both Edwards and Rahner, then, use a dispositional soteriology in so far as they ground justification primarily in the disposition of the human person. However, while Rahner's (saving) disposition highlights obedience to one's conscience,[42] Edwards's (saving) disposition is centered in religious consciousness — awareness of sin and one's need for divine mercy. Another difference between the two is

---

42. Karl Rahner, S.J., "Anonymous Christians," in *Theological Investigations*, vol. 6 (Baltimore: Helicon Press, 1969), p. 397.

that Rahner rejects "primordial revelation" and locates revelation to non-Christians in the unreflexive and unobjectified "depths of [their own] being,"[43] while for Edwards revelation to non-Christians has come historically in propositional form through the Jews and the fathers of the Gentile nations.

A fourth class of people who enjoyed salvation without explicit knowledge of Christ were those we might call holy pagans. In his 1739 sermons on the history of the work of redemption, Edwards surmised that conversion to true religion, justification, and glorification have occurred in all ages of the world since the Fall, and cited examples of such holy pagans living outside of Israel: Melchizedek, the posterity of Nahor (Job and his family), Job's three friends, including Bildad the Shuhite, and Elihu.[44] These were individuals outside the national covenant with Israel and of course without explicit knowledge of Christ who nonetheless seem to have been regenerate.

In correspondence during his last years, he wrote of a group of Onohquaga Indians residing in Stockbridge for a time as excelling "in religion and virtue" and "far the best disposed Indians we have had to do with, and [who] would be inclined to their utmost to assist, encourage, and to strengthen the hands of missionaries and instructors, should [any] be sent among [them]."[45] It is not at all clear from the letters that these Indians were all converted; the opposite is more probable. But it is significant that Edwards said they excelled in both religion and virtue. In both his sermons on charity and the "Miscellanies" he criticized pagan moralists who sometimes had good ideas about religion and virtue but failed to live virtuous or religious lives.[46] But Ed-

43. Rahner, "Jesus Christ in Non-Christian Religions," in *Foundations of Christian Faith* (New York: Seabury Press, 1978), pp. 315, 313; Rahner, "Anonymous Christians," p. 394.

44. *Works of Jonathan Edwards*, 9, *History of the Work of Redemption*, ed. John F. Wilson (New Haven: Yale University Press, 1989), p. 179. Edwards also said in these sermons that after Abraham God rejected all other nations and gave them up to idolatry; ibid. That Edwards is speaking of collective groups and not individuals is clear from several discussions in his notebooks, including the one mentioned in the next paragraph of this text.

45. Letter to Secretary Andrew Oliver, April 12, 1753, pp. 4-5 in *Works of Jonathan Edwards*, 16, ed. George S. Claghorn, *Letters and Personal Writings* (New Haven: Yale University Press, 1998), p. 583..

46. *Works of Jonathan Edwards*, 8, *Ethical Writings*, ed. Paul Ramsey (New Haven: Yale University Press, 1989), pp. 310-11; "Miscellanies," nos. 965, 1357.

wards praised these Indians not for the truth of their ideas but the quality of their lives, just as Luke had commended Cornelius for the quality of his practice. In this letter and another during that period he described two other tribes of Indians who "have a great desire that the gospel should be introduced and settled in their country."[47] Perhaps, in the twilight years of his career, Edwards thought he had found holy pagans who, like Cornelius, were sincerely seeking the gospel.

6. God's Expectations

If there were grounds to think that these different sorts of people could be saved without explicit knowledge of Christ, and if salvation is based on dispositions, what does God expect of a saving disposition? We have already seen that a sense of sin and trust in God's mercy are required. But how was that to be manifested? For Edwards, God's expectations vary according to the degree of revelation available. All human beings have received revelation, but revelation is progressive (*History of the Work of Redemption,* passim; "Miscellanies," nos. 160, 439, 489). Its principal lineaments were given to the fathers of the nations, who handed them down by traditions to their descendents, but at any given time its extent varied because of the law of religious entropy: different times and different places were affected by different degrees of sin's corruption.

Hence, while the basic conditions for salvation remained the same in every place and period, God's expectations varied according to the conditions of extant revelation. "Though holiness or spiritual image of God be in its principle and habit the same[,] yet the circumstances . . . the different relations to God . . . different manner of God's dealing with us and discovering himself to us and the work he appoints us and the views and expectations given us and pursuits that are appoint'd us . . . the exercises of it be most diverse" ("Miscellanies," no. 894). Therefore the "duties" pertaining to salvation differ because of the "different state of the church and revelation" ("Miscellanies," no. 439; see also "Miscellanies," no. 246). God expects the same principle and spirit, but varying exercises and explicit acts.

Edwards states as a general rule that God's expectations are al-

47. Letter to Rev. John Erskine, April 14, 1753, p. 2, in *Works,* 16, p. 595.

ways in "just proportion" to the degree of revelation present. Since eighteenth-century New England had been so flooded with revelation, God expected "vastly" more than even in New Testament times. "A man now in order to a being perfectly holy or coming up to his duty now must be vastly more holy[,] must love God in an unspeakably higher degrees [sic]. . . . Then a man is perfectly holy when his love to God bears a just proportion to the capacities of his nature under such circumstances with such manifestations as God makes or his loveliness and benefits that he receives from him" ("Miscellanies," no. 894). Edwards went on to say that more is expected of us than of Adam. If Adam were transported across time to the modern era, he would be considered "earthly minded in a sense"; if modern Christians were to behave as he did, they would be thought "corrupt and abominable."

Because God's expectations depend on the degree of revelation available, and the heathen have received so much less than those in the Christian world, the heathen are nowhere so displeasing to God as the unregenerate in Christian lands. After all, Edwards preached, the heathen never had a choice to receive Christ explicitly; they aren't as hardened and are more free from prejudice. They have "a principle of enmity against God and rebellion against God," but a "gospel sinner" has a "habit" of rejecting God. Sinners who have heard the gospel, then, have a habit or disposition to reject the gospel, but sinners in heathen lands do not (sermon on Matthew 11:21, before 1733, 13).

Just before he was ejected from his pulpit, Edwards told his congregation that most of them were "more provoking enemies to that Lord they love and adore, than most of the very heathen" (*An Humble Inquiry*, 255). Nearly a decade later he wrote that the Christian world is more "hateful to God and repugnant to true virtue, than the state of the heathen world" before Christ (*Original Sin*,[48] 183).

7. A Possibility of Reconciliation

The implications of Edwards's use of his dispositional ontology for his soteriology can now be articulated. While a saving disposition was nearly always a disposition to receive Christ, he also considered explicitly several classes of persons who can have a saving disposition with-

48. *Works*, 3, p. 183.

out faith in the historical Christ. And he surmised that some heathen knew more about virtue and divinity than Old Testament figures who were saved. After Edwards reached these conclusions, he reflected late in his career, tentatively but positively, on the eternal possibilities of the heathen. In "Miscellanies," no. 1162, after explaining that heathen philosophers had said "such wonderful things concerning the Trinity [and] the Messiah," he asked whether they might have been inspired by the Holy Spirit. Yes, he figured, but then reminded himself that this is not so high "an honour and priviledge as some are ready to think." For "many very bad men have been the subjects of it." Some were idolators such as Balaam. Nebuchadnezzar, "a very wicked man," received a revelation about the Messiah and his future kingdom. Even the devil at the oracle at Delphi was "compelled to confess Christ."

But in any event, of what use were the revelations given to Socrates and Plato "and some others of the wise men of Greece," who were just as inspired as the wise men from the East? These philosophers did not use these revelations to lead their nations toward the truth, so God must have had other intentions. Edwards suggested four: to dispose heathen nations in the future to converse with and learn from the Jews, to prepare the Gentiles for their future reception of the gospel, to confirm the truths of Christianity, and (in what is one of Edwards's most cryptic comments in the thousands of pages of his private notebooks) to benefit their own souls: "We know not what evidence God might give to the men themselves that were the subjects of these inspirations that they were divine and true . . . and so we know not of how great benefit the truths suggested might be to their own souls." Edwards is hesitant and tentative, but he nevertheless clearly opens the possibility that these heathen can use revelation for their own spiritual benefit — a notion that is incoherent unless it means they can be saved. When it is recalled that Edwards wrote this entry during a period in which he was frequently quoting from writers who explicitly argued for the salvation of the virtuous heathen, it is difficult to believe that Edwards did not include salvation among the possible benefits to heathen souls.[49]

49. It should also be noted that Cambridge Platonist Henry More, who according to Wallace Anderson had "an early and lasting influence upon Edwards' thought," wrote that the heathen can be saved by grace through "Faithfulness to that Light and Power which God has given them." *Works*, 6, p. 21; Henry More, *An Explanation of the Mystery of Godliness* [orig. 1660], in *The Theological Works of the Most Pious and Learned Henry More* (London, 1708), 10.6, p. 352.

Near the very end of his life, in a notebook entry ("Miscellanies," no. 1338) arguing against deist notions of reason, Edwards asserted that reason can confirm many religious truths but cannot discover them on its own. Then he considered the deist objection that most humans have not had the benefit of revelation. There is a "possibility," he replied, of the heathen being "reconciled" to God and thus receiving the benefit of divine revelation, for "the greater part of the heathen world have not [been] left merely to the light of nature." They have received revelation by tradition from their ancestors and have borrowed from the Jews. Since the means of revelation were available, it was theoretically possible that some could have had a saving disposition and been reconciled to God. But their "extreme blindness [and] delusion" suggested that few had taken advantage of the "benefit of revelation."

Once again, we see Edwards's familiar response to deists: revelation is both necessary and pervasive. God has revealed himself to humankind, and not just to the Jewish and Christian communities. The history of the world is the history of the work of redemption, the exploits of which were reported to most human ears. Because of this transmission of the good news to almost all human societies, salvation was available for those among the heathen who would pursue the leads they were given from the *prisca theologia* and the Jews.

8. Typology

In yet a third way of considering salvation for some heathen, Edwards fitted the religions into his massive typological scheme. Although the elaboration of this scheme is beyond the scope of this essay,[50] suffice it to say here that while previous scholars have shown that for Edwards not only the Old Testament but also nature and history are types of the divine, it should now be said that the history of religions is also typological. To give just two of many examples, Edwards believed that many non-Christian traditions contain types of the Messiah in their depictions of the sufferings of a second divine person — Mithras, Osiris, Apollo, Adonis, Hercules, Kiun Tse (*Book of Controversies*, 232). He also wrote extensively of how the heathen learned about Christ's

---

50. I have explicated it in chapter six of *Jonathan Edwards Confronts the Gods.*

ultimate sacrifice through their own traditions of sacrifice, which stem from original revelations from God.[51]

Edwards's typology, into which he integrated the religions, sheds further light on his soteriology by showing a deeper level at which he believed revelation had come to the heathen. In this way they had even greater access to saving knowledge, and by the same token greater responsibility for rejecting "the true Light, which lighteth every man that cometh into the world."

9. A Comfortable Agnosticism

But if Edwards was convinced that, *contra* deism, God's revelation had been made available to most of the world, he was not sure that it had indeed reached every last person. On this point he was agnostic. But his agnosticism did not bother him. For he was convinced, on other grounds, that the Scriptures were true and therefore that God was just and good. Edwards was never persuaded by the deists that God's justice had to be completely comprehensible in human terms, or that divine justice must be coordinate to human justice by some rational calculation. He was so convinced by the beauty and coherence of the Christian drama of redemption that he was happy to permit divine justice — which he conceded is finally incomprehensible by human minds — to serve as the standard by which human justice and goodness are to be judged.

At the end of his career Edwards twice reflected at some length on this question. In "Miscellanies," no. 1299, he acknowledged that for most of those who don't have the Scriptures, reconciliation with God is "very improbable." The preacher of "Sinners in the Hands of an Angry God" was too convinced of general depravity to think otherwise. But reconciliation was not impossible, for if people really sought the truth, they could find it. If for some it was "next to impossible" (here he seems to concede that some are bereft of truth and perhaps even revelation), however, one must not hastily conclude that God is not good or just. For if God's distribution of spiritual benefits does not seem eq-

---

51. *Works*, 9, pp. 135-38, 152-53, 164, 182, 198, 204, 225, 318, 331, 361; *Works of Jonathan Edwards*, 11, *Typological Writings*, ed. Wallace E. Anderson and Mason I. Lowance (New Haven: Yale University Press, 1993), pp. 193, 308.

uitable, neither does his distribution of temporal benefits. Different people have different foods and animals and kinds of clothing. Some have no glass or "loadstone" (an eighteenth-century word for a piece of iron used as a magnet) at all. Even rain and sun are apportioned unequally.

Hence the mere fact that God's gifts are not distributed universally does not prove God's meanness to some. It shows only that God is discriminate in how he demonstrates his goodness. Edwards refused the deist inference that God must be unjust if his gifts are not distributed equally. By his lights, the goodness of the world in general and the objective reality of redemption in Christ have already proven God's good intent. If we cannot calculate how God's goodness coheres with distributive justice that is not by our reckoning absolutely equal and universal, so be it. The God of the spider may seem arbitrary to human eyes, but Edwards was so taken by this God's beauty that he could not imagine that his God was not also finally just to all.

A short time later ("Miscellanies," no. 1340), Edwards responded to the deist insistence that what is mysterious cannot be believed. "It may be expected that as in the system of nature, so in this system of revelation, there should be many parts whose use is but little understood, and many that should seem wholly useless, yea and some that should seem rather to do hurt than good." In fact, Edwards allowed, some parts of Scripture seem to do more harm than good.

But such problems should not be surprising, Edwards replied. This is to be expected in a revelation that unveils a reality that is infinitely complex and often paradoxical. Like Joseph Butler, whose *Analogy of Religion* was perhaps the most effective response to deism, Edwards argued that the difficulties and mysteries of revelation are analogues to their counterparts in nature, to whose pedestrian clarity the deists religiously appealed. "It may well be expected, that there should be mysteries, things incomprehensible and exceeding difficult to our understanding; analogous to the mysteries that are found in all other works of God, as the works of creation and providence."

So Edwards did not presume to explain all the mysteries of revelation and salvation. Instead he claimed that the vision of Christian redemption is so compelling that we are obliged to work within the bounds of that vision, reconciling as best we can its features with the world we experience. In the process we will make new discoveries because the Spirit continues to give new illumination of written revelation. But we must not insist on full understanding of every part, as the deists did, because revelation, like life, abounds with mystery and paradox impervious to human comprehension.

10. A Curious Tension

We are left with a curious tension in Edwards's thinking about the salvation of the heathen. On the one hand, in most of his explicit commentary on the heathen, he took a negative view characteristic of his Reformed predecessors. While appreciating the religious truth known by the "wiser heathen," for example, he never tired of recording the "absurdities of the worship of the heathen." The later Miscellanies contain frequent references to human sacrifice, religious prostitution, fornication, sodomy, castration, and cannibalism. At times it seems that Edwards revelled in the titillating details. From Skelton's two volumes Edwards was careful to copy passages that poked fun at the Greek philosophers who made dangerous journeys by sea to visit the "celebrated Prostitutes of their time," let out their own wives "for Hire," kept mistresses and gave the world "the strongest reasons to think them guilty of greater crimes, than it was possible to commit with the other sex." Aristotle, Edwards dutifully recorded, was a fob, a debauchee, a traitor to Alexander his master. Xenophon kept a boy lover. Sometimes Edwards's choice of extracts bordered on the ridiculous: "The most solemn act of worship performed to the Syrian Baal by his ordinary devotees, was to break wind and ease themselves at the Foot of his Image" ("Miscellanies," no. 1350).

Edwards was his most uncompromising in his sermons. In an early Northampton sermon (Rev. 3:15, before 1733) he identified immorality and idolatry as characteristically "heathenish" (13). God had forsaken and withdrawn his gracious presence from heathen lands. They were "Lost Nations" and the heathen were the devil's people (30). In a particularly vivid passage, Edwards said "the devil nurses them [the heathen] up as swine in a pen that he may fill his belly with them in another [world]. . . . They are his prey when they die. That dragon[,] that old serpent[,] then Got 'em into his own den and sucks their blood and feeds upon their bowels and vitals" (30). And there seems no hope, for "those that die heathen he will prey upon and Exert his Cruelty Upon forever" (31).

Even in his last decade at Stockbridge preaching to Indians, Edwards seems to have held out little hope for the heathen. While in these sermons he emphasized those heathen (Indians) who had heard the gospel and rejected it, the implication in most discussions was that *heathen* and *lost* are synonymous. In a sermon on Proverbs 15:24, for example, he proclaimed, "They that Trust in graven Images or in mahomet or Pagan priests to save them . . . take a sure course to destruction" (4). And in a sermon on Matthew 7:13-14 he declared that "all they are going in the way to destruction who are Heathens and worship the sun and moon and worship the devil and dont worship the true God" (2).

But that is not the whole picture. Edwards made a series of important theological moves beyond his Reformed predecessors that could have opened the door for a more hopeful view of the salvation of the heathen. The advances he made in typology, the extensive use he made of the *prisca theologia,* and his development of a dispositional soteriology prepared the theological way for a more expansive view of salvation. Edwards used these developments primarily to argue for a greater knowledge of religious *truth* among the heathen than his favorite Reformed predecessors had allowed — greater, for instance, than Francis Turretin (1623-87), Petrus van Mastricht (1630-1706), and, for that matter, John Calvin (1509-64), all of whom conceded knowledge of God the Creator but not knowledge of God the Redeemer among the heathen.[52] On the question of salvation, he usually only conceded the *possibility* that heathen could be saved, and never spoke in the expansively hopeful terms of a Watts, Ramsay, or Skelton, or even a Baxter or Wesley.[53] So while he built the theological foundations upon which a more hopeful soteriology could quite naturally have been erected, Edwards himself never chose to construct a superstructure.

Perhaps Edwards reasoned that such concessions would yield too much ground to the enemy. Robert Breck had concluded that since there

---

52. Turretin, *Institutes,* 1:9-16; Mastricht, *Theoretica-practica theologia* (Utrecht, 1724), I.i.xxii-xxv; Calvin, *Institutes* 1.1-5.

53. Baxter forthrightly granted salvation to those (outside the "Jewish church") who did not have "knowledge of Christ *incarnate,*" and Wesley said pagans just need to live up to the light they are given. Richard Baxter, *The Reasons of the Christian Religion* (London, 1667), pp. 201-2; Wesley, Sermon 68, "The General Spread of the Gospel," in Wesley, *Works,* 9, p. 234; see David Pailin, *Attitudes to Other Religions: Comparative Religion in Seventeenth and Eighteenth Century Britain* (Manchester: Manchester University Press, 1984), p. 48.

can be salvation without profession of Christ, it was not absolutely necessary for people to believe that Christ died for sinners. Their motive did not matter as long as they "forsake sin and lead moral lives."[54] Edwards knew that this was the deist and Arminian position which proposed a self-determining will and considered sincerity sufficient in the absence of disinterested virtue. The American theologian retorted that mere sincerity was not enough ("Miscellanies," no. 1153). Self-love and fear of damnation could produce a sincere desire to be virtuous without a will to virtue. To affirm the salvation of the heathen on the grounds of moral sincerity alone would have conceded the argument to the Arminians and deists on the freedom of the will.

This may explain Edwards's puzzling reversal in his interpretation of John 1:9 ("That was the true Light, which lighteth every man that cometh into the world" [King James Version]). In the early 1730s, before the Breck incident, Edwards explained the meaning of John 1:9 in universal terms. Every one who was ever enlightened, he wrote in his Blank Bible, was enlightened in no other way "but by Jesus Christ." This light enlightened not only the Jews but "indifferently Every man[,] Let him be of what nation soever." Hence this was a "general" light. Edwards reminded himself at the close of the entry to "see a parallel Expression Col. 1.23 'the gospel . . . which was preached to every creature which is under heaven.'" The upshot of this comment is that non-Christians who had religious truth had been given it by Christ himself.

But nearly a decade later, after the Breck controversy had subsided, Edwards restricted the meaning of this text (John 1:9) to groups of people rather than individuals. In his Book of Controversies (135), he wrote, "What is really intended is only universal with Respect to Kinds and without limitation by any Rule. Or being limited or Restrained from any one Individual Person by any Rule Given." It was as if Edwards worried that William Turner may have been right, that undisciplined speculation about "the Variety which appears in Religion" might lead indeed to "Scepticism and Atheism and Impiety in the world."[55] Breck had demonstrated what damage mischievous use of the religions could do.

Breck's position was also perilously similar to that taken by Ed-

---

54. *A Letter to the Author of the Pamphlet,* p. 159.
55. *The History of All Religions in the World* (London, 1695), "To the Reader" (no pagination).

wards's opponents in the communion controversy that led to his ouster from Northampton.[56] Not coincidentally, Breck sided with these opponents and cast the deciding vote on the clerical council. Edwards's opponents also argued for moral sincerity without full-hearted "ownership" of Christ as sufficient for admission to the sacrament. Edwards kept insisting that the conviction that one possesses Christ and therefore true virtue is necessary for such admission. Once again, to preach the salvation of the heathen based on an internal disposition without profession of Christ could too easily be co-opted by his opponents, to the ruin of his church. Ironically, the integrity of his church was ruined anyway, and he was banished to preach to the heathen.

More likely, however, Edwards saw no irony or tension in his position. For him there was no inconsistency whatsoever between the possibility of reconciliation for the heathen (because of the *prisca theologia*, God's types in the religions, and a dispositional soteriology) and the probability that only a precious few of the heathen had ever been saved. For this was the testimony of Scripture as he understood it. The sacred authors of the Bible, by the inspiration of the Holy Spirit, portrayed a world in which God had shown himself directly through Jewish history and Jesus Christ. Salvation was available to all, but only through the events of that Jewish-Christian history. News of those events had been heard by most of the world, but few had listened. Hence the world's darkness and delusion were tragic but not unfair. History was a mirror of the human soul: able to perceive cosmic truths but disinclined to appropriate those truths.

Furthermore, the beauty of God that he saw in the history of redemption convinced him of the justice of God the Redeemer. The aesthetic ecstasy he had experienced as a teenager had been repeated and confirmed in the years since as he contemplated the deity's manifold excellencies displayed throughout the history of the work of redemption.[57] For Edwards, seeing the beauty of God in the work of redemption was the best proof possible that this deity was true and real.[58] And

56. The most accurate review of the controversy is Hall's introduction to *Works*, 12, pp. 1-90.

57. "Personal Narrative," in Simonson, ed., *Selected Writings of Jonathan Edwards* (Prospect Heights, IL: Waveland Press, 1992), pp. 40-41.

58. Michael J. McClymond, *Encounters with God: An Approach to the Theology of Jonathan Edwards* (New York: Oxford University Press, 1998), chs. 1 and 5.

since for him the beautiful was the good — the drama of redemption as climaxed in Christ was aesthetically excellent precisely because it described the apogee of love — there was no quarrelling with God's redemptive maneuverings. Every last question (Why did revelation extend only to a majority of pagans rather than to all? Why was grace for repentance not given to more heathen?) did not have to be answered. A glimpse of the divine glory was intrinsically self-validating. This deity was beautiful and therefore just. To demand that it stand before the human bar of justice was an act of unconscionable hubris. It made no philosophical sense. It would be comparable to asking how many inches are in a pound, or whether yellow is round or square.

Therefore the fact that God had provided revelation for the majority of the heathen was sufficient to exonerate divine justice. We should be content with that peek into the otherwise inscrutable sanctum of the divine wisdom, and trust that the balance of the divine economy — while baffling the canons of human probity — was finally just. Hence the deist reproach, Edwards reasoned, had been turned back, and the deity's glory but further magnified.

List of Contributors

Harry S. Stout, Jonathan Edwards Professor of American Christianity, Yale University, and General Editor of *The Works of Jonathan Edwards*

John E. Smith, Clark Professor of Philosophy Emeritus, Yale University, and former General Editor of *The Works of Jonathan Edwards*

Sang Hyun Lee, K. C. Han Professor of Systematic Theology, Princeton Theological Seminary

Stephen H. Daniel, Professor of Philosophy, Texas A & M University

Roland A. Delattre, Professor of American Studies Emeritus, University of Minnesota

Allen C. Guelzo, Grace F. Kea Professor of American History and Dean of the Templeton Honors College, Eastern College

Walter V. L. Eversley, Professor of Systematic Theology, Virginia Theological Seminary

Helen P. Westra, Associate Professor of English, Grand Valley State University

Robert W. Jenson, Senior Scholar for Research, The Center of Theological Inquiry

Gerald R. McDermott, Associate Professor of Religion and Philosophy, Roanoke College

Index

Pinker, Steven, 96, 107
Pinnock, Clark, 101, 102
Plantinga, Alvin, 100
Plantinga, Cornelius, Jr., 54n.18,
55n.22
Plato, 48, 180, 186, 194
Possibility, 81, 169-70
Postmodern, 45-46, 48, 51, 53, 57-58,
64, 110, 169
Potentiality, 26
Power, created, 89, 109-10; divine,
26, 67-68, 74-75, 77
Pragmatism, 97-100, 104, 107-8
Preaching, 132, 134-35, 140, 155. *See
also* Sermons
Predestination, 90, 174
Predication (of qualities to a sub-
ject), 49, 58, 60
Premodern, 110
Prideaux, Humphrey, 177
Prisca Theologia, 178-83, 195, 199,
201
Process theology, 24-25, 49, 51, 57,
63, 72, 100
Profession of faith, 116, 118, 125,
127, 152-53, 201
Proportion, 70, 71, 167, 170
Proudfoot, Wayne, 117
Providence, 132-35, 138-40, 143,
145-47, 149, 151, 153, 155, 197
Psychology, 87, 89, 106, 117
Public life, 80, 84, 87
Punishment, 93, 139, 145, 189

Rahner, Karl, 53, 57, 63, 166, 190,
191n.43
Ramsay, Chevalier (Andrew Michael), 177-78, 199
Raschke, Carl A., 59n.37
Realism, 2, 7-8, 18, 102, 107, 168,
201; of habits and dispositions,
18, 26; of physical universe, 25; of
resistances, 27-28
Reason, 5, 90, 195-97
Reconciliation, among persons, 121;
with God, 63, 195-96, 201

Redemption, 10-11, 34, 42-43, 63,
118, 132-33, 135, 137-39, 154, 186,
191, 195-97, 201-2. *See also* Salvation; Soteriology
Redwood, John, 175n.7
Regeneration, 187-90. *See also* Revival
Relationality, 39, 54, 57, 68, 76, 77,
82
Religion, 2, 141, 144, 146, 149, 150,
153; true, 139, 152, 155, 179, 181,
184, 186, 191
Religions, 68-69, 176-80, 195-96, 200
Repentance, 120, 149, 152, 155
Responsibility, 33, 68, 81-83, 88, 103,
105, 109, 196
Revelation, 35, 48, 50, 53, 55, 57-60,
63-64, 175, 178, 180-83, 185, 189-
97, 200-202; and nature, 35-36;
progressive, 192; propositional,
191; and Scripture, 6
Revival, 4, 74, 119, 126, 131-32, 135-
40, 143-44, 150-54, 156. *See also*
Regeneration
Revivalism, 113-17, 119-22, 129-30,
138-39, 155; techniques of, 119,
139
Rhetoric, 139, 141-44, 149
Roman Catholicism, 178, 187-88,
190
Ross, Dorothy, 96n.18
Rowbotham, Arnold H., 179n.20
Royce, Josiah, 97
Rupp, George, 33

Sacramentalism, 113-14, 117, 125,
127, 129
Sacraments. *See* Baptism; Communion
Saints, 43, 75, 92, 122, 142, 187, 189-
90. *See also* Elect
Sale, George, 177, 178n.18
Salvation, 60, 63, 173-74, 178, 182-
92, 194-96, 198-201. *See also* Redemption; Soteriology
Salzberg, Sharon, 82n.25